Using Effectiveness Data for School Improvement

Data metrics in schools are becoming increasingly complex and, despite their best efforts, teachers and academics generally find them something of a 'black box'. This book lifts the lid on that box, exploring the provenance and problematisation of existing techniques and developing new algorithms for measuring the more oblique aspects of in-school performance.

Using contextual value-added measures in England as a foundation – they have become the template of choice for policy-makers around the world and a basis for some excellent school effectiveness research – the book explores the potential of performance and progress data to guide student and teacher self-evaluation, to set targets and allocate resources, to evaluate initiatives and identify good practice, to assess and reward staff responsibility, and to inform policy in relation to emerging issues such as school choice, equality of opportunity and post-compulsory progression.

Chapters are sectioned in three parts – 'Past', 'Present' and 'Future' – and cover:

- the historical journey from raw-threshold to refined-contextual measures of school effectiveness
- research and policy on pupil attainment and value-added data
- the leading UK government and Fischer Family Trust models
- issues relating to differential effectiveness and the interpretation of data
- how best to blend data from different sources
- new non-cognitive metrics for assessing social and emotional aspects of learning (SEAL) and staff responsibility
- managing data for school improvement and understanding professional attitudes to it.

Using Effectiveness Data for School Improvement brings together for the first time in one place the various metrics and models, and their basis in research. A full technical specification is included so that 'data experts' and 'data novices', academics and practitioners, can use the book to understand and maximise what is potentially a hugely transforming but under-utilised resource and an increasingly important aspect of school and curriculum management.

Anthony Kelly is Professor of School Improvement and Political Economy and Director of Research in the School of Education, University of Southampton, UK.

Christopher Downey is Lecturer at the School of Education, University of Southampton, UK.

Using Effectiveness Data for School Improvement

Developing and utilising metrics

Anthony Kelly and Christopher Downey

Routledge
Taylor & Francis Group

LONDON AND NEW YORK

First edition published 2011
by Routledge
2 Park Square, Milton Park, Abingdon, Oxon, OX14 4RN

Simultaneously published in the USA and Canada
by Routledge
270 Madison Avenue, New York, NY 10016

Routledge is an imprint of the Taylor & Francis Group, an informa business

© 2011 Anthony Kelly and Christopher Downey

The right of Anthony Kelly and Christopher Downey to be identified
as authors of this work has been asserted by them in accordance with
sections 77 and 78 of the Copyright, Designs and Patents Act 1988.

Typeset in Garamond by
Pindar NZ, Auckland, New Zealand
Printed and bound in Great Britain by
CPI Antony Rowe, Chippenham, Wiltshire

British Library Cataloguing in Publication Data
A catalogue record for this book is available from the British Library

Library of Congress Cataloging-in-Publication Data
Kelly, Anthony, 1957-
Using effectiveness data for school improvement: developing and
utilizing metrics / Anthony Kelly and Christopher Downey.—1st ed.
    p. cm.
 1. Educational evaluation—Data processing. 2. Educational
equalization. 3. School improvement programs. I. Downey, Christopher. II. Title.
  LB2822.75.K48 2011
  371.2'070285—dc22   2010026670

ISBN13: 978-0-415-56277-5 (hbk)
ISBN13: 978-0-415-56278-2 (pbk)
ISBN13: 978-0-203-83436-7 (ebk)

Contents

Illustrations

Figures

Tables

1 Introduction

On 12 March 2010, the *Times Education Supplement* (TES) in London screamed: 'Fraught heads spend half-term in data hell'. It is one of many recent articles in the media reflecting the growing view of many in the profession that teaching and school management in England have become overloaded with impenetrable data from such a wide variety of sources that practitioners cannot keep track of what is available, never mind use it to effect the change for which it was produced. At system level, education in England is characterised by an almost manic obsession with tinkering (and acronyms), which over the last couple of decades has reached operatic proportions, and data measures have not been immune. Many government policies, driven (critics would say) by the hubris of politicians who lack the conceptual apparatus to discern the difference, have confused improvement with change and left many in the teaching profession foundering in the wake of ever-increasing complexity: data is collected centrally but at a significant time-cost locally to schools; it is analysed prescriptively by third parties who are perceived to lack empathy with teachers; it is interpreted by a priesthood of expertise that alienates practitioners; and it is generally underutilised in classrooms by those charged with improving educational outcomes. Accountability has likewise been abandoned to the fetish of the market as authorities sidestep the norms of robustness[1] to elevate performance to a level that defies analysis by befuddled professionals. It is not a situation unique to education, of course – health service provision has similarly suffered – but it reflects the desire of successive governments to put data into the hands of stakeholders across a wide range of public services to inform choice about quality and access.

Yet despite these shortcomings – or perhaps *because* of them – the UK is now a major player – if not *the* major player – globally in terms of school and student data. Its collection and analysis, not to mention the opportunities it provides to academics to carry out good-quality school effectiveness research, has become the template of choice for policy-makers from countries as far

---

1 See, for example, Tymms and Dean (2004) and Ray (2006: 34).

afield as Australia (Downes and Vindurampulle 2007) and Poland (Jakubowski 2008). Over the past decade, various measures for gauging pupil attainment and progress in schools have been introduced: from simple threshold measures of raw academic attainment (such as the percentage of pupils obtaining a particular set of examination grades) to the latest complex contextual value-added (or 'intake adjusted') models that take account of a wide range of factors outside the control of schools. These developments have, by and large, been greeted favourably by teachers, and rightly so, though they have sometimes been made to serve two masters simultaneously: to inform school improvement through target setting and to facilitate the government's accountability agenda through the publication of performance data. However, there are obstacles to extending the use of data even within a profession that welcomes it, one of which is the fact that the terminology used carries with it a context-specific lexicon whose terms and cognates, while straightforward to those familiar with their provenance, have different shades of meaning in everyday life. To a modest extent, this book seeks to prise open that 'black box' and explain the concepts, terminology and processes behind the collection, analysis, interpretation and utilisation of data in schools: from measures of attainment and progress, to non-cognitive metrics for social and emotional aspects of learning and staff responsibility. It is an ambition best served (we think) by considering in depth the English system, which leads the field, rather than describing in lesser detail many systems from different countries, though of course *all* data systems share some common features. For one thing, there is an obvious 'flow' to data processes, from collection through analysis and interpretation to utilisation (see Figure 1.1), and it is a simple matter to represent in each system the typical learning feedback cycles within that flow: *systemic practice learning* (1) when the experience of *utilisation* is fed back to those who decide what data to collect; *systemic technical learning* (2) when the experience of *analysis* is fed

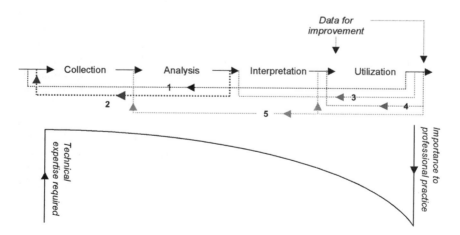

Figure 1.1 The data journey from collection to utilisation, with learning loops

back; *professional learning* (3) when the experience of utilisation informs new interpretative approaches; *personal learning* (4) when utilisation leads to *better* utilisation; and *institutional learning* (5) when the experience of utilisation leads schools to new ways of analysing the data passed to them by outside agencies. Additionally, most systems share the fact that the *collection* and *analysis* of data both require high levels of *technical* expertise, and engagement with the *interpretation* and *utilisation* of data (where it can most effectively be used for improvement) requires higher levels of *professional* expertise (see Figure 1.1).

The introduction of complex data systems in England, as elsewhere, is the culmination of years of sustained public argument about how best to measure pupil performance in a way that takes context into account, and sheds light on progress as well as on standards. This book explores the limitations of current arrangements in light of these arguments, and explores the potential of various measures to guide student and teacher self-evaluation, to set targets for pupils, teachers, schools and local authorities,[2] to target resources, to hold schools publicly responsible for underperformance, to evaluate the efficacy of remedial initiatives, to identify good practice, to assess and reward responsibility, and to inform policy in relation to emerging issues like school choice, equality of opportunity and post-compulsory progression. Of course, all school data systems suffer from the disadvantage of being processed mechanistically by the algorithms of the chosen model, so they cannot operate obliquely to answer the all-important question of how best to educate young people and deploy staff so that no one is disadvantaged, nor can they use differently prioritised metrics to capture the diverse ambiguity of school life. They *can* cope directly and technologically with one aspect at a time, but it requires the human touch to put them all together and interpret the results as a way of guiding practice. So we have included chapters on developing metrics for social and emotional learning and assessing staff responsibility, to take account (respectively) of how pupils *feel* about their own learning and what teachers and managers *think* about their work and how it is rewarded.

We have written *Using Effectiveness Data for School Improvement* with a wide readership in mind:

- School practitioners: not just those with responsibility for interpreting and using school effectiveness data as part of their leadership roles within schools – head teachers, school data managers, heads of department and the like – but more widely among classroom practitioners, to reflect the growing importance of data in official professional standards. For them, we hope the book will facilitate a more critical engagement with data at every level of practice.

---

2 The (approximate) equivalent to a school district in the US.

- Those working for local government, and commercial and third-sector organisations offering services to schools as school improvement partners and professional development providers. For them, we hope the book will provide material to stimulate more informed, effective and innovative uses of data, and make a significant contribution to the crucial process of self-evaluation in schools.
- Those individuals and groups who are motivated to contribute to new systemic initiatives like Charter Schools, Academies, 'Free' Schools and Voucher Schemes, and those who hold schools to account for their impact on the academic outcomes of young people: members of school governing bodies, school inspectors, and politicians at local and national level. We hope the book will provide them with food for thought about the insights that attainment data can provide and the limitations inherent in using such data to draw conclusions about the effectiveness of schools and teachers.
- Academics engaged in educational research, specifically in the fields of educational effectiveness, school improvement and school leadership.

There are many ways in which the contents of a book like this can be organised. We have settled on a chronological sequence and the chapters are sectioned in three parts: 'The past: why data is used', in which we consider the research and policy background from which effectiveness measures emerged; 'The present: how data is interpreted', in which we explore the technical aspects of the two most widely used models for school effectiveness data in England; and 'The future: why data is important', in which we use the principles of school effectiveness measures and a range of school improvement techniques to illustrate the way new metrics can be developed, employed and managed.

In the 'Past' section, Chapter 2 discusses, in research terms, the historical journey from raw-threshold to refined-contextual measures of school effectiveness, and Chapter 3 is a review of research and policy on pupil attainment and value-added data. In the 'Present' section, Chapter 4 describes and examines UK government models, Chapter 5 deals similarly with Fischer Family Trust models, Chapter 6 debates issues relating to differential effectiveness and the interpretation of data, and Chapter 7 explores how best to blend data from different sources. The final 'Future' section suggests some new metrics in Chapter 10 for dealing with social and emotional aspects of learning and in Chapter 11 for assessing staff responsibility for data-related tasks, and discusses ways of managing data for school improvement (Chapter 8) and understanding professional attitudes to it (Chapter 9). The book finishes (Chapter 12) by challenging the complexity of some current measures and the extent to which they are fit for purpose.

While the chronological framework is our way of structuring the book's wide-ranging content, for some readers who are already familiar with the technical aspects of effectiveness measures, the 'Future' section will be a place to engage with stimuli to current practice and organisation. For those readers wanting to deepen their technical understanding around the issues and contradictions of effectiveness data, the 'Present' section will provide the insights they are seeking. For most, the 'historical' first section, charting as it does the development of the tools described in the middle and final parts, will serve as a guide through the maze of literature in the field. Overall, we hope the book makes a contribution to school improvement; specifically, to the role that effectiveness data can play in informing classroom practice and management. We feel that teachers need the confidence to look beyond the superficial acceptance of data as analysed and interpreted *by others*. It is the essence of being a professional to be conscious of this need, even when it is accompanied by a fear of the consequences. Myth, no matter how beguiling, is the most treacherous of all sources of evidence – it becomes the thing it pretends to be – but it cannot sustain professional practice in any meaningful way for any length of time, so teachers and school leaders must be able to look real evidence steadfastly in the eye and if necessary abandon that which was previously secure. The analysis and interpretation of data is the mechanism by which the truth about performance of (and in) schools is acquired, as long as the technical mechanisms and shortcomings are understood to the extent that they can challenge the unproven certainties of convention. While local context shapes the perception of effectiveness, the demand for it is universal. We suggest that the knowledgeable utilisation of data in schools can go some way to meeting that demand.

Part I

The past

Why data is used

2 The journey from raw to refined measures of school effectiveness

A research-informed view of the practicalities of value-added models in England

Introduction: getting the measure of school effectiveness and school improvement

The development of value-added (VA) measures of school effectiveness could be said to have progressed along twin tracks, reflecting their use for both accountability and school improvement purposes. The latter has its origins in the field of School Effectiveness Research (SER): a quantitative, school-focused approach that seeks to measure school output, correct for input and circumstance ('context'), and assign a scalar to the value the school adds to the learning experience of its students (Kelly 2008: 517). School Effectiveness Research began in earnest in 1979, following earlier research by Coleman *et al.* (1966) and Jencks *et al.* (1972). Edmonds (1979) and Brookover *et al.* (1979) in the USA, and Rutter *et al.* (1979) in the UK, produced seminal studies which found that schools have a 'small but significant' effect on pupil attainment. School-level factors which were found to have impact included the balance of able and less-able students, the presence or absence of reward systems, the physical environment, the opportunity for students to take responsibility, and having strong leadership with democratic decision making. Among the factors found *not* to be correlated with effectiveness were class size and school size. In the 1980s, Reynolds, Creemers, Scheerens and others added to the list of factors affecting outcomes: a high proportion of students in positions of authority, low levels of institutional control, high expectations, a low ratio of pupils to teachers, a safe and orderly school climate, and regularly evaluating student progress (Teddlie and Reynolds 2000). With the advent of more sophisticated statistical approaches (and software), School Effectiveness Research was then able to adjust its models to account for these factors, considered to be beyond the control of the school, in order to come closer to 'the school effect' – the contribution that the school makes to the academic progress of its students – and to cater for the fact that in reality students are clustered within schools and are not single entities independent of their peers.

One of the aims of School Effectiveness Research is to identify effective schools so that their characteristics can be determined and studied to ascertain whether, and to what extent, they can be mimicked by others less effective. In

School Effectiveness Research, 'effectiveness' itself is narrowly and deliberately defined as the progress students make in the academic, cognitive and scholastic elements of their schooling. It does not dispute that schools are concerned with *more than* academic progress, and indeed strands of it are concerned with developing additional *non-cognitive* measures of school effectiveness (see Chapters 10 and 11). For this reason, the field has long been closely allied to School Improvement, which is a developmental approach to understanding how and why schools change or remain static over time. Whereas School Effectiveness Research tends to be cross-sectional, output-focused and empirical, School Improvement tends to be longitudinal, process-focused and evangelical. It holds that all schools *need* to be improved and that all schools *can* be improved, though they operate under different sets of circumstances, produce different outcomes and need to be judged 'effective' using a variety of metrics. Whereas School Effectiveness Research is disinterested in the propriety of aims, School Improvement seeks to interpret and evaluate the appropriateness of policy and the effect of practice at different systemic levels. It seeks insights rather than correlations; it is attitudinal and tactile.[1]

School Improvement followed in the wake of School Effectiveness Research (1979) so its provenance can be traced to the 1980s, though there was earlier work on developing curriculum resources to improve student outcomes that could be included in the genre (Hopkins and Lagerweij 1996). The early emphasis was on improvement of out*put* resulting from government fiat, but in later years this shifted to process and out*come*-focused research, and became naturalistic, grounded and practitioner-based. If School Effectiveness Research is about *measuring* difference, School Improvement is about *generating* it. The former sees itself as 'doing the science' that allows the latter to endure and in that sense it lights the way, though School Improvement must additionally be guided by influences external to the school: in society, in communities and among policy-makers. And although School Effectiveness Research and School Improvement differ in respect of their relationship with theory – the former is essentially experimentalist and *testing* of theory; the latter seeks to coalesce what is known and is *developing* of theory – some of the most insightful long-term

---

1 Kelly (2008: 518), while praiseful of the field, suggests that SER can be criticised on a number of counts: (1) that schools are 'complicated palimpsests' and the idea that they are homogeneous entities, while convenient for policy-makers, does not ring true with parents and practitioners; (2) that because SER focuses on measurables it tends to ignore 'difficult-to-measure' but important factors like the impact of competitor schools on each other, teacher satisfaction and societal culture, the last of which makes international comparisons 'difficult to make and sometimes nonsensical'; (3) that the act of measurement itself affects what is being measured so that schools learn to limit their engagement to those activities that produce the most visible 'public' effects; (4) that while SER is good at listing and ranking influencing factors, it is not so good at understanding the processes 'without which practical efforts at improvement become futile'; nor does it (5) provide an accurate account of the 'waxing and waning of everyday life in schools'.

School Effectiveness Research projects have been those giving feedback on 'improvement initiatives' directly to national governments, local authorities, school districts and schools (e.g. Sammons, Thomas *et al.* 1997; Van Damme *et al.* 2002; Thomas *et al.* 2007).

Accountability and school performance tables

The accountability track has its origins in the political realm and in the need to be able to demonstrate that schools are effectively discharging their duties (or not) in terms of their responsibly to the public. School performance indicators provide a means by which schools can be held accountable to a wide range of stakeholders such as parents, school governors, the local community and other taxpayers, which of course presumes that *suitable* indicators of school performance exist: the original ones were simply measures of raw attainment, such as the percentage of students in a school reaching or exceeding a particular qualification threshold. A reliance on unadjusted threshold measures like these has been reviewed and critiqued in detail (e.g. Fitz-Gibbon 1990), but despite their limitations they are still published for schools in England, in the form of the percentage of pupils achieving five or more General Certificate of Secondary Education (GCSE)[2] passes at grades A* to C, or the percentage of pupils attaining a particular National Curriculum (NC) level. For an educational system in a society as diverse as that of the UK, such 'raw' measures are considered unfair as they are not adjusted for the local context that influences the demographics of a school, such as ethnicity and socio-economic status, nor is the impact of student prior attainment on entry to the school taken into account. In other words, raw attainment measures ignore the very variables considered to be beyond the control of the school that School Effectiveness Research seeks to control so that the *effect of the school* can be isolated and gauged. It is not surprising then that development of more refined school performance indicators should have become intertwined with the efforts of School Effectiveness Research to find more robust and methodologically precise measures for the school effect. In retrospect, it has been a journey from the 'unadjusted' to the 'contextualised'; from the 'raw' to the 'refined'.

Figure 2.1 presents the timeline for the development of value-added measures in the UK alongside some of the developments in data collection and tracking of students that facilitated their introduction. At the end of the 1980s, the then Conservative Government was pursuing policies to increase the accountability of all public sector bodies with the introduction of its Citizens' Charter. The Citizens' Charter covered three areas of public sector delivery: transport

---

2 The 'General Certificate in Secondary Education' is the examination taken by virtually all 16-year-old pupils in England after (typically) five years of secondary schooling.

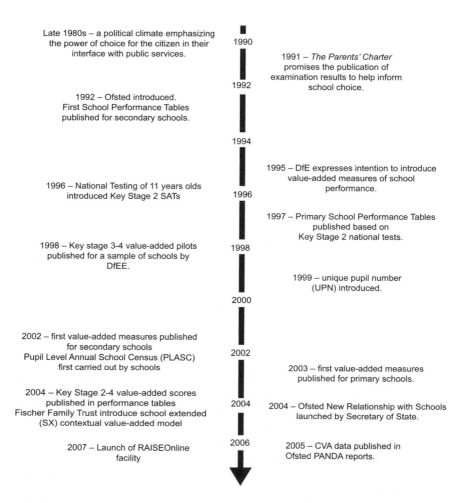

Late 1980s – a political climate emphasizing the power of choice for the citizen in their interface with public services.

1990

1991 – *The Parents' Charter* promises the publication of examination results to help inform school choice.

1992

1992 – Ofsted introduced. First School Performance Tables published for secondary schools.

1994

1995 – DfE expresses intention to introduce value-added measures of school performance.

1996 – National Testing of 11 years olds introduced Key Stage 2 SATs

1996

1997 – Primary School Performance Tables published based on Key Stage 2 national tests.

1998 – Key stage 3-4 value-added pilots published for a sample of schools by DfEE.

1998

1999 – unique pupil number (UPN) introduced.

2000

2002 – first value-added measures published for secondary schools Pupil Level Annual School Census (PLASC) first carried out by schools

2002

2003 – first value-added measures published for primary schools.

2004 – Key Stage 2-4 value-added scores published in performance tables Fischer Family Trust introduce school extended (SX) contextual value-added model

2004

2004 – Ofsted New Relationship with Schools launched by Secretary of State.

2007 – Launch of RAISEOnline facility

2006

2005 – CVA data published in Ofsted PANDA reports.

Figure 2.1 Timeline showing the development of VA measures in England and Wales

(the 'Passengers' Charter'); health (the 'Patients' Charter'); and education (the 'Parents' Charter'). The Parents' Charter, first published in 1991, reflected the desire on the part of the then government to put information into the hands of parents to enable them to make an informed choice in relation to schooling. The charter contained five promises to parents, two of which related to direct government information: the publication of raw examination results as a measure of school performance, and the publication of school inspection reports. The following year saw the introduction of school performance tables and the establishment of the Office for Standards in Education (Ofsted),[3] both of which had a major impact on how secondary schools were viewed by those within and without the system. Specifically, Ofsted was introduced to provide qualitative reports for every state school in England[4] and to make them available to parents through publication.

Secondary school performance tables were originally published in the form of percentages of pupils obtaining five or more GCSE grades A* to C. The tables were presented by the (then) Department for Education as alphabetical listings of schools, but these were then adjusted by newspapers to a 'league table' format with the schools *ranked* on their percentage of 5+ A*–C grades at GCSE. Immediately, schools were identified as belonging to 'top' or 'bottom' performing groups and intense focus was placed on the schools at either end of the tables with little attention paid to the difference in raw scores separating the top schools from those at the bottom. This practice of ranking schools still continues despite the development of refined school performance measures. The BBC News website, for example, allows its visitors to 'sort' schools in particular local authorities using both raw examination data and value-added scores, all at the click of a mouse, as well as publishing reviews of the 'best' and 'worst' performing schools with links to 'schools that add the most value'. Schools were clearly the testing ground for wider public sector performance and accountability indicators since it was nearly a decade before similar rankings for health providers were released – in the form of 'high level' and 'clinical indicators' for National Health Service (NHS)[5] hospitals in 1999, and 'star ratings' for hospitals in 2001 – since when league tables generated from performance rankings have become the ubiquitous measure of public sector performance.

Using raw data to compare schools

It soon became clear that raw measures of school performance were not popular with schools or teachers in England as they failed to compare 'like with like'. Selective (grammar) schools were ranked in the same tables as non-selective secondary modern and comprehensive schools with no consideration given to the prior attainment of pupils on entry, and inner-city schools were ranked with those in leafy suburbs with no account taken of the socio-economic background of students despite a strong body of English and international effectiveness research evidence suggesting that it was strongly correlated with academic attainment.

3 Ofsted is the English schools' inspectorate. Originally, it was the 'Office for Standards in Education', thus the acronym. Its full title now is the 'Office for Standards in Education, Children's Services and Skills'.
4 The Welsh equivalent is 'Estyn: Her Majesty's Inspectorate for Education and Training in Wales'.
5 The National Health Service is the UK's system of public hospitals and healthcare.

The publication of school league tables based on raw examination results had been foreseen by various school effectiveness researchers (e.g. Smith and Tomlinson 1989) and their eventual publication provoked a critical response from schools themselves and from the school effectiveness community, which had for some time been arguing convincingly for a distinction to be made between 'standards attained' and 'progress made' by students. For example, Gray *et al.* (1986) had posed key questions about the circumstances under which one school could be considered to have done better than another, and in answer to such questions a growing number of school effectiveness researchers were arguing for a more sophisticated statistical model to account for both context and the hierarchical or clustered nature of the data (reflecting the fact that students are nested within schools so that any set of students in the same school are more similar to each other to the general population of students). One such statistical technique is a variant of regression analysis known as 'hierarchical linear' or 'multilevel' modelling (MLM) and this has since become the tool of choice in the field.

The government responded to the criticisms of raw unadjusted attainment measures of school performance in different ways. In 1995 the Department for Education expressed its intention to develop 'value-added' measures that adjusted for the prior attainment of pupils before they entered secondary school, and an extensive period of consultation began which culminated seven years later in the first publication of valued-added measures in school performance tables. One key aspect of the consultation was the Value-Added National Project (Fitz-Gibbon 1997) commissioned by the Schools Curriculum and Assessment Authority (SCAA)[6] and conducted by the Curriculum Evaluation and Management (CEM) centre at the University of Durham.[7] The project's final report made a comprehensive set of recommendations regarding the reporting of value-added progress measures for both internal school improvement and external accountability purposes. In essence, it argued for a system based on the following.

- School value-added scores as the simple mean of the scores of individual pupils.
- Residual Gain Analysis (RGA) based on ordinary least squares (OLS) regression methods.
- The *omission* of further contextualising variables such as gender and socio-economic proxy variables like the percentage free school meal entitlement (FSM), to prevent stereotyping and the lowering of expectations, but *some*

---

6 SCAA was the forerunner to the Qualifications and Curriculum Authority (QCA), now the Qualifications and Curriculum Development Agency (QCDA).
7 The CEM centre had been producing well-respected value-added analyses to aid school improvement and self-evaluation (e.g. its Advanced Level Information System, ALIS) since 1983.

consideration to be given to schools with *disproportionate* numbers of students from such groups (such as boys-only schools or schools with more than 60 per cent FSM).

- The external publication of value-added measures summarising the progress of at least three cohorts of students to counter inherent year-on-year instability.
- The adoption of minimum threshold numbers on roll, below which value-added scores would not be published for these (small) schools.
- The publication of both subject-specific and syllabus-specific regression lines to facilitate interpretation of confounding effects due to the variety of subjects and syllabuses available in the UK examinations system.

Additional recommendations in the report covered a wide range of issues, from the need to develop statistical literacy among teachers as part of initial teacher training courses to enable them to understand and interpret value-added analyses, through to the rigorous monitoring of the examinations and assessment system to ensure comparability of outcomes between subjects and examinations. Fitz-Gibbon also called for an acknowledgement of the narrow view of education that value-added measures represent, calling for *other* measures of educational outcomes to be developed.[8]

In Annexes C and D of the report, there is some technical coverage of whether multilevel regression techniques, which adjust for the clustered nature of school performance data, are preferred over the less complex OLS methods recommended by the report. This section of the report is largely based on earlier work by Fitz-Gibbon (1991) in responding to criticisms of the CEM centre's development of value-added analyses like 'ALIS' (its A-Level Information System). It concludes that MLM presents little statistical benefit over the simpler OLS techniques, especially for schools with reasonably sized cohorts, and that the corresponding complexity introduced by MLM makes it more difficult for teachers and school leaders to understand the statistical procedures employed. Fitz-Gibbon identified two flaws in the calls to employ MLM in value-added analysis. The first is that the use of 'school' as the upper level in the data hierarchy is not valid; if MLM is to be employed, Fitz-Gibbon suggests that it is 'class' or 'teaching group' that should be the upper level in the hierarchy. The second issue is around the shrinkage factor applied to residuals in the analysis. The shrinkage factor enables more robust parameter estimates to be calculated for schools with small cohorts by 'borrowing strength' from the larger data set, though the resulting (shrunken) estimates for small schools are drawn closer to the mean as a result.

---

8 And, in a small way, this is what this book attempts in Chapters 10 and 11.

Refining the measures

While the value-added consultation was under way, the Department for Education and Ofsted continued to employ benchmarking techniques – the grouping of similar schools – to adjust the school effectiveness measures for prior attainment and socio-economic status, but only for data intended for *internal* self-evaluation purposes via the Performance and Assessment (PANDA) reports given directly to schools and local authorities by Ofsted. Figure 2.2 shows a typical PANDA analysis of the percentage of pupils attaining National Curriculum Level 5 and above in nationally administered tests (KS3 SATs)[9] for the National Curriculum core subjects of English, science and mathematics. The upper table shows the KS3 outcomes for the school, benchmarked *against all schools nationally*. The intervals *between* national thresholds for performance at the 95th – 75th – 60th – 40th – 25th – 5th percentiles are allocated the grades A, B, C, D and E respectively to aid interpretation (since they have been used for many years in schools). Performance above the 95th percentile scores an A* grade while that below the 5th percentile scores an F grade.

The lower table on Figure 2.2 shows the same KS3 outcomes for the school benchmarked against *a narrower set of* schools; namely, those admitting pupils with a similar below-average prior attainment at the end of KS2. It is clear that the comparative performance of the school improves considerably. Outcomes in science, in the lower quartile when compared with *national* outcomes [53 per cent on the third row, upper table], are around the mean when compared to outcomes for schools with similar prior attainment [53 per cent between 40th and 60th quartiles on the third row, lower table]. Similarly, Level 5 and above outcomes in KS3 English place the school's performance around the mean compared with all schools nationally [66 per cent on the first row, upper table], but this becomes upper-quartile performance when compared to schools with a similar prior attainment range [66 per cent on the first row, lower table]. The grades A to E given under the heading 'Interpretation' correspond to the position of the attainment for each subject on the percentile ranges.

Notwithstanding the debate in England over statistical modelling techniques raised by the SCAA consultation, when value-added scores were *eventually* published in 1998 for a pilot group of schools, the methodology used was different to that recommended by Fitz-Gibbon. A simple 'median model' was employed rather than the ordinary least squares approach recommended by

9 Compulsory schooling in England is divided into 'Key Stages' (KS): KS1 (Years 1 and 2) for ages 5–7; KS2 (Years 3–6) for ages 7–11; KS3 (Years 7–9) for ages 11–14; KS4 (Years 10 and 11) for ages 14–16. At each Key Stage, all children in state schools study certain subjects, following the requirements of the National Curriculum.

   SATs are 'Statutory Assessment Tests' or more formally 'National Curriculum Teacher Assessments and Key Stage Tests'.

Comparison with national benchmarks for *all* schools
Percentage of pupils reaching Level 5 and above

Percentile	95th	Upper Quartile	60th		40th		Lower Quartile		5th	Interpretation
English	97	82	75	**66**	65		56		35	C
Mathematics	98	82	77		68	**60**	60		44	D
Science	98	81	75		65		57	**53**	37	E

Schools that achieved a KS2 average point score of at least 25 but less than 26 in 2000
Comparison with benchmarks for schools in similar context (prior attainment, level)
Percentage of pupils reaching Level 5 and above

Percentile	95th		Upper Quartile		60th		40th	Lower Quartile	5th	Interpretation
English	72	**66**	61		55		49	44	32	A
Mathematics	69		62	**60**	58		54	50	42	B
Science	66		58		54	**53**	49	44	36	C

Figure 2.2 Extracts from a typical PANDA report showing the effect of benchmarking (in this case, by prior attainment) on the judgement of school effectiveness (The grades given under the heading 'Interpretation' correspond to the position of the percentage attainment for each subject on the percentile ranges.)

Fitz-Gibbon or the multilevel regression approach used by school effectiveness researchers.

In Figure 2.3 the curve represents the *median* performance of *all pupils nationally* in KS3 SATs (on the vertical axis) based on their prior attainment at the end of KS2 (on the horizontal axis). The outcomes for four typical pupils have been plotted on the figure showing how their value-added scores are calculated. The *school's* KS2–KS3 value-added score is then simply the *mean* of the pupil VA scores with a value of 100 added for cosmetic reasons so that all school VA scores are positive, at least in the mathematical sense.[10] Assuming for the purposes of illustration that the four pupils on Figure 2.3 constitute *the whole school* at KS2–KS3, then the School VA score is:

$$[(7 + 3 + 0 - 6) / 4] + 100 = 101.0$$

10 100 is also added to KS1–KS2 value-added scores and 1,000 is added for KS2–KS4 value-added scores as GCSE outcomes are scored on a different scale. Of course, a school getting less than 100 for its KS2–KS3 value added has a '*negative*' VA in the vernacular sense of the word.

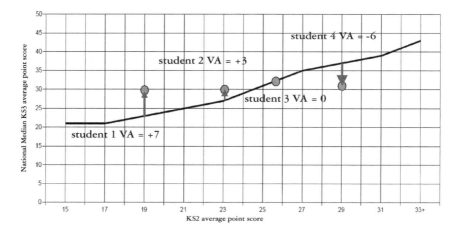

Figure 2.3 A KS2–KS3 median value-added plot showing how student value-added scores are calculated (data source: DfES 2004 with annotations added)

One consequence of this mix of *median* and *mean* in the methodology is the apparently odd result that the mean of all schools' VA scores is often less than 100 (or 1,000 for KS2–KS4 value added). This was seen by some critics as evidence of a slide in standards, but the more likely explanation is 'ceiling' and 'floor' effects are skewing the distribution of scores. Others have argued that the important thing is simply to adopt a consistent approach, either mean or median, throughout (e.g. Critchlow and Coe 2003).

The first UK school performance tables incorporating school value-added scores based on this 'median model' were published in 2002. The key advantage of the median VA method was its simplicity: as soon as median lines are published, teachers can calculate VA scores for their own students and, from the student scores, calculate their own school VA scores. Teachers are also able to interact with the data to calculate VA scores for *groups of* students – class cohorts, students with special educational needs and so forth – and they can check the accuracy of the scores and gauge the influence of 'outliers' on the overall result. Eventually, an electronic tool called the Pupil Achievement Tracker (PAT) was developed to help schools carry out these in-house analyses (DfES 2004).

Emerging critiques

Despite being heralded as an advance in measuring school performance, with an adjustment for prior attainment that allowed schools to be compared on a more like-for-like basis, the median VA metric soon had its critics. In a paper entitled 'Value added is of little value', Gorard (2006) argued that school VA scores tell us little (if anything) more about school effectiveness than raw attainment measures. He provided evidence for this claim in the form of measures of association between VA scores and the national GCSE benchmark of percentage of pupils obtaining $5+A*$–C passes at GCSE, finding that the two measures had a Pearson correlation coefficient (r)[11] of 0.84, signifying that 71 per cent of the variance[12] in VA scores could be explained by the raw attainment measure. He argued that such a high correlation between the old and the new measures is evidence that VA scores add little to our understanding of school performance: '[T]here is a clear pattern of low attaining schools having low VA, and high attaining schools having high VA. Value-added scores are no more independent of raw-score levels of attainment than outcomes are independent of intakes' (Gorard 2006: 240).

Gorard concluded that such measures were therefore 'worse than pointless' as they could mislead politicians and families about the relative effectiveness of schools, and was also critical of calls to add further complexity to value-added models by using MLM and introducing contextualising variables that 'masked, but did not solve' the problems.

An earlier but more wide-ranging critique by Moody (2001) of the rationale behind the development of value-added indicators and the use of predictive models for target setting had concluded that value-added measures were 'driven by political necessity, and by the desire to "prove" that educational standards were rising, rather than by any demonstrable evidence of their predictive validity or reliability' (Moody 2001: 100) and warned against the use of such measures to formulate judgements on schools, teachers and students. Moody pointed out that an initial report on the VA feasibility study carried out by SCAA in 1994 had concluded that NC levels should *not* be used as baseline predictors of attainment as they could lead to unreliable predictions due (at least in part) to concerns about the parity of levels across Key Stages. The SCAA study had recommended that some finely differentiated but unspecified prior attainment measure be used instead. Three years later, about the same time as the change in government from Conservative to New Labour, an about-turn had occurred when SCAA (1997: 5) stated that standardised tests were no longer necessary as the KS2 tests were 'now sufficiently established and reliable to lend confidence to their results', although the report did note that KS2 levels were 'not equivalent to the same levels at KS3'. Moody criticised the Fitz-Gibbon (1997) report of the (SCAA-sponsored) national study on VA measures, which he said represented:

---

11 Pearson's correlation coefficient – sometimes called Pearson's 'r' – between two variables is defined as the covariance of the two variables divided by the product of their standard deviations. It is a measure of the linear dependence between the two variables and can take any value between $+1$ and -1 inclusive. Pearson's 'r' does not reflect *the slope* of a linear relationship, nor does it capture anything of a *non*linear relationship.

12 The value of r^2.

a classic case of using a range of statistical methods to examine data, and then choosing the method which produces the outcomes which 'prove' that the existing preconceptions are well founded, while at the same time rejecting outcomes which tend to undermine, challenge or complicate those preconceptions.

(Moody 2001: 84)

However, it seems in retrospect that Moody harboured some misunder-standings of the differences between OLS and MLM – possibly confusing multiple regression with multilevel modelling – and with related issues such as shrinkage inherited from earlier SCAA reports that had been criticised by Goldstein (1997a) at the time for employing 'weak statistical procedures'. Moody sought to demonstrate that the results of the Cognitive Ability Tests (CAT) developed by the National Foundation for Educational Research (NFER) gave a better baseline predictor of KS3 performance than either KS2 National Curriculum levels or teacher assessments. Moody's study was limited by the fact that the data was based predominantly on an analysis of two years of inputs/ outcomes in a single, rural, girls-only comprehensive school, but nevertheless the debate about the suitability of NC test data as a baseline measure is an important one, not just for the reason highlighted by Moody – that of implied transferability of NC levels between Key Stages – but for other reasons: the objectivity of the process by which level thresholds are set for the tests; the subjectivity of the marking process, especially for English tests; and the fact that an entire school's test papers are allocated to a single marker rather than randomly distributed between many markers.[13] Allocating all a school's papers to a single marker may result in greater internal consistency between scores within a cohort, thus facilitating some aspects of *internal* self-evaluation, but it raises questions of reliability when making comparisons *between* schools. This is particularly important when fine-grade decimalised levels are used to calculate the input prior attainment measures for the most recent incarnations of value-added measures because when the measures are used to produce comparative indicators (such as percentile rankings for subgroups of students), the differences between decimalised scores and their associated percentile rankings can be very fine indeed.

A more methodologically focused critique by Prais (2001) of the 1998 KS3–KS4 median value-added pilot examined the perils generated by ceiling effects and the *spread* of data when trying to compare different school types using VA scores.[14] Prais also raised the issue of assigning a *continuous* points

---

13 Which would be possible if the papers were scanned and marked electronically, as is the case with an increasing number of GCSE and A-level examinations (taken by most students at age 18).

14 In the case of Prais, the focus was on a comparison between the relative performance of comprehensive schools and grammar schools.

score scale to an *ordinal* scale of GCSE grades, which would assume that the GCSE grade spectrum represents a continuum of challenge. As Prais noted, the points score scale makes no distinction between a pupil who achieves an F grade rather than a G grade, and one who achieves an A* rather than an A. Which of these 'one-GCSE-point' value-added scenarios represents the greater improvement may depend on individual circumstances reflecting issues of motivation as well as academic challenge.

While the median VA model did adjust for prior attainment at the pupil level, it made no adjustment for other pupil and school context variables (like socio-economic status) that were being incorporated gradually into alternative models by school effectiveness researchers at the time. In order to address this, Ofsted, in its PANDA reports to schools, started to employ a benchmarking approach similar to that used previously with raw attainment data. In the example shown on Figure 2.4, a school with a KS1–KS2 value-added score of 100.1 is, as shown in the uppermost of the three tables, positioned exactly on the 60th percentile

Value-added measure: in comparison with national distribution

Percentile	95th	Upper Quartile	60th	40th	Lower Quartile	5th	Interpretation
KS1-KS2 VA score	102.1	100.6	100.1	100.1	99.4	98.8	97.5	B

Non-selective schools with more than 21% and up to 35% FSM
Value-added measure: in comparison with similar schools (FSM)

Percentile	95th	Upper Quartile	60th	40th	Lower Quartile	5th	Interpretation
KS1-KS2 VA score	102.7	100.1	99.5	99.1	98.6	98.2	97.0	A

Schools that achieved a KS2 average points score of at least 25 but less than 26 in 2000
Value-added measure: in comparison with similar schools (prior attainment)

Percentile	95th	Upper Quartile	60th	40th	Lower Quartile	5th	Interpretation
KS1-KS2 VA score	100.9	100.1	99.8	99.3	98.8	98.3	96.9	A

Figure 2.4 Extracts from a typical PANDA report showing the effect of benchmarking of value-added scores by SES (percentage FSM entitlement) and by mean prior attainment on entry

when compared to all schools nationally. When benchmarked with other (non-selective) schools with a similar percentage FSM entitlement, as shown in the middle table, it is positioned between the 75th and 95th percentiles. In the bottom table, the school's VA score has been benchmarked against schools with similar prior attainment and the school is similarly positioned between the 75th and 95th percentiles, which at first glance may appear to be double counting since by definition VA scores are *already* adjusted for prior attainment, but in the median model the adjustment for prior attainment is *only at level of the student* whereas in the PANDA report the mean prior attainment of *the whole cohort* is used to select the benchmarking set of schools.

Emerging complexity

While school VA scores based on the median model were being published in school performance tables, work was going on behind the scenes to develop the more sophisticated models of value-added used by school effectiveness researchers. A group of school effectiveness researchers had been reflecting on the methodological developments of the 1980s and drawing conclusions about what they felt were the essential components of a good value-added model, and as early as 1991, in a piece written for the *Times Educational Supplement*, Nuttall (1991) gave a checklist, which included:

- measures of prior attainment;
- a range of outcome measures and not merely 5+ A*–C at GCSE (say);
- socio-economic variables;
- analyses of differential effectiveness;
- allowance for the possibility that school results are not stable over time;
- use of MLM as the statistical technique of choice.

A report for the National Commission for Education (McPherson 1992), which defined value-added explicitly as a 'calculation of the contribution that schools make to pupils' progress', contained a similar checklist. In its view, VA models should cater for:

- prior attainment;
- the longitudinal nature of progress;
- the multilevel nature of schools;
- the multivariate nature of the factors involved, especially 'non-school factors that boost or retard progress' (such as pupils' socio-economic background);
- differential effectiveness for different groups of pupils.

The National Commission report also stated that performance measures based on *raw examination results* should have their place in the great scheme of things, but that they can lead to 'mistaken judgements, needless anxieties and fruitless "further investigations" . . . triggered by false signals'. It highlighted the potential tension between providing useful information to parents and giving teachers evidence for raising attainment in their schools, noting that value judgements needed to be made by all stakeholders. 'Any attempt to improve schooling by means of informing choice presupposes that parents are capable of understanding at least the complexity of an adjusted outcome score. To reject that possibility is to reject the possibility of informing parents' (McPherson 1992, cited in Saunders 1999: 251).

The report concluded by saying that issues of complexity should not necessarily prevail over the need to develop the best possible indicator, but that optimism was not shared by the school effectiveness researchers involved in developing the methodology. Two eminent UK school effectiveness researchers, Goldstein and Thomas (1995), were less than sanguine about the capacity of SER-based value-added models to differentiate between schools on the basis of performance. They pointed to the 'historical' nature of VA measures – they are, by definition, based on *past* data rather than *contemporary* practice or policy – and concluded that 'research into school effectiveness is a useful activity in our attempt to obtain knowledge about the process of education, but a very poor tool for holding schools to account' (p. 37).

Saunders (1999) has summarised the situation at the end of the 1990s by stating that while the *principle* of value-added was comprehensible, the increasingly rigorous *analysis* only served to reveal the complex and inconsistent nature of effectiveness that lies at its centre. Drawing her words from the recommendations of the SCAA (1994) report, Saunders argued that 'better information' and 'public consumption' are incompatible purposes, especially if public consumption depends on 'simple and straightforward' measures of progress, a conclusion that some school effectiveness researchers had already reached: 'Research emphatically demonstrates that the measurement of progress or value added . . . is neither simple nor straightforward' (Thomas and Goldstein 1995: 17).

Despite these concerns about the complexity of school effectiveness and the statistical models it employs, the UK government pressed on with its plans to develop more sophisticated models. As Ray reflects in his review:

> Views of a selection of academics in the field were sought on the future direction of the value added work and, although there was no consensus of opinion, there was strong support from some for the development of more complex models that used the new data.
>
> (Ray 2006: 10)

The 'new data' to which Ray refers comes from the Pupil Level Annual School Census (PLASC), which the DfES[15] began gathering in 2002 in order to

---

15 The 'Department for Education and Skills', formerly the DfEE, now the DfE.

facilitate the development of contextual value-added (CVA) models. PLASC returns require schools to gather, store and return to the relevant government department a wide range of demographic data on students: gender; date of birth; ethnic background; level of Special Educational Need (SEN); whether students are in the care of the local authority or speak English as an additional language (EAL); and whether students made late entry into a particular Key Stage ('mobility'[16]). All this information is gathered *at the level of the individual student* alongside classic contextualising information such as FSM entitlement, the much-criticised proxy measure of socio-economic deprivation that is further entrenched in the CVA model with the addition of another government-produced measure known as the Income Deprivation Affecting Children Index (IDACI).[17] The CVA model makes substantial use of the data gathered from PLASC, although some data, such as that collected on absences and exclusions, is *not* included in the model because although it would improve its explanatory power, in the CVA model 'schools should to some extent be responsible for the factors' (Ray 2006: 21).

The 2005 pilot CVA model included all the variables listed in Table 2.1 and multilevel modelling techniques were employed to account for the clustered nature of the data. The majority of the variables are pupil-level factors, but two additional school-level factors were included to capture peer effects: the *mean* and the *spread* of the prior attainment of the school cohort.

In line with the approach used when the median VA model was piloted, both the old VA scores (adjusted only for prior attainment) and the new CVA scores for the pilot schools were made publicly available the following year, which presented an opportunity to carry out an analysis, similar to that conducted by Gorard (2006), into the association between the raw attainment data,[18] the old VA measure and the new CVA measure (Downey and Kelly 2007a).

Figure 2.5 shows the association between raw attainment [on the vertical axis] and the old KS2–KS4 value-added measures [on the horizontal axis].[19] The Pearson correlation (r) for the two measures is 0.772, similar to Gorard's

---

16 Mobility is based on pupils' dates of entry to a school. The mobility indicator shows whether a student was in the school for the whole of that Key Stage; for KS2 (say), that is Year 3 to Year 6 inclusive. Where schools have recently merged or opened, dates of entry are set to the school's date of opening or later. In such cases, mobility may appear to be low.

17 IDACI is calculated by the Communities and Local Government department and is based broadly on the student's home postcode. It is a measure of the proportion of children under 16 living in families in receipt of at least one of a specified range of social support measures which include income support, job seeker's allowance, working families' tax credit and disabled person's tax credit. The Index (which ranges in value from 0.0 to 1.0) is linked to the student's postcode but the area of measurement is much wider. The lower-level super output area (LLSOA) has on average a population of 1,500 people and subsumes a number of postcodes (National Statistics 2006).

18 Benchmarked using the percentage of students obtaining 5+ A*–C grades at GCSE.

19 For the KS2–KS4 CVA pilot schools only; n=370, not including special schools.

Table 2.1 Factors included in the first DfES/Ofsted CVA multilevel model

Factors at the student level

Mean intake test level for student based on fine grade (decimalised) National Curriculum levels

Subject variations (take into account differential attainment in English, mathematics and science)

Gender

Month of birth

English as an Additional Language (EAL)

Free School Meal entitlement (FSM)

Special Educational Needs (SEN) stage or Statemented for SEN

Ethnicity

Mobility (late entry to the Key Stage)

In-care at current school

Deprivation indicator (IDACI score)

Factors at the school level

Mean test level *of cohort* on intake

Range (standard deviation) of test level *of cohort* on intake

finding (r=0.84) for the equivalent association using the 2004 data.

When the association between raw attainment and the *new* school KS2–KS4 *CVA* measure is examined (Figure 2.6), the Pearson correlation (r) is found to be much lower at 0.367. Thus, less than 14 per cent of the variation (r^2) in CVA scores for schools in the pilot is explained by the raw attainment measure, which suggests that CVA, for a substantial number of pilot schools, is presenting a *different* picture of performance than that presented by the raw measures; in other words, CVA *is* telling schools 'something they don't already know' from the raw data.[20]

The Pearson correlation between the two value-added measures (the KS2–KS4 CVA and the KS2–KS4 VA) for the pilot schools is 0.718, suggesting a moderately strong association between the two, though the DfES made its comparison, not by using Pearson correlations, but by considering the impact

20 Forty-one schools had 80 per cent or more 5+A*–C grades at GCSE. Only one of these had a KS2–KS4 VA score less than the national average (1000) (range 1042.5–998.6; standard deviation = 11.3) whereas 14 schools had a CVA score below the national average (1000) (range 1048.2 – 984.1; standard deviation = 15.9).

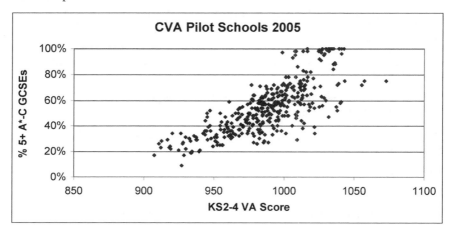

Figure 2.5 The association between KS2–KS4 VA and raw GCSE attainment (the percentage of students obtaining 5 + A*–C grades) for the 2005 CVA pilot schools (source: DfES 2006d)

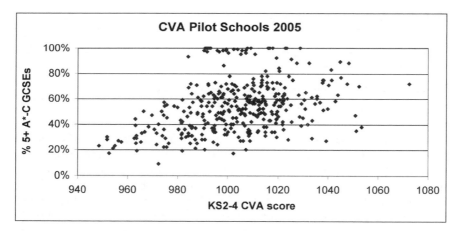

Figure 2.6 The association between KS2–KS4 CVA and raw GCSE attainment (the percentage of students obtaining 5 + A*–C grades) for the 2005 CVA pilot schools (source: DfES 2006d)

of the extra contextual variables *on the relative rankings of schools*. Both measures of association found similarly: that the switch from VA to CVA *does* have an impact. In ranking terms, while just over half the schools remained within the same broad ranking band,[21] it caused approximately 25 per cent of schools to

21 The ranking bands selected were top 5 per cent, next 20 per cent (upper), middle 50 per cent, next 20 per cent (lower) and bottom 5 per cent.

move up one or more bands and 21 per cent to move down (DfES 2006a).

The pilot of the KS2–KS4 CVA model was considered successful enough to release CVA scores for *all* secondary schools as part of the 2006 school performance tables, and also in that year to conduct further pilot studies for KS1–KS2 and post-16 CVA.[22] Table 2.2 shows that the Pearson correlation coefficients for the association between a range of KS2 raw outcome measures and the scores from the two value-added models (KS1–KS2 VA and KS1–KS2 CVA).[23] The proportion of variance explained by the raw measures varies between 14 per cent ($r=0.372$) [bottom row; column 2] and 24 per cent ($r=0.494$) [bottom row; final column].

These results also show that (for the pilot schools) even the simple KS1–KS2 VA measures already in use were giving a very different picture of school performance than the raw, unadjusted KS2 attainment measures. The addition of the further contextual variables in the KS1–KS2 CVA model therefore had less *additional* impact in explaining variation between schools than in the case of KS2–KS4 progress measures.[24] Not surprisingly, the Pearson correlation between the KS1–KS2 VA and KS1–KS2 CVA scores is high at 0.939.

Accepting uncertainty

A further refinement of school performance measures was introduced with the publication of KS2–-KS4 CVA scores; that of 'confidence intervals'.[25] The use of (95 per cent) confidence intervals became a major part of the way the new CVA measures were presented both to schools in their PANDA reports and in the school performance tables published by the government. Their use in CVA

22 The post-16 (or KS4–KS5) CVA is for students pursuing post-compulsory qualifications between the ages of 16–18 in schools and Further Education colleges. For the data relating to all the CVA pilot groups, see the DfE school and college achievement and attainment tables at www.dcsf.gov.uk/performancetables/

23 APS on Table 2.4 stands for 'Average Point Score'. For a school at KS2, it provides a picture of the *overall* KS2 attainment of all pupils in the school. Two schools with similar percentages of pupils achieving Level 4 and above may have different APS since the APS includes the attainment of pupils below the Level 4 threshold.

24 This is confirmed by examining the proportion of unexplained variance between schools compared to the variance within schools (known as the variance partition coefficient). For the KS2–KS4 CVA pilot model only 7 per cent of the unexplained variance was between schools, for KS1–KS2 CVA models it is typically around 25 per cent when the KS2 average points score (APS) is used as the outcome measure.

25 Confidence intervals (CI) are commonly used in inferential statistical analyses that involve random samples being drawn from a larger population. The value of any estimates from the analysis will depend on the exact sample drawn from the population and so the CI represents the reliability of an estimate taking into account the effects of chance in the sampling process. Increasing the confidence level widens the confidence interval. The calculation of CIs requires assumptions to be made, usually about the distribution of the population from which the sample came.

Table 2.2 Pearson correlation coefficients for KS1–KS2 VA and CVA scores and a range of raw attainment measures for the 2006 KS1–2 CVA pilot schools

	KS2 APS	English		Maths		Science	
		%L4+	%L5	%L4+	%L5	%L4+	%L5
KS1–KS2 VA	0.501	0.401	0.427	0.412	0.408	0.473	0.493
KS1–KS2 CVA	0.493	0.372	0.412	0.410	0.406	0.468	0.494

Source of data: DfES 2006c.

calculations helps to express the uncertainty inherent in claiming that a CVA score measures the effectiveness of a school, either for all its pupils or for those in a particular subgroup.[26] With their addition it was hoped that the discussion would shift away from the crude ranking of schools on absolute values, towards whether schools were performing above or below the national mean. Thus schools were divided into three categories: those in line with the national average CVA score;[27] those with significantly above average CVA; and those with significantly below average CVA. However, the media refused to play ball and simply developed yet more ways to rank schools in league tables!

The government maintains (correctly) that *it* does *not* publish league tables – its online 'School and College Achievement and Attainment Tables' (formerly 'School Performance Tables') only list schools *in alphabetical order* by local authority – but admits that the media *does* use its data to rank schools for public consumption. School effectiveness researchers investigating the use of multilevel models to produce school CVA scores had also warned against using data – specifically, the use of MLM residuals – to produce league tables and stressed the importance of applying confidence limits when interpreting them. 'Only schools in which, taking account of intake, results are significantly ($p<0.05$) better or significantly worse than predicted on the basis of intake relationships calculated for the whole sample can be distinguished' (Sammons and Smees 1998: 400).

Although the use of 95 per cent confidence intervals puts schools in one of only three categories of significance – 'average', 'significantly above' and 'significantly below' – there is obviously a region close to the mean where a small change in the confidence limit can produce a crucial change in the designation of significance. It is likely that a number of schools with non-significant values will have confidence intervals that overlap with schools in the 'significantly

---

26 This application of confidence intervals is controversial among those who hold that CVA scores should be based on whole populations rather than on sampled data and therefore see their use as inappropriate (see Gorard 2007 and in response Hutchison and Schagen 2008).

27 '100' for KS1–KS2 CVA and '1000' for KS2–KS4 CVA, KS3–KS4 CVA and KS4–KS5 CVA.

above the mean' or 'significantly below the mean' categories, making it difficult to distinguish between them. Understanding the difference between 'a significant difference' in score and 'a change of statistical significance' renders the interpretation of residuals a fairly fraught exercise for many, aside from the fact that there are many loaded expressions in terms of the colloquial use of the term 'significant'.[28] The use of value-added indicators in the public domain is already very 'high stakes' for schools, teachers and pupils, and for this reason some research – for example, that by Sammons and Smees (1998) on the use of pre-school baseline assessment – suggests that they only be used within a strict code of conduct and on the basis of voluntary participation. School effectiveness researchers generally have been consistent in criticising the public ranking of schools based on value-added analyses, and Goldstein and Cuttance (1988) have suggested that the specific method employed to calculate value-added will, at least in part, determine the rankings. Saunders (1999) interprets this as covering both the choice of outcomes (used to differentiate between different groups of pupils, for example) as well as the type of statistical methodology used. As Saunders notes, there have been calls for CVA models to include as many factors as possible that affect school performance, but this, Saunders argues, while understandable, fails to appreciate the difference in purpose between school effectiveness research and value-added analysis. The latter is essentially 'eliminative rather than an accumulative', aiming deliberately to exclude from consideration those factors that are extraneous or part of the 'noise'.

Despite value-added measures finally coming into line with the complex contextual multilevel models used in school effectiveness research, Goldstein, whose work has done much to influence the development of the current methodology, has been one of the most vocal and long-standing critics of (what he continues to call) league tables, and it is instructive to follow his arguments and note his consistency over the years. In several wide-ranging critiques of pupil and school performance measures and the plethora of uses to which they are put, he has discussed the benefits and limitations (relative to raw attainment measures) of the value-added systems that were being introduced at the time, but his strongest criticism has been reserved for the use of such measures to bolster 'politically driven' policies relating to accountability – teacher performance management, target setting and annual league tables

28 A result is 'statistically significant' if it is unlikely to have occurred by chance. The use of the word 'significant' in statistics is different from its everyday use which suggests 'important' or 'meaningful'. Some research findings can be statistically significant, but the difference might be so small as to be trivial and of no practical use. *Statistical* significance says nothing about *practical* significance. One of the common problems in significance testing is the tendency for multiple comparisons to yield spurious significance even when the null hypothesis is true, and the converse is also true: failing to find evidence of a difference does not prove that there is no difference.

– with no reference to their limitations in terms of statistical uncertainty and appropriateness. He concludes one paper by saying: 'What is required is a commitment to phasing out current procedures which serve a purpose which is largely politically driven, which is widely viewed as irrelevant and which, in its misleading nature, may be doing fundamental harm to education' (Goldstein 2001: 442).

Three years later, after basic value-added measures had become established, Goldstein was still highly critical of their use for public accountability purposes (Myers and Goldstein 2004), stating that: 'the best use of value-added comparisons is for [local authorities] and schools to provide additional information, in confidence, about school performance, set alongside, and not dominating, other factors, especially when disaggregated to individual school subjects or departments'.

And a further three years on, after the publication of school KS2–KS4 CVA scores as measures of secondary school progress, Goldstein (2007) remained critical, though perhaps less strident in tone. He acknowledged the inclusion of key contextual factors in the model and also the publication of (95 per cent) confidence intervals in the official DfE[29] tables, but despite these advances stated that 'there remained considerable problems' (Goldstein 2007: 4) centred around the continued publication of value-added measures in the public domain and referred to a 'league table culture' that gives rise to numerical data being used 'sometimes unscrupulously, sometimes in ignorance, as a substitute for serious and well-informed debate' (Goldstein 2007: 5).

Overall, in academic terms, Goldstein's criticism is an impeachment, not of the methodology or of the models, but of the quasi-political use to which they are put. However, it is also partly a critique of the type of School Effectiveness Research which accepts that *a single measure* of effectiveness can capture the performance of an individual school, ignoring the fact that schools probably differ as much *internally* as they do relative to each other. A decade before the first value-added pilot, hinting at this differential effectiveness within schools, Goldstein and Cuttance (1988: 198) had argued that a comparison of school averages:

> tells us nothing about the relative achievements of different types of pupils within schools. . . . Consequently schools which perform well relative to other schools for the average pupil in the population may perform less well for disadvantaged or advantaged pupils.

This was a view reiterated with a more methodological slant by Nuttall *et al.* (1989) when they stated that:

---

29 The Department for Education, formerly the Department for Children, Schools and Families (DCSF).

school effectiveness varies in terms of the relative performance of different subgroups. To attempt to summarise school differences, even after adjusting for intake, sex and ethnic background of the pupils and fixed characteristics of the schools, in a single quantity is misleading. . . . [T]he concept of overall effectiveness is not useful.

(pp. 775–6)

Sammons and Smees (1998) also found statistically significant evidence of differential effectiveness within schools; in their case, based on gender and FSM eligibility. While the Sammons and Smees sample was self-selecting due to the voluntary participation clause in their code of conduct, the findings do suggest that the use of a single measure to capture the effectiveness of schools across a range of outcomes masks a great deal of fine detail, which, as previously suggested by Goldstein and Cuttance (1988) and Nuttall *et al.* (1989), questions the usefulness of a single school VA score as a performance indicator.

VA and CVA scores, despite the criticisms, have become a key part of the public accountability framework for English schools, informing such varied and wide-ranging decisions as local and national government funding allocations, inspection judgements, performance management of teachers, and of course the initial driver for such performance indicators, to inform parental choice. Through their publication first in school PANDA reports and the PAT, and then their inclusion (since 2007) in the sophisticated online improvement database known as RAISEonline,[30] school leaders have become accustomed to using them as key tools for self-evaluation and school improvement, though the twin purposes of accountability and improvement do not always sit well together. In Chapters 4, 5 and 6, the technical details of the main value-added models used in England – those from DfE and the Fischer Family Trust – will be discussed, including some key issues surrounding their use for school improvement purposes.

30 RAISE stands for Reporting and Analysis for Improvement through School Self-Evaluation. RAISEonline was launched by the DfE and Ofsted in January 2007 as a web-based portal providing access to a standard set of analyses of school-level and pupil-level data. It replaced the paper-based documents previously issued annually to schools; namely the *Autumn Package* and PANDA reports. RAISEonline is part of Ofsted's New Relationship with Schools, which aims to ensure that both schools and inspectors have access to the same set of data on which judgements of school performance are made. RAISEonline also contains a suite of tools and analyses to use the same data for student and school target setting and school self-evaluation, which sets up a particular tension as the same data is used for both accountability and improvement purposes.

3 Pupil attainment and value-added data

A research-informed view of policy

Introduction

In 1986, the UK Conservative government under Margaret Thatcher decided to publish secondary school examination results as simple percentages of pupils achieving the highest grades in GCSE and A-level examinations, which the media then used to rank schools. While the purpose of publishing the examination results was not to rank schools per se, it cannot be doubted that it was a consequence known in advance by policy-makers. Academic commentators at the time pointed out the shortcomings of league tables, citing research that demonstrated the need to adjust them for school-intake characteristics – what became the value-added model – and the need to provide confidence intervals to capture their inherent uncertainty (Goldstein 2008). McPherson (1992) has defined 'value-added', a term borrowed from economics, as the contribution a school makes to pupil progress, adjusted for differences between schools in the attainment of pupils upon entry. It is the relative progress pupils make in a school compared to the progress of all pupils with similar prior attainment (Demie 2003) – the 'boost' a school gives to a child's previous level of attainment – which examination results cannot measure because schools differ from each other in terms of pupil intake, school type, gender, denominational composition, location, and ethnic and social mix. This is not to say that raw unadjusted results are useless – after all, they do reflect *actual* attainment – but they should at a minimum be accompanied by information on the school's contribution to pupil progress. And as McPherson points out, schooling is a process that takes place *over time* as schools maintain or fail to maintain their effectiveness. 'Any pupil can have a bad day, any school a bad year. Sensible judgements will therefore be based, not on snapshots, but on repeated measures of pupils and schools' (McPherson 1992: 2, column 2).

Driving the development of value-added data

The systematic use of data – that is to say, its collection and analysis using appropriately defined methodologies – is core to coalescing and interpreting professional experience, without which the power to advance existing theory and change policy is seriously curtailed. In education, the collection and analysis of hard data, and research in the related area of school effectiveness, is often seen (unfairly) as too accepting of the accountability agendas of governments; an apparent acquiescence in agendas that seek to control what teachers do and how they do it. Gray, a leading researcher in the area, commented in 1996 that while interest in value-added approaches to judging effectiveness was high, progress was faltering. He suggested that some considerable obstacles needed to be overcome if a national value-added system in the UK was to become properly established. Over the years, Gray has frequently and consistently addressed the important issue of fluctuation in school performance over time, but the issue has rarely been addressed by government policy. In 1997 the DfEE,[1] as the DfE then was, published its *Excellence in Schools* white paper (DfEE 1997). It was one of the first white papers to be published by the newly elected Labour government and it outlined the government's intention to raise standards over the course of its first five years in office. The approach to involving parents, teachers, governors, businesses, local government and communities in implementing policy was *underpinned* by six principles – education at the heart of government, policies designed to benefit *all* pupils, a focus on standards, intervention in inverse proportion to success, and zero tolerance for underperformance – and *predicated* on gathering data from assessment of all children starting primary schools, improved Ofsted inspections to increase school accountability, and numeracy and literacy hours as part of a national programme to raise standards. The approach hoped to 'estimate the value schools were adding' and help teachers 'check the rate of pupils' progress', while assessment was to be 'based on teachers' own observation' and 'introduced on the basis of partnership', not 'confrontation'.

Excellence in Schools recognised that standards generally rise faster when schools take responsibility for their own improvement with the right mix of pressure and support from government, but that schools 'must have annual plans for improving performance . . . based on the results they are already achieving' (DfEE 1997: 24–5). It acknowledged that one of the most powerful underlying reasons for low performance in schools is the fact that they fail to stretch the most able pupils and identify and push poor performance, and suggested that the comprehensive pupil attainment data that exists for each school at each Key Stage of the National Curriculum could be further improved in terms of its collection, dissemination and utilisation. It went on to advocate the publication of even more performance data for the benefit of parents and as a spur to improvement:

1 The Department for Education and Employment, which became in turn the DfES, the DCSF and most recently (May 2010) the DfE.

We will publish more such data than ever before. We need to provide parents and others with better information by supplementing 'raw' results with a measure of the progress which pupils have made. Data on prior attainment, which could form the basis of a true measure of 'value added', are not yet available consistently for every Key Stage but better information can be introduced into performance tables progressively from 1998.

(DfEE 1997: 25)

The intention was to oblige local authorities to provide schools with comparative data to look at differences in performance between cohorts and between local schools, and to encourage 'the use within schools of reliable and consistent performance analysis to enable teachers to assess progress' (DfEE 1997: 27) and change teaching strategies as and when required. A year previously, Thomas and Mortimore (1996) had presented results of a value-added study of the 1993 GCSE examination results in Lancashire. Their study evaluated a variety of different multilevel models for measuring school effectiveness on the basis that the publication of raw examination results on their own was not a good enough guide, and that a fairer and more accurate method was to take account of the characteristics of pupils attending each school (what we now call 'context'). Thomas and Mortimore matched more than 8,000 GCSE results from 79 schools to additional information on gender, age, prior attainment, ethnicity, FSM entitlement, SEN, length of time in UK secondary schools, and pupil mobility. They found that gender difference was *not* significant, but that large differences appeared between students with different prior attainment scores, particularly in verbal (as opposed to non-verbal) tests.[2] Students eligible for free school meals were also found to have lower GCSE scores than those not eligible, and a very substantial average decrease in examination performance was found for pupils who had received fewer than five years of UK secondary education. Students attending more than one secondary school also scored poorly and substantial differences appeared across ethnic groups. Taken together, this 'basic' model of school effectiveness, using an aggregated outcome measure of attainment across a number of subjects, found that 10 per cent of the variation in examination scores was attributable to schools once pupil background factors had been taken into account.[3]

Although the overall correlation (r) of raw and VA scores in the Thomas and Mortimore study was relatively high at 0.73, they investigated the efficacy of alternative models. A number of pupils and schools were tested individually against 'the basic model' and through a structured procedure of eliminating

2 Suggesting that language skills are important in pupil attainment across all subjects.
3 Using overall examination scores as the only measure of school effectiveness is not unproblematic as significant subject differences can be masked.

non-significant variables, only two pupil census measures improved the fit of the model and these were included in a refined value-added model. Seven measures relating directly to each school were tested: school size, school status, whether or not the school was co-educational, the percentage of pupils entitled to free school meals, the percentage of Asian pupils, the percentage of low-attaining pupils on entry, and the percentage of high-attaining pupils on entry. By comparing the significant explanatory variables of different value-added models, the findings showed that when prior attainment data is missing, other pupil background and school context information explains a substantial proportion of the variance in *school* performance but is less useful in predicting *pupil* outcomes. However, when prior attainment data *is* available, no school context factors are significant and the fit of the model is substantially improved. Therefore the conceptual rationale for including school context factors in the analysis of school effects is sound, though Thomas and Mortimore suggested that: 'this issue requires further research as it has important implications as to whether socio-economic data (at the pupil or school level) or other pupil characteristics (such as gender or ethnicity) should be included in value-added models of school effectiveness' (p. 27).

The best models of measuring school effectiveness clearly control for the prior attainment of pupils, and the evidence strongly suggests that there is a substantial benefit in providing a range of different VA measures for each school in terms of overall examination scores, individual subject scores and the scores for different groups of pupils. The Thomas and Mortimore study also sought to demonstrate that schools could collaborate to provide a better database of pupil outcomes and background information so that examination results could be interpreted in a wider context than just individual schools. Such partnerships, they suggested, if established and continued over time, could provide a mutually beneficial stimulus for investigating and identifying the mechanisms of effective school improvement. Goldstein and Spiegelhalter (1996) also studied the limitations of school performance indicators, acknowledging that the focus on quantitative comparisons between individual institutions was part of a wider attempt by government to introduce accountability into public sector activities like education and health. Like Thomas and Mortimore, they argued for a proper contextualisation of outcome indicators by taking account of individual institutional circumstances and designing an appropriately specified statistical model. They used the term 'adjusted comparison' rather than 'value added' in judging whether a school had 'enhanced its members between their entry and exit' (Goldstein and Spiegelhalter 1996: 387).

A number of years earlier, the OECD (1992) had been active in developing performance indicators *for national education systems*, which included measures of pupil attainment to complement other *school-level* indicators, and had identified a shift from the use of *input* indicators like expenditure, to a concern with *outputs* like student achievement, but had shown little interest in *process* indicators like curriculum organisation or pedagogy. OECD assumed, like most others at the time, that raw unadjusted comparisons of pupil attainment across countries allowed inferences to be drawn about the relative merit of their educational systems, but even by then the mood had shifted towards a recognition that all meaningful comparisons, whether school or systemic, must be contextualised at least to the point of taking into account prior attainment, even though, according to Goldstein and Spiegelhalter, adjusted league tables inherit many of the deficiencies of unadjusted ones (like statistical uncertainty). Goldstein and Spiegelhalter considered it clear-cut to treat comparisons between schools as *suggestive* rather than *definitive* and to be aware that for any given set of variables, there is often a choice of models each of which may fit the data equally well but give different estimates; the implication is that policy-makers should be concerned that data users are properly informed of the data's shortcomings. For Goldstein and Spiegelhalter, the continuing official publication and ranking of unadjusted scores lends them an authority they do not have. As we say in the previous chapter, Goldstein himself has been consistent in highlighting the shortcomings of performance tables over more than a decade of groundbreaking research in the area. In 2007, he called for the inclusion of confidence intervals in performance tables in the (forlorn) hope that their publication or that of some other marker of statistical significance would be taken up by the media in their league tables. While the DfE rose to the challenge, the media did not reciprocate[4] so that in some ways the optimal public use of its measures is hindered by the government's own drive towards greater complexity.

The 1998 Sammons and Smees report on the use of baseline assessment at the start of primary schooling and how it could be used to measure value-added in KS1 described the ways in which schools in one local authority in the UK were using data to improve delivery and, in that sense, their project provides a snapshot of data usage at the time of New Labour's ascent to power (1997). Surrey local authority had introduced baseline screening for all Reception pupils in September 1993 to assist schools in identifying at-risk pupils, to enable it to distribute funding to schools on the basis of need, to monitor pupil progress, and to provide a basis for judging future performance. The assessment covered five main areas – language, literacy, mathematics, drawing skills and social skills – and produced an individual profile for each child. The local authority published guidelines to assist schools and teachers in their use of data, but the initiative was very much about improving pupil outcomes rather than enabling public accountability. Sammons and Smees examined the

---

4 Goldstein, whose work has done much to shape the development of CVA, has expressed his frustration at the absence of confidence intervals in the league tables published by the major UK newspapers and the media. While he praised the BBC website for giving a balanced overview of the issues relating to the use of CVA scores in league tables, the same website also contained interactive tables of CVA and 'raw' threshold measures against which schools could be sorted against any of the measures at the click of a mouse, *without* a confidence interval.

links between the baseline assessment results, the impact of pupil background factors and subsequent KS1 performance. They found that the association between performance in Reception and KS1 results was weak but significant and positive, though the fact that many teachers quite properly use low entry scores to focus on those children most in need of help reduces the statistical correlation with later performance.[5]

Nationwide baseline assessment was, in fact, introduced the year following the Sammons and Smees research, at the start of the 1998/9 school year. It was welcomed by parents, local authorities and schools at the time, and by researchers who wanted to conduct meaningful international comparisons, but there were concerns (which remain today) that parents do not understand the subtleties enough to make full use of the data. Its purpose was to plan the measurement *of future progress* and to ensure the 'equal *entitlement* for all children to be assessed on entry to school' (QCA 1997: 3) (emphasis added). (The assumption that a national system of assessment is an 'entitlement' rather than an imposition in the lives of four year olds, their parents and teachers was perhaps a harbinger of the developments that were to follow!)

Many other studies have similarly demonstrated that pupil background characteristics are related systematically to cognitive attainment by age seven (e.g. Sammons, West and Hind 1997), but few studies examined the impact of *pre-school* experiences on KS1 results as Sammons and Smees had done.[6] Their results have important 'equity' implications for practitioners and policy-makers. They found that age and gender are consistently related to better performance and all forms of pre-school experience have a positive impact relative to *no* pre-school experience. Other factors were found to be associated with *poorer* performance; namely, having English as a second language and eligibility for free school meals. In line with findings from other earlier studies (e.g. Brandsma and Knuver 1989; Tymms *et al.* 1997), Sammons and Smees also found that schools exert a proportionally greater influence over subjects 'primarily taught at school' than 'over reading which appears to be relatively more susceptible to home background influences' (p. 399) . . . which means subtly that raw league tables are even more misleading for reading, due to the relatively greater impact of background factors.

It is difficult to draw any conclusions about the stability over time of school effectiveness measures and as was mentioned at the end of the previous chapter, it is widely known that schools exhibit *within-school* variation too. The value-added working group in the Sammons and Smees project decided that feedback of VA results in terms of simple divisions like 'significantly above expectation'

---

5 This is an important issue regarding research on teachers' use of data; that in using it to guide classroom practice, it impacts on the research that provides the guidance.

6 Although Davies and Brember (1997) reported on a cross-sectional study that indicated positive effects for some pre-school experience.

and 'significantly below expectation' is a good starting point for evaluating performance and identifying areas of strength and weakness. This 'keep-it-simple' strategy encourages school improvement initiatives, which Creemers and Reezigt (1997) argue also offer valuable ways of testing the validity of effectiveness research (though Goldstein (1997b) urges caution).

In 1999, Yang *et al.* carried out two longitudinal studies in Hampshire local authority: one from Reception Year to the end of Year 2; and another from the end of Year 2 to the end of Year 6 (the final year in primary school). The core of the research was to analyse approximately 11,000 pupil records from 275 schools, but also to seek ways to communicate the results to head teachers in ways that 'were meaningful without destroying the underlying complexity of the relationships uncovered' (p. 469). It is one of the first methodological recognitions of the tensions inherent in working with pupil attainment data; that which exists between understandability (for improvement purposes) and complexity (to capture adequately the relationships between the variables). In order to provide individual schools with data that allows them to 'make valid comparisons of their performance' (p. 476), Yang *et al.* suggested three criteria:

- The information provided to each school was confidential to that school (and to the local authority). Summary information about the performance of all local schools was provided only for comparative purposes.
- The data system evolved over time in light of feedback from users, the availability of new data and national developments.
- It was acknowledged *ab initio* that VA estimates have uncertainty attached to them and that this needed to be taken into account in any interpretation.

Only a minority of schools were found by Yang *et al.* to be significantly different from the mean and only about a third of all comparisons yielded significant results, which suggests that the use of such data for the public ranking of schools in league tables is problematical. Internally, of course, schools use data as they see fit – to compare subjects or Key Stages perhaps – but Yang *et al.* recommended a programme of in-service training, initially for head teachers and local authority advisors, to familiarise them with interpretation and the limitations of results. In fact, a programme to evaluate the use of results was also set up following the research.

The Hampshire value-added project demonstrates that it is both feasible and useful to provide sensitive analyses of student progress for school improvement purposes, that complex multilevel models *can* be presented in ways that are accessible to users without sacrificing the essential components of the analyses, and that over time, as the number of yearly cohorts increases, the data and its analysis becomes better and more useful to practitioners. Yang *et al.* also found that effective analysis and presentation of pupil attainment and progress data emphasises the uncertainty surrounding results. The provision of uncertainty bands poses no real interpretational difficulties for users, but there are a number of other limitations which need to be understood:

- That residual estimates are derived from a model that uses only *available* data. It is possible that there are other factors which ought to be included but for which data is *not* available.
- That predictor variables with low reliability can affect both residual estimates (value-added scores) and parameter estimates (the effect size of the various contextual factors) (see also Woodhouse *et al.* 1996).
- That students can change school during particular phases of education, and analysis shows that the number of previous schools and the length of time in the final school are linked to academic progress. In principle, analyses should incorporate information about *all* schools attended and apportion student progress between them (Hill and Goldstein 1998), but such data is difficult to acquire.

These limitations need to be borne in mind when making interpretations. Yang *et al.* suggest that the strength of good data analyses is that they 'provide a *further*, quantitative indicator that schools can use in their judgements of how well they are functioning' (p. 481) (emphasis added). They can indicate when problems are present, and where, but it is not a precise diagnosis and in particular the use of pupil attainment data as a public accountability measure in the form of league tables may be inappropriate and lack 'credibility and usefulness'. When league tables become high stakes, they 'inevitably become distorted and no longer reflect any underlying reality of school performance' (p. 481).

Challenges to utilising value-added data

Saunders (2000) uses the phrase 'the psychology and sociology of numbers' to describe reservations in relation to the use of VA measures by senior and middle management staff in schools. Saunders acknowledges that measures are well-developed and sophisticated, but suggests that there are still conceptual and ethical issues when interpreting and using effectiveness data for school improvement purposes. She suggests that the fact that the range of parties interested in VA extends widely, 'from politicians to school senior managers, and from academic researchers to lay governors' (pp. 241–2), necessitates a continuing discussion about how the different expectations and requirements of different stakeholders and users can be met.

The paper by Saunders is interesting for its summation of value-added measurement in England. Before the introduction of the national value-added system, various methods had been developed for producing information to be used, on the one hand, to assess the relative effectiveness of different schools and local education authorities, and on the other to provide diagnostic assistance for managers and staff (e.g. Gray *et al.* 1990; Schagen 1991; Mortimore *et al.*

1994; Jesson 1996). Quite understandably, the focus of research has been on methodological accuracy – from conceptualising the statistical model appropriately to collecting the right data in the right form[7] – but what head teachers and staff *do* with the analysis when it arrives in schools is something that is largely taken for granted. Saunders suggests that the emphasis in VA performance data has now shifted to supporting and improving the quality of teaching and learning, and cites Dudley's (1999a) view that teachers' use of quantitative data is 'uniquely powerful' in the way they are prepared to trust and act on it. For teachers and heads, value-added data is valid in a number of ways:

> First, because people are prepared to act on the basis of the data, it . . . has a strong 'validity of consequence'. Second, in measuring pupil progress rather than merely learning outcomes, value-added data . . . has a strong 'construct validity'. . . . Value-added data enjoys this validity and currency almost entirely because of such psychological affective factors as trust and perceived fairness.
>
> (Dudley 1999a: 113)

However, not all school staff can easily acquire an accurate understanding of value-added. Maw (1999) argues, for example, that the media's coverage of value-added has largely been in the context of publishing controversial tables, and that coverage of key issues concerning the measurement and presentation of VA data has not been coherent. Various research-based approaches have provided empirical evidence in relation to schools' use of VA data via a number of 'services'; for example, the ALIS system from the University of Durham and the QUASE[8] system from the National Foundation for Educational Research. Data from ALIS was made available to schools over a decade ago and its developers researched how schools made use of it when it was a relatively new system. The picture that emerged was of a 'very peripheral level of awareness' and a tendency 'to read reports sparingly and to take no action on reports once read' (Williamson and Fitz-Gibbon 1990: 40). A little later, the picture had changed for the better (Williamson *et al.* 1992), but levels of awareness (of ALIS data) varied considerably among schools using it, impact on practice had been minimal, the statistical nature of the data remained a serious obstacle to engagement and there was a general lack of within-school systems to ensure that data was acted upon. ALIS was, of course, established at a time when the use of performance indicators for monitoring and feedback was at an early stage of development, but nonetheless the findings indicate that the *active use* of data supplied to schools, even when they are paying it, is not something that can be taken for granted.

---

7 See Saunders and Thomas (1998) for a summary of the issues.
8 QUASE is an acronym for Quantitative Analysis for Self-Evaluation.

Research on the use of QUASE data (e.g. Harris *et al.* 1997) suggests very similar issues and difficulties to those found by the ALIS team earlier in the decade. Wikeley (1998), for example, revealed problems in disseminating and sharing good practice because staff felt that the system had been imposed from above by senior management and that the data told them nothing new, and even staff in departments that had positive VA felt that being identified as such was divisive within their schools. Wikeley also found a general tendency to distrust external quantitative data and that people tended to be much more critical of statistical analysis than they were of professional judgement, especially when there was a lack of other robust data to test (confirm or refute) VA findings.[9] It confirms the view that teachers are generally not familiar with the technical nomenclature of value-added and sometimes fail to appreciate that VA analysis produces losers as well as winners. Some staff want primarily to 'predict' GCSE pupil results from baseline data; others want to inform school organisation, curriculum design and pedagogy. Most do not differentiate between one set of statistics and another, which limits the active utilisation of the data in schools. In the case of the QUASE data, five factors were found to be positively correlated with utilisation: active support from senior management; the 'championing' of data by a senior member of staff; incentives based on a school's overall relative effectiveness; length of time using the data; and previous exposure of staff to guidance on data interpretation (Saunders and Rudd 1999). The lesson today, more than a decade later, is that policy-makers need to pay attention to how data is perceived by managers and teachers. While many schools and local authorities are highly numerate and are increasingly 'aware of what different kinds of value-added analyses can tell them and, just as importantly, what they cannot' (Saunders 2000: 245), there are still many in the profession, at management and classroom level, for whom such data presents difficulties of acceptance, understanding and utilisation.

Dudley's research (1997, 1999a, 1999b) on how teachers respond to feedback from pupil data suggests that teachers respond to it as either 'good news' or 'bad news', and that this stimulates one of the following four reactions: an action-orientated positive response to improve the issue behind the data (equally likely to be provoked by either good-news data or bad-news data); a passive 'filing away' of the issue behind the data; a passive rejection of the issue; an active denial or rejection of the issue. Other research has similarly found that psychological and sociological aspects are important in attitude to data. Head teachers in particular feel that they have a public relations function to fulfil around managing published data and to use it to lift the school's reputation and expectations. In a market characterised by high accountability, a head teacher's

---

9 Wikeley's research was a small-scale qualitative project in nine secondary schools. It studied the ways in which staff at different levels within school hierarchies were (or were not) given access to, and enabled to use, performance data.

role involves 'talking the school up' (Saunders 2000) rather than engaging in (or overwhelming teachers with) the fine detail of data.

At department level, performance data has potentially an even stronger role to play than at senior management level and there appears to be a range of feelings about the proper place of data in teaching, which Saunders (2000: 251) tries to capture on two perpendicular axes: *emotional* feelings ranging from 'cold' to 'hot', representing the subject's degree of enthusiasm for the potential contribution of data to teaching and learning; and *intellectual* stances towards the use of data, from 'literal' at one extreme to 'provisional' (the view that data is necessary but only useful if professional judgement is brought to bear on it) at the other, representing teachers' degree of reliance on data as a manifestation of pupil ability. This typology therefore creates four quadrants to describe different combinations of intellectual and emotional responses to the use of data: *unengaged, technicist, sceptical* and *heuristic* (see Figure 3.1).

- The '*unengaged*' quadrant is characterised by a resistance to making use of data, often because it is perceived as not intrinsically relevant to pedagogical needs. It places teachers' professional judgement and data in opposition to each other.
- The '*technist*' quadrant is characterised by an enthusiastic reliance on performance data, which is seen as problematic only with regard to its accuracy. It is also characterised by a dedication to gathering and recording large amounts of data.
- The '*sceptical*' approach is marked by a resistance to the literal use of data rather than to its rejection per se.

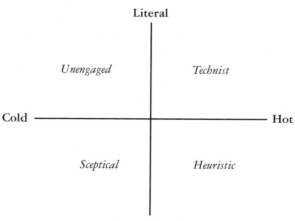

Figure 3.1 A model for categorising teachers' responses to the use of data (from Saunders 2000)

• The '*heuristic*' approach is one that accepts and values data, which typically is then used for raising questions rather than making judgements.

Saunders's classification suggests that teachers' own beliefs and values about teaching and learning are highly implicated in data usage:

> Performance data generally may be impartial in intention, but are rarely perceived as neutral in effect. Value-added data in particular are complex, relatively new and often 'high stakes'; it can therefore represent an overt threat or at least a felt disturbance to some kinds of school, departmental and/or group culture.
>
> (Saunders 2000: 254)

Data does not speak for itself. It depends on a series of prior decisions about *what* has been measured and *how* it has been measured; decisions which necessarily involve value judgements as well as technical ones. Some staff are unduly sceptical about performance data to the point of wanting to dismiss it; others are over-optimistic about what it can tell them. It may or may not be championed by a 'data manager' who mediates its more technical aspects for colleagues, but the research evidence suggests that the interpretation of data emerges from an 'interaction' between it and teachers' own values, attitudes and expectations. For Saunders and others, this raises the question of whether performance data acts as a 'locus' for conversations staff want to have (or anxieties they want to express) about their professional work, in which case whoever controls access to it holds the key. Some schools are unsure how to make the best use of data and let departmental heads manage it, which can lead to inertia on the one hand and overuse on the other. Others are more confident and know what they want from the data. Research suggests that the extent to which schools make use of data depends on whether or not they have a strong extrinsic incentive to use it, so that external in-service training and support is necessary. The use to which data is put seems to follow 'existing contours' of management style, and the introduction of data *of itself* does not bring about a culture supportive of self-review and improvement. It seems to us rather the other way round; that school culture determines what use is made of the data.

Data needs to be interpreted with caution: sometimes 'obvious' and widely held views are unfounded, and predicting future performance from past trends can often be unreliable. Gray *et al.* (2001) investigated the implications of using past performance as a guide to future success – or 'charting', as it is called in financial markets – noting that a mixture of external and internal forces act to put pressure on schools to match (and if possible, exceed) previous performance. International research suggests that there is significant stability – 'inertia' would in some situations be a better word – in school performance over time (Teddlie *et al.* 2000; Scheerens and Bosker 1997), though these studies have typically only examined data from two adjacent years and as Gray and colleagues noted in a previous study (1996), some degree of *instability* is necessary for schools to improve. Studies of consistently improving schools (e.g. Gray *et al.* 1999; Thomas *et al.* 2007) have found that three years of continuous improvement represents 'a good run for a school' before performance levels off, but for a school to have a step change in effectiveness, four or five years of sustained improvement is necessary, which is something very few schools can sustain (Gray *et al.* 2001). A study by Thomas in 2001 of nearly 200 schools in London and Lancashire found similarly – that irrespective of improvement in raw performance, very few schools were able to improve their effectiveness (relative to that of other schools) for long – though this type of research is not without its critics (e.g. Pugh and Mangan 2003) who condemn the unproblematic and deterministic way in which the notion of 'trend' is treated. Gray *et al.* (2001) ask whether, and to what extent, we are justified in extrapolating an early upward trend in school performance and to what extent momentum exists for improvement. The problem is complex and multi-layered – at A-level, for example, the majority of schools in England have seen results improving on a year-by-year basis because of national trends and grade inflation, and post-16 performance is quite stable anyway because schools with A-level provision attract similar sorts of (university-ambitious) students each year – but such trends as *do* exist are relatively short-lived and come in bursts, and very few schools manage to lock into cycles of continuous improvement.

Goldstein *et al.* (2000) considered the use of value-added data in judging school performance over time. In practice, of course, value-added analysis is only possible when and where linked prior attainment data is available down to the individual pupil level, but Goldstein *et al.* studied the possibility of *approximating* to a full value-added analysis using data only available at the point of measurement; in this case at the end of KS2.[10] They compared such proxy models with the results of unadjusted mean attainment scores, and with a full value-added analysis (including prior attainment at the pupil level) in order to see the difference this makes to judgements about individual schools. They found that even when full value-added adjustments are made for prior attainment, there still remains uncertainty surrounding estimates for individual schools and only extreme schools can be statistically separated from the average. It is possible that even the best models lack key 'contextualising' variables so that additional caution needs to be taken with interpretations. Goldstein *et al.* indicate that there is little to be gained by the use of 'proxy' measures: they offer only a very small improvement over *raw* scores, and when compared to a full value-added analysis provide quite different (and inferior) classifications for certain schools.

It is a recurring theme throughout the research literature that value-added models are best used for the (formative) purpose of school improvement rather

---

10 This means including contextual factors such as entitlement to free school meals and gender at KS2, but only aggregate school-level measures of prior attainment at KS1.

than the (summative) purpose of public accountability. Research in New Zealand by Robinson *et al.* (2002) suggests that standards-based systemic reform should also be driven by student achievement data in terms of how it can improve the quality of instruction and not how it can comply with external accountability requirements. They propose an approach based on professionally motivated commitment to iterative data use, where accountability can be delivered in parallel by holding school leaders responsible for using internally and externally generated data to improve teaching, identify strengths and weaknesses, and evaluate the impact of changes made. In New Zealand, where teachers enjoy a high level of autonomy, there is little support within the profession for building capacity in data-based curriculum review. Robinson *et al.* claim that removing accountability pressures would create that support, but their findings suggest that schools already collect a considerable amount of evidence about students in the normal course of events but have difficulty interpreting it correctly, and in any case routines for the storage, retrieval and dissemination of data are inadequate. As elsewhere, this situation limits learning and stunts reform in that schools tend to use data to evaluate students without evaluating programmes and without examining whether their rates of progress are good enough. Robinson's research suggests that building local capacity to use data to review programmes requires a combination of central policy, local support and school-based expertise. Policy itself 'cannot drive local learning' and schools need support in their learning from both externally and internally generated data.

Demie (2003) suggests that data, particularly value-added data provided by external sources like governments and inspection agencies, is not widely used in schools (and not just in New Zealand) because it is not presented in a way that is accessible or easily interpreted, and that guidance is lacking as to how classroom teachers can use it effectively. Value-added data is essential to enhancing teachers' abilities to analyse their own effectiveness in terms of pupil progress and enabling them to take the necessary steps for improvement. Best practice suggests that local authorities and school districts should support schools through school-focused training courses on the use of performance data for self-evaluation and target setting, and different types of feedback at different stages of analysis. Demie and others claim that the willingness of schools and local authorities to engage with data and act as 'critical friends' is growing, but statistical analysis – whether it is based on raw or CVA data – should *not* be the final verdict on a school's performance. It should be *the starting point* for asking questions.

Using data is a major part of large-scale school reform efforts too (Earl and Fullan 2003),[11] but in *all* reform situations school leaders experience 'multiple

11 The large-scale reforms in this research were the National Literacy and Numeracy Strategies in the UK, the Manitoba School Improvement Program and the Ontario Secondary School Reform programme.

dilemmas' as they negotiate their relationship with data about their own schools. Unsurprisingly, the use of data is variable across jurisdictions – for example, it is more widely used in England than in Canada – but is usually mandated as part of a 'centrally directed reform agenda'. In some cases, the nature of its use is more home-grown and localised in individual schools, which Earl and Fullan suggest creates insecurities about not having the necessary skills and training to interpret it. However, they found that where schools do gather and summarise their own data, they regard it as important for making decisions and are more at ease with interpreting and applying it.

One of the recurring dilemmas in the literature is whether data is used by leaders for teaching and learning or as a mechanism for surveillance. The evidence suggests that school leaders become more comfortable with data as they move further away from targets and progress reports, and the rapid shift from *no data* to *mountains of data* has an effect on how (and what) leaders communicate and what evidence they use. When they receive data that is also made available to the public in league tables, leaders feel the 'story' gets 'out of control'; as Earl and Fullan succinctly put it, 'transparency means vulnerability' in many situations. Data on its own has no meaning – turning it into knowledge is what makes it worthwhile – and the function of a school leader is to become an expert consumer of data in order to create the conditions for others to generate improvement. Hemsley-Brown and Sharp (2003) looked at how school leaders and teachers use research findings for school improvement and how teachers use research findings in their own practice. They analysed publications between 1988 and 2001 using a 'best evidence approach' – in other words, by prioritising findings from the best and most authoritative studies – and found that head teachers (mostly in the US and Australia) generally hold a positive view of research and tend to use data from it in their decision making largely as a result of having received postgraduate training. Teachers, on the other hand, typically consider research credible only when it matches their personal experience (e.g. Zeuli 1994) and this lack of applicability and ambiguity are barriers to its use (Castle 1988). Findings from Israel (Shkedi 1998) suggest that very few teachers use research to expand their professional knowledge. They perceive it as unhelpful and overly theoretical, they lack the time to engage with it and they lack the knowledge to make sense of it.

Hemsley-Brown and Sharp also investigated whether medical practitioners make greater use of research than practitioners in education. Compared with surgeons, both GPs and teachers are less involved and less interested in research, which probably reflects the relative importance of research to advancement in their respective careers.[12] McIntyre (2005) has argued that the

---

12 Physicians typically choose sources of information that are easily accessible and applicable to a problem, whereas general practitioners typically rely on indirect sources of information about research, such as discussions with colleagues (Haug 1997).

gap between educational research and educational practice (i.e. teaching) is the result of having two contrasting *kinds* of knowledge – that needed by classroom teachers in their everyday work ('knowledge how'), which of its nature must be pragmatic and context-specific; and that generated by researchers ('knowledge that'), which prioritises the clarity and coherence of arguments and which cannot easily be translated into pedagogical knowledge. Others (e.g. Schagen and Schagen 2005) have suggested (optimistically perhaps) that the growing rich national data sets in England, coupled with developments in MLM techniques, will give teachers new opportunities to carry out objective research, though other studies suggested that there may be risks to that (e.g. Noortgate *et al.* 2005). In 2006, Cousins *et al.* took an in-depth look at research and how it relates to a school's capacity to learn. They found that decision making, policy development and problem solving are supported by data, insight and informal/ subjective knowledge. They observed a wide range of purposes for research in schools – including needs assessment, strategic planning, monitoring, program evaluation and school improvement – but that most inquiry in schools (and most data) remains informal, observational and qualitative. Rarely are results reported in a technical format or using data displays; they are usually reported verbally during staff meetings or in newsletters.

Cousins *et al.* noted a wide variety of benefits to schools with regard to their engagement with research; in particular, using it as a basis for reflection and planning, to motivate and focus staff, to inform structural decisions, to enable a better systemic analysis of issues and to develop new insights into complex social phenomena within the school context. Research can also lead to further interest in exploring issues through empirical means, but Cousins *et al.* warned that 'data-*use* can lead to data-*valuing*' and that not having well-developed data skills and research capacity can thereby become an impediment to improvement. There are also some concerns about the reliability and validity of data. Wiliam (2000; 2001a, 2001b, 2001c) found that standardised test data, which might be reliable for assessing average abilities for *groups* of children, has questionable reliability for assessing (and tracking) the attainment of *individual* children. And the reliability of standardised tests in general, and English national tests in particular, has been questioned by others (e.g. Morrison and Wylie 1999; Doyle and Godfrey 2005) who have called for England to adopt codes of standards similar to the American Educational Research Association's (AERA) Standards for Educational and Psychological Testing.

Timperley (2005) reported on the use to which data is put in New Zealand and the challenges for school leaders in developing internal systems for promoting professional learning from it. Timperley suggests that problems about teachers' expectations of pupil achievement are lessened by the availability of data, though suspicion might still remain about its usefulness. Teachers' motivation to acquire new skills depends on their perception of the data's likely benefits, but one of the ways in which data is most powerful is in changing previously held beliefs.

Research shows that there is a high correlation between the nature of the pupil intake to a school and subsequent examination results, and the majority of the difference between schooling outcomes is directly attributable to the prior attainment (and thereby to the socio-economic characteristics) of its pupils rather than to the work of the school itself. Schools can produce good outcomes simply by attracting high-attaining students, and as we saw in the previous chapter, some commentators have suggested that, in order to show that a school has improved, it should have to demonstrate an improvement in test scores that cannot be explained by a change in the nature of the intake. Multilevel modelling has the ability to help in this regard, taking advantage of the hierarchical nature of data and being computationally efficient in considering pupils, classes and schools as random effects. Classes and schools in any data set are regarded as samples of their populations, but there are disadvantages from the practitioner point of view. Teachers are happy enough to regard one year's pupil cohort as a sample of all the cohorts progressing through the school, but this is not the case for individual schools in a local authority or for class groups within a school, and teachers want to know not what schools and classes *would have* done hypothetically, but how they *actually* did. From the outset, Fitz-Gibbon (1997) has argued that it is easier to explain and interpret VA data using Ordinary Least Squares residuals than using complex multilevel models, and the latter yields the same results even when the data is hierarchical, but it is difficult using OLS residuals to allow for variations from one class or school to another. Others have expressed concerns about using pre-test and post-test scores to derive value-added measures of effectiveness because it means adopting a fairly restricted definition of 'effectiveness'. As Goldstein (1997b: 371) remarked, while 'we may be able to establish that differences exist within schools, we cannot, with any useful precision, decide how well a particular school or department is doing'. Practitioners are particularly likely to be dismayed by this since 'deciding how well a particular school or department is doing' is exactly what they want to know (Sharp 2006). While multilevel analyses that include class/teacher groups as an intermediate level (e.g. Luyten 2003) suggests that schools may be as important in explaining variance as class groups, this is only true 'in a statistical sense' and even then 'teachers must still be the mechanism by which influence is exerted' (Sharp 2006).

In 2007, Sun *et al.* developed (from 31 case studies in eight European countries) a theoretical model for 'effective school improvement' to capture the relationship between goals (student outcomes and school improvement), pressure (central control, external evaluation, market mechanisms and school accountability) and support (time, financial and human resources, local support and autonomy). Their research suggests that clear, prescriptive policy goals are important for schools in relation to pupil achievement, and using data to raise it can only be achieved if there is a strong monitoring, evaluation, feedback and reinforcement system.

Goldstein (2008) also considered the relationship between policy and research. Reflecting on whether policies in the UK were based on best research evidence insofar as the use of data was concerned, he suggests that governments *are* taking some note of it and that current official school performance tables in the UK *do* go some way to meeting the technical concerns of academics working in the field. Nevertheless, according to Goldstein, the league table culture is symptomatic of a deeper problem; namely, that the superficial precision 'associated with numerical data is used, sometimes unscrupulously, sometimes in ignorance, as a substitute for serious and well-informed debate' (Goldstein 2008: 398). On the technical side, leading researchers in mainland Europe like Kyriakides and Creemers (2008) have investigated the effect on attainment measurement of *all* the teachers that a student may have had during a given period, and found that the *long-term* effect of teachers is *underestimated* by not taking into account the effect of all teachers that students have had, while the *short-term* effect of teachers is *overestimated* (by not taking into account the effects of all teachers). In early school effectiveness research, when a school was rated effective, the assumption was that it would remain effective the following year, or would remain effective with another cohort of pupils, or across all subjects, but it is now recognised that the difference between cohorts and subjects can be considerable and the effects unstable (e.g. Scheerens and Bosker 1997). Kyriakides and Creemers argue that it is more important to identify factors that explain *differences* in effectiveness over time than search for *stability* in school/teacher effects, and that the inconsistency found in research investigating long-term effects may be attributable to the fact that most of the studies did not take into account effects of particular teachers or previous schools. Goldstein and Sammons (1997) similarly found that research on value-added in secondary schools after controlling for students' initial level *but not for their past school* may be seriously deficient. In studies on long-term school and teacher effects, all the teachers and schools that a student has had during the period are likely to have had an impact on final attainment, and for this reason should be included in any analysis. Similarly, policy-makers should not give so much emphasis to the measurement of school effectiveness at any given point *in time*, but should instead concentrate on developing mechanisms to support improvement *over time*.

A US study by Palardy (2008) investigated, using a multilevel latent growth curve, differential school effects in low, middle and high social-class schools, and whether the average socio-economic status of a student body moderates the association between student/school factors and student learning. Palardy (2008) argues that having a representative sample of a broad population is important for producing generalisable results, but that subpopulations can exist which differ substantially from the general population in ways that impact on both the school's effectiveness and the relationship between certain school factors and student outcomes. A one-size-fits-all approach which assumes that effects apply across a population of students or schools is inferior to one that examines differential effects of subgroups of students or schools. The results of the Palardy study suggest that student learning in socially disadvantaged schools is more sensitive to school factors than student learning in middle and high social-class schools where differences in learning rates are more random and unrelated to the school's variables. The findings also provide significant evidence of a differential effect regarding teacher salary: it has a significant positive association with learning in low social-class schools, but was *not* associated with learning in middle and high social-class schools. Palardy also found that at low social-class schools, monetary resources matter more – at least those that are spent on teacher salaries – suggesting that in those countries, districts or school systems where rates of pay are not fixed on a set scale, increasing salaries in schools serving disadvantaged areas can have a positive impact on learning and help to reduce the learning gap with schools serving better-off communities (probably by aiding the recruitment and retention of high-quality staff).

Shen and Cooley (2008) also considered the allocation of financial resources as one of the critical issues in using data in schools. They noted that although pupil attainment has become *the* barometer of effectiveness, data itself is not a panacea for school improvement and unless data-informed decision making is closely aligned with other systems, it will just be 'another band-aid'. Data should be a tool to connect pupil attainment with the curriculum, teaching with teacher development, and the allocation of resources to school improvement. Echoing earlier suggestions by Hemsley-Brown and Sharp (2003), Shen and Cooley note that data is routinely used as a basis for making decisions in many professions outside education, and the authors suggest that while educators often maintain that schools, students and communities are too complex to rely on data, they accept that it can help improve decision making. Shen and Cooley, like so many others before them, conclude that current attempts to use data have been overly focused on accountability and not on teaching and learning, and as a result 'the promise of data usage has not been realised'. They identify several features of data-informed decision making in the US, which include:

- an over-emphasis on achievement data based on standardised tests, at the expense of a more balance approach using a variety of data sources;
- the current emphasis on data *of* learning, rather than data *for* learning, driven by the publication of performance data for accountability purposes that magnify its political dimension;
- a lack of intersection between student achievement data and other streams of data [They use Bernhardt's (1998) concept of intersectional analysis to describe how four types of data – demographic, perceptual, student achievement and school process – should be combined to identify the cause of the problems that impact on learning.];
- a lack of technological infrastructure in schools and local authorities/ school districts to facilitate data analysis for efficient and effective use by practitioners;
- the presence of local- and school-level competition and the politics of data, which can compromise effectiveness and result in teacher education programmes failing to meet the needs of teachers.

Shen and Cooley capture much of the argument about data use when they say that the human element and human judgement cannot be divorced from the process. Data must have 'a face'. They support the argument advanced by Knapp *et al.* (2006) that data should *inform* rather than *drive* decisions, and echo many of the points made by Wohlstetter *et al.* (2008), although the latter's research sought to improve understanding of data-driven decision-making strategies initiated at system level by applying principal–agent theory to identify strengths and weaknesses. Shen and Cooley suggest that data-driven decision making involves an implicit contract between 'the centre' and schools whereby the local authority assists in the collection and analysis of data, but the responsibility for interpreting it (and developing solutions from it) is devolved to schools and individual teachers. Data-driven decision making is not a reform that can be implemented in isolation, and time and resources are needed to build a solid foundation for change. There is also a need to diminish 'information asymmetry' between schools and the centre, so that systems need to collect information from practitioners on *their* needs, strengths and weaknesses, and develop capacity-building plans around it. This 'bottom-up information flow' in and between schools recognises that those closest to students usually have the most accurate and complete information about what is needed to leverage improvement.

On a similar theme, Ozga (2009) sought to connect *systems* to the changing nature of data and its use, and to explore what these developments reveal about relations between the centre and the local in education in England. One constant feature identified by Ozga is the rapid growth of data *produced by new agencies* involved in public service provision and the related growth in the *demand* for more information. The dependence created by central regulation through data use has established patterns of interaction between the centre and schools that 'invoke the rhetoric of self-evaluation but retain key elements of managerial accountability' (Ozga 2009: 152). Ozga suggests that, at the core of the growth of data in England since the 1980s lies the linked activities of measurement of attainment and national setting of performance targets. In this brave new world, data is king and the capacity to develop data-rich networks the new order of the day. Local authorities have been reconstituted as data-distributors and 'calculating devices' to facilitate direct data-flow between schools and central government, and in the absence of local democratic accountability, the development of data use has dominated the systemic reconfiguration. As Ozga puts it, 'the local is a partner, but not in government' (p. 158).

In continental Europe, similar research on the use of data was conducted, but at the level *of the individual school* rather than the local authority or school district. Verhaeghe *et al.* (2009), for example, focuses on the design, development and implementation of a school performance feedback system (SPFS) in Flanders/Belgium and heads' perceptions of factors that promote or hinder its use. The SPFS gives schools data feedback on a confidential basis and enables teachers and principals to understand their value-added scores relative to a reference group of some 6,000 children from a representative sample of Flemish primary schools. Interestingly, no prior statistical knowledge on the part of the nearly 200 school principals was required; they were simply required to interpret the results for their school and receive individual pupil feedback. Verhaeghe *et al.* found that SPFS was only used on a limited basis in schools: sometimes reports were not read, or read and nothing done with the information; at other times, the data was deliberately not given to teachers. In a finding that echoes experience in England and elsewhere, principals found that engagement with the interpretation of data is a time-consuming and difficult activity. They confirmed that they could not interpret or understand the information correctly, which is a problematic situation for schools as the interpretation phase is crucial for developing policy. Verhaeghe *et al.* found that the interpretation phase also has a strong impact on the diagnostic phase, if indeed that phase and the subsequent 'action phase' are reached at all. Some schools feel that feedback information does not offer enough starting points for direct action and most staff claim not to have the necessary statistical know-how. Whatever statistical knowledge they do have is acquired during initial teacher training and in later professional development courses, but this does not seem to be sufficient to work with modern school performance data.

A common theme throughout the research is that head teachers and teachers are willing to search for explanations if data is up to date and presented in a way that suits their needs (which of course differs from school to school). Some are interested in pupil performance data; others in the social and emotional aspects to learning. Teachers want pupil-level feedback and material to support their pupils; policy-makers prefer aggregated information. And not unnaturally, data is most likely to be perceived as valid and reliable when it is congruent with other data and teachers' professional judgement. When this is not the case, research suggests that low performance is too easily attributable to external factors.

Part II

The present

How data is interpreted

4 The government contextual value-added model and RAISEonline

Introduction

As we have seen in the previous two chapters, over the last few decades successive UK governments have sanctioned the development of an increasingly sophisticated suite of school effectiveness measures for schools in England. As a result, schools now have access to value-added metrics that utilise advanced statistical techniques, drawing on many years of international School Effectiveness Research designed to provide robust and reliable measures of the value added by individual schools to the academic outcomes of their students. Through their publication in school PANDA reports, their incorporation into the Pupil Achievement Tracker and as part of the development of RAISEonline, school leaders and classroom teachers are actively encouraged to use these value-added measures to evaluate their institutional and personal effectiveness. Schools have become data-rich environments equipped for an era of 'intelligent accountability' (Miliband 2004). However, as we have also discussed, Miliband's phrase 'intelligent accountability' also refers to another agenda; that of using value-added measures to hold schools and teachers accountable for the educational outcomes of students. The original, raw attainment metrics – typically, the proportion of pupils crossing the particular threshold of 5+ A*–C grades at GCSE – were developed for publication in School Performance Tables, more commonly known as 'league tables', and have always been used by Ofsted for accountability purposes. As more refined and sophisticated value-added measures have been developed, these too have been adopted for accountability purposes: Ofsted uses them to inform pre-inspection hypotheses and schools are ranked by value-added scores in league tables published by the national news media.

The move away from the simple median value-added model to the complex multivariate multilevel models used today to calculate school CVA scores has generated issues around the understandability and interpretability of the measures. This chapter aims to 'lift the lid' on the CVA model in order to explore the way the model is constructed and some of the technical issues related to interpretation and understanding how CVA data can be used to inform school improvement.

Using regression modelling to generate the CVA model

As we saw in Chapter 2, the earliest value-added model was based on a national median line: the equivalent of plotting a graph of prior attainment against outcome for all students nationally and then joining the central data points for each prior attainment score. The median line therefore represents a type of average for the national data set. Regression methods use a different technique to determine the line that represents the average outcome. One of the most basic is Ordinary Least Squares regression, which essentially produces an average line that represents the best fit of all the data points.[1] The line forms a model so that the specific point for any individual student can be calculated by knowing some information about the line and the residual for the student. The residual represents the difference in score between that given by the model (the line) and that actually achieved by the student, so that in equation format:

Data = model + residual

In the KS2–KS4 CVA model, the prior attainment *independent* variable is the Average Points Score in KS2 National Curriculum tests in English, mathematics and science at age 11. The *dependent* variable is the 'capped' GCSE points score which records the best eight pass grades in GCSE examinations five years later, at age 16. Table 4.1 shows how GCSE grades and KS2 National Curriculum level outcomes are converted to point scores.

An example of how OLS regression can be used to generate a value-added model, simply adjusted for prior attainment, is shown in Figure 4.1. This model was generated using the KS2 APS and GCSE capped points score data for approximately 4,000 pupils from a single cohort and is similar to the modelling conducted in the calculation of national VA models, but on a much-reduced scale for the sake of clarity. The left side of Figure 4.1 shows the regression line which forms the value-added model and two individual data points; one with a positive residual above the line (representing a positive VA score for the pupil) and one with a negative residual below the line (representing a negative VA score). The right side of Figure 4.1 shows the individual pupil data points on which the value-added model is based. An interesting point to note is that there is much greater variation in the 'low outcome – low prior attainment' area (bottom left quadrant). This is, at least in part, due to the fact that the *lowest* points score that can be awarded in the National Curriculum tests at KS2 is 15, even for those pupils who were not awarded a level in the test (as per Table 4.1).

Conversely, in the 'high outcome – high prior attainment' area (top right), there is an *upper* limit to the amount of value that can be added in this system as only the points from the best eight GCSE passes are included in the (capped GCSE) points score used as the outcome measure for the (KS2–KS4 CVA)

---

1 Technically speaking, this line is the one that produces the smallest sum of all the squared residuals.

Table 4.1 Points scores for GCSE grades and KS2 National Curriculum tests

GCSE grade	Points score	KS2 test level	Point score
A*	58	5	33
A	52	4	27
B	46	3	21
C	40	2	15
D	34	Below level 2	15
E	28	Level not awarded	15
F	22		
G	16		

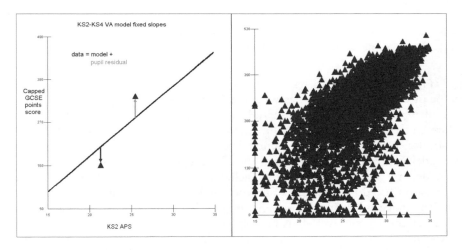

Figure 4.1 An OLS value-added model (adjusted for prior attainment only) for a single cohort of approximately 4,000 students

model. Together, these two issues give rise to what are known as 'floor' and 'ceiling' effects for data at the extremes of the range, where the model would otherwise predict outcomes outside the range possible for pupils to attain. Through recent developments of the CVA model, adjustments have been made to take account of such effects and in any case the ceiling adjustments only apply to 2 per cent of the national cohort (Ray *et al.* 2009), though there will be a disproportionate number of these students in selective schools.[2]

---

2 Schools that select on the basis of attainment/entrance tests on entry are known as 'grammar' schools in the English system.

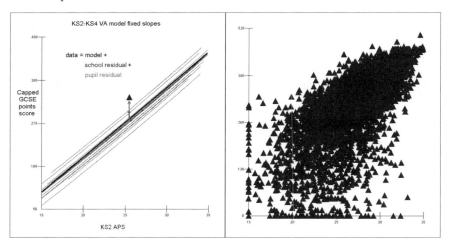

Figure 4.2 A multilevel value-added model (adjusted for prior attainment only) for a
single cohort of approximately 4,000 students

Figure 4.2 shows the results of a multilevel value-added model (adjusted
for prior attainment only, as with the OLS model). The key difference in a
multilevel model is that the analysis takes into account the fact that students
are clustered (or 'nested') within schools and are therefore likely to be more
similar to their peers in the same school than to those in other schools. The
model is divided into two parts: the 'fixed' effects, which for VA and CVA
models are the explanatory factors included in the model (i.e. the independent
variables listed in Table 2.1); and the 'random' effects, which in the case of
CVA models is restricted to the amount of variance located at the student level
and at the school level. This random part of the model results in a process
known as 'variance partitioning' and provides information on how much of the
unexplained variation in student outcomes is located *within* schools (i.e. at the
student level) and how much is located *between* schools (i.e. at the school level).
This is critical information since the proportion of the variance that is 'between
schools' is in essence 'the school effect'; in other words, the contribution
schools make to student outcomes (assuming the unexplained variance at
school level is not due to any factors not included in the model that are still
beyond the control of schools). As a result of the random part of the model,
the multilevel approach produces two sets of residuals: one for each school and
one for every student. Thus, the formula for calculating an individual student's
data is:

Data = model + school residual + pupil residual

Unlike the OLS model, the school VA score is not calculated as the mean of its
students' scores, but is calculated directly from the model itself as the school

residual. Figure 4.2 shows the regression lines for each of the schools in this analysis.[3]

Some schools contribute less data to a model than others because they have fewer students in the cohort under study. In such cases, MLM applies a process known as 'shrinkage' in order to produce more reliable estimates for the residuals (the VA scores). This process is akin to 'borrowing' data – what Kreft (1996) describes as borrowing *strength* – from *all* the schools in the model in order to calculate a better estimate of the residuals for smaller schools. The result is that *all* the school residuals are drawn closer to the overall mean, *but the effect is greatest for smaller schools*, but shrinkage can create some issues for interpreting small-school VA scores produced by the model.

The multilevel model described here is simply adjusted for prior attainment – a 'plain' VA model – but the principle for adding additional contextual variables to produce CVA scores uses the same approach. It is worth noting at this point that the model makes the very important assumption that the value added by a school is constant across the range of prior attainment, which is shown on Figure 4.2 by the fact that the school regression lines are parallel. This type of model is known as a 'random-intercept, fixed-slope' model (or simply 'fixed-slope'). It is appropriate for calculating single overall school-level VA/CVA scores. It is possible to allow the slopes of the school regression lines to *vary* across the range of prior attainment by allowing the slope estimate to be in the random rather than in the fixed part of the multilevel model. This produces what is known as a 'random-intercept, random-slope' model (or simply 'random-slope'). The lines from a random-slope model can be compared to determine whether some schools add more value than others *at different parts of the prior attainment range*, which provides evidence of differential effectiveness where it exists. (This is discussed in greater detail in Chapter 6.)

By taking into account the nested nature of students within schools, MLM produces more robust estimates of the school residuals. Figure 4.3 shows the residuals (the triangular data points) together with 95 per cent confidence intervals for each of the 20 schools in the Figure 4.2 analysis. The horizontal dotted line represents the average value-added for the whole model. Only those schools with confidence intervals which do *not* overlap the average can be considered to have a VA score *significantly* different from the average. In Figure 4.3 two schools have significantly high VA and three schools have significantly low VA. Other schools have upper or lower limits of their confidence intervals that *only just* cross the average line. For these schools, a small change in their VA scores would potentially move them into the group of

3 There are only 20 schools in this analysis, which is considered to be less than the minimum number required for the efficient calculation of a two-level model. Simulation studies conducted by Maas and Hox (2005) suggest that the efficient (unbiased) calculation of multilevel models requires more than 50 schools as Level 2 units. As the model here is used only for illustrative purposes, that is not a concern.

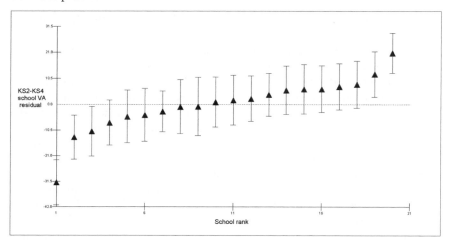

Figure 4.3 School residuals and 95 per cent confidence intervals produced by a
multilevel value-added model

schools with statistically significant scores, which suggests that the designation
of schools as having a positive or negative CVA needs to be interpreted with
care. This is also the reason why CVA scores are only released in the public
domain after schools have an opportunity to validate their data.

Although the schools are presented in rank order from lowest to highest VA,
it can be seen that the difference between many of the VA scores is very small[4]
and a number of schools, especially those at the centre of the distribution,
could easily move several places in the ranking with relatively small changes
in their residuals. Those schools towards the ends of the distribution would
require larger changes in their residuals to move up or down the order. This
situation can be likened to the spread of runners in a long distance race: those
in the middle can exchange places with little effort, but for runners at the tail
to catch runners in the pack or for runners in the pack to catch those in the
leading group, a much great expenditure of effort is required.

The confidence intervals for many of the schools overlap. Where this is the
case, it is not possible to say that their residuals are significantly different from
one another. Thus, some of the schools with VA *not* significantly different from
the average are also not significantly different from those schools which *do*
have significantly high/low scores. And smaller schools have larger confidence
intervals so it is *less* likely that their scores will be significantly different from

4 The difference between the lowest and highest school residual (VA score) shown in Figure
   4.3 is approximately 50 GCSE points. Since each GCSE grade has a value of six points, this
   is equivalent to students in the lowest performing school in this set attaining one grade less
   in all eight of their best GCSEs than those in the highest performing school.

the average or from those of other schools. These issues make interpreting the statistical significance of VA scores quite challenging and lend weight to the argument that the untrained use of VA/CVA scores to rank schools is questionable and can be misleading.[5]

A closer look at the original 2005 KS2–KS4 CVA pilot model

We concluded our look at the developments that led to CVA in Chapter 2 with the KS2–KS4 CVA pilot that was conducted in 2005. Having considered the technicalities of multilevel and OLS regression models, we are now in a position to consider the KS2–KS4 CVA pilot model in detail. A list of the factors included in this model is summarised in Table 2.1, but the list gives no indication of the contribution each factor makes to the overall CVA score or the statistical significance of each factor.

The estimates for the parameters produced by the 2005 KS2–KS4 CVA pilot model are summarised in Table 4.2. The estimates for the random components show the proportion of the variance located at the student level (*within*-school variance) and at the school level (*between*-schools variance). The variance partition coefficient is the proportion of the variance that is located at the school level; in this case only 7 per cent of the total. This proportion of the total unexplained variance located 'between schools' is the *school effect*, the value of which varies from model to model depending on the particular Key Stage and whether the model is for mainstream or special schools.[6] Table 4.3 summarises the value of the school effect for various CVA models. Inspection reveals that the school effect is largest in primary schools (i.e. between KS1 and KS2) and appears to diminish as pupils progress through secondary schools. Nevertheless, all the school effects, even those for progress during KS4 and KS5, are both statistically and practically significant.

The 'log-likelihood'[7] parameter shown on the bottom row of Table 4.2 is a

---

5 See Goldstein and Leckie (2008) and Leckie and Goldstein (2009) for a discussion of the implications of this for ranking schools on CVA league tables and using CVA to inform parental choice.

6 Special schools are schools specifically for pupils with special education needs/learning disabilities.

7 A 'log-likelihood' test is used to compare the fit of two models, one of which is nested within the other. Both models are fitted to the data and their log-likelihood recorded. The log-likelihood, D, is twice the difference in these log-likelihoods:

D = −2 [ln (likelihood for first model) − ln (likelihood for second model)]

= −2 ln [likelihood for first model/likelihood for second model]

The model with more parameters will always fit at least as well; i.e. have a greater log-likelihood. Whether it fits better and should therefore be preferred can be gauged by calculating the probability of D, which can be approximated by a chi-square distribution with (df1−df2) degrees of freedom, where df1 and df2 are the degrees of freedom of the first and second models respectively.

Table 4.2 Output of the 2005 pilot KS2–KS4 CVA multilevel model showing parameter estimates, standard errors and significance values

Explanatory factor/variable	Estimate	Std. Error	P-value
Intercept	147.81	13.20	0.00**
Prior attainment			
KS2 student APS	−8.55	0.24	0.00**
KS2 APS (using fine grades) – squared	0.45	0.00	0.00**
KS2 English points score deviation	1.94	0.07	0.00**
KS2 Maths points score deviation	−0.32	0.07	0.00**
Deprivation/SEN			
Does student have FSM?	−21.36	0.30	0.00**
Deprivation indicator – IDACI score	−65.14	0.70	0.00**
Does student have SEN – Action Plus or statement?	−64.02	0.42	0.00**
Does student have SEN – school action?	−37.91	0.35	0.00**
Mobility/Gender/Age/EAL			
Student joined other than Jul/Aug/Sep?	−27.09	0.44	0.00**
Student joined within last two years?	−74.98	0.67	0.00**
Gender – Is student female?	15.80	0.20	0.00**
Age within year	−14.20	0.31	0.00**
Language – Is English not the student's first language?	23.83	0.65	0.00**
Ethnic group/in care			
Is the student White Irish?	−0.40	1.48	0.79***
Is the student a White Irish Traveller?	−43.76	6.84	0.00**
Is the student White Gypsy/Roma?	−43.05	4.50	0.00**
Is the student White other?	14.68	0.79	0.00**
Is the student Mixed White/Black Caribbean?	−1.25	1.05	0.24***
Is the student Mixed White/Black African?	4.91	2.19	0.02*
Is the student Mixed White/Asian?	7.78	1.49	0.00**
Is the student any other Mixed ethnic group?	6.08	1.09	0.00**
Is the student Indian?	22.58	0.85	0.00**
Is the student Pakistani?	24.50	0.91	0.00**

(*continued on next page*)

Explanatory factor/variable	Estimate	Std. Error	P-value
Is the student Bangladeshi?	30.92	1.27	0.00**
Is the student any other Asian ethnic group?	27.06	1.41	0.00**
Is the student Black Caribbean?	17.13	0.84	0.00**
Is the student Black African?	34.22	1.02	0.00**
Is the student any other Black ethnic group?	8.07	1.49	0.00**
Is the student Chinese?	29.01	1.66	0.00**
Is the student any other ethnic group?	25.44	1.27	0.00**
Is the student in an unclassified ethnic group?	−11.82	0.60	0.00**
In care – Has the student ever been in care at this school?	−32.85	1.35	0.00**
School level factors (Peer Effects)			
Level of school prior attainment KS3 APS (using fine grades) for CVA	3.04	0.36	0.00**
Spread of school prior attainment std dev of KS3 APS	−5.45	0.95	0.00**
Random components			
Between school variance	351.16	9.63	
Within school variance	4444.83	8.51	
Variance partition coefficient	0.07		
Overall model parameters	Log likelihood = 6,168,797	n=548 222 pupils	

* = sig. at 95% (p<0.05); ** = sig. at 99% (p<0.01); *** = not sig. even at 95%.

Source: Data from Ray 2006: 37–8.

Table 4.3 School effects calculated for various CVA models from 2003 to 2009

Model	2003–2006	2007	2008	2009
KS1–KS2 CVA	20.1–20.8%	18.8%	19.3%	20.4%
KS2–KS3 CVA	10.7–11.4%	11.5%	–	–
KS3–KS4 CVA	6.6–7.4%	–	–	–
KS2–KS4 CVA	6.8–7.4%	7.2%	8.4%	7.8%
KS4–KS5 CVA	–	8.0%	8.1%	7.4%

Source of data: Documents accompanying the scores published in the School and College
   Achievement and Attainment Tables available at www.dcsf.gov.uk/performance
   tables/.

measure of how well the CVA model fits the data compared with the simpler,
'prior-attainment-only' model. Though it is not shown here, the 'prior-
attainment-only' model has a larger log-likelihood value than the CVA model
value [6,168,797] shown on Table 4.2. The fact that the CVA log-likelihood
figure is *smaller* confirms that the CVA model *better* fits the data because the
additional contextual factors explain more of the variance in pupil outcomes.[8]

Although the majority of variables are statistically significant in the model,
either at the 95 per cent level (* $p < 0.05$) or 99 per cent level (** $p < 0.01$), this
is expected as the rationale for including factors is that they have been shown
previously to be significant in models used in School Effectiveness Research.[9]
The two non-significant ethnicity variables (denoted by ***) were retained in
the model for political reasons (Ray 2006).

Examining the individual factors in the CVA model

Although the graphs below refer to an earlier (2003) KS2–KS4 CVA model
produced retrospectively, they illustrate how individual factors contribute to
the CVA score for a pupil.

The chart and the equation in Figure 4.4 show that prior attainment at KS2
is a major explanatory factor in the KS2–KS4 CVA model. The 2005 KS2–KS4
CVA pilot model used KS2 average points score and subject deviations for

---

8 This extra explanatory power was also demonstrated by inspecting the r^2 values for OLS
   versions of both the VA and CVA models (Ray 2006), which show that the prior-attainment-
   only model explains 49 per cent of the variance in student capped GCSE outcomes, whereas
   the CVA model explains 57 per cent.
9 The p-value is the probability of obtaining a test statistic at least as extreme as the one that
   was actually observed, assuming that the null hypothesis is true. The *lower* the p-value, the
   less likely the result, and assuming the null hypothesis, the *more* significant the result. One
   rejects a null hypothesis if the p-value is less than 0.05 (say), corresponding to a 5 per cent
   chance of an outcome at least that extreme, given the null hypothesis.

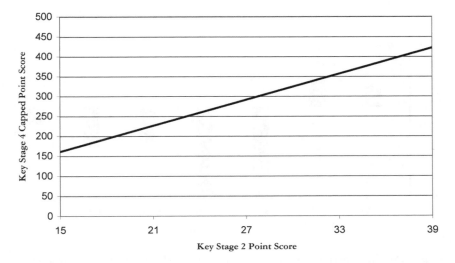

Figure 4.4 The contribution of prior attainment to KS2–KS4 CVA (source: Evans 2005)

English and mathematics, whereas the 2003 model described in Figure 4.4 uses individual subject point scores, though in reality these approaches are mathematically equivalent. The quadratic term ($KS2_{APS}^2$) is included to adjust for the fact that the relationship between KS2 APS and GCSE capped points score is not linear. It is not surprising to note that English is the major contributory factor in prior attainment.

Figure 4.5 shows the contribution that a number of pupil-level variables make to the CVA model. The estimates show that girls achieve higher outcomes than boys; approximately a grade higher overall in each of three subjects in terms of the capped (best eight) GCSE points score. Speaking English as an additional language (EAL) is similarly associated with an increase in progress. The result of these adjustments in the model means that any girl or pupil who speaks English as an additional language who did not make this additional progress would have a negative residual, showing they had made lower-than-average progress and thus would have a lower-than-average CVA score.

Special educational need is considered at two levels: those with the highest level of SEN average just over a grade lower in all eight GCSEs, whereas those with the lower level of SEN score just under a grade lower (on average) in all eight subjects. Entering late to the school year or to the Key Stage (mobility) or being eligible for free school meals results in on average just under half a grade less progress in each of the eight GCSEs. Finally, those who were older in the school year make slightly *less* progress in their GCSE outcomes than their younger peers with the same prior attainment. Thus, any of these pupils who make better progress than these factors suggest they should would have a positive residual and therefore a higher-than-average CVA score. In the 2005 KS2–KS4 CVA pilot and subsequent CVA models, the Income Deprivation

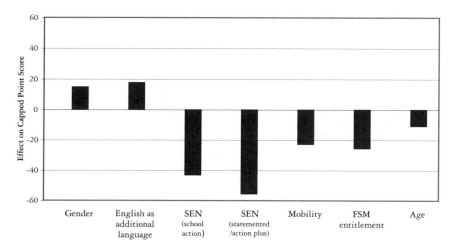

Figure 4.5 The contribution of a number of pupil-level contextual variables to KS2–KS4 CVA (source: Evans 2005)

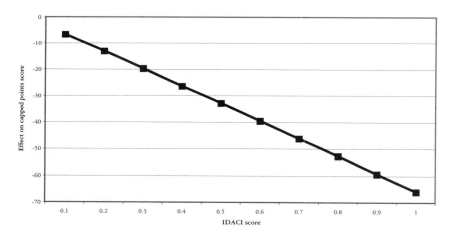

Figure 4.6 The effect of the Income Deprivation Affecting Children Index (IDACI) score on KS2–KS4 CVA

Affecting Children Index was also included as a contextual variable related to socio-economic status at the pupil level. The effect of IDACI score on KS2–KS4 CVA is shown in Figure 4.6.[10]

---

10 Based on the value of the coefficient estimate for IDACI score in the 2006 KS2-KS4 CVA model. (Data source: www.education.gov.uk/performancetables/pilotks2_06/24Jan07CVA PupilCalcKS2-4-06.xls)

Figure 4.7 shows the effect of a pupil's ethnicity in the KS2–KS4 CVA model. Here, White British is the reference group (effect equal to zero) against which the progress of pupils with others ethnicities is evaluated. The average progress for most other ethnicities is higher than progress for those in the reference category, so a pupil from one of these ethnicities making similar progress to their White British counterparts (if similar in all other respects) would have a negative CVA score, all other factors being equal.

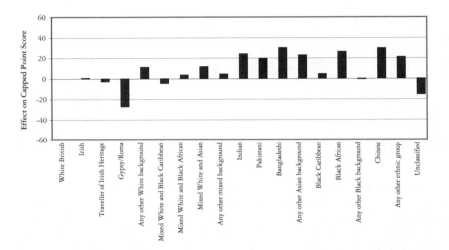

Figure 4.7 The contribution of a pupil's ethnicity to KS2–KS4 CVA (source: Evans 2005)

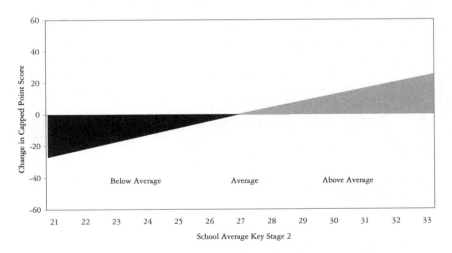

Figure 4.8 The contribution of the cohort's mean prior attainment to KS2-KS4 CVA (source: Evans 2005)

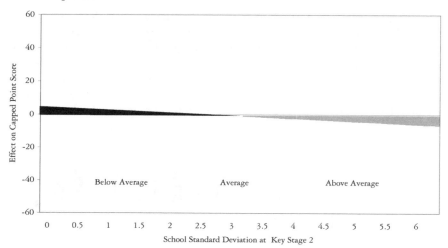

Figure 4.9 The contribution of the cohort's spread of prior attainment to KS2–KS4 CVA (source: Evans 2005)

Figures 4.8 and 4.9 illustrate the peer effects of the *mean* and *spread* of prior attainment in each school. High average prior attainment in the cohort is associated with higher outcomes at GCSE, as is a narrower spread of prior attainment around the mean (as measured by standard deviation). These peer measures only include pupils in the cohort under study and *not* all those in the school at the time.

Differences and developments in the CVA models

In Chapter 2 we saw that the KS2–KS4 CVA model was the forerunner of a suite of CVA models to evaluate progress across all Key Stages: KS1–KS2, KS2–KS3, KS3–KS4 and KS4–KS5.[11] Although the resulting data from these models has always been made available to schools for improvement purposes, some of the models have also been used (as with the KS2–KS4 CVA model) to provide accountability measures; especially the KS1–KS2 CVA data, to evaluate the progress of pupils in primary schools.

The other CVA models are very similar to the KS2–KS4 CVA pilot model described in Table 4.2. The key differences are:

- KS1–KS2 CVA: Neither of the peer effects of mean and spread of prior attainment are included.

---

11 KS1–KS2 covers the ages 6–11, KS2–KS3 ages 11–14, KS3–KS4 ages 14–16 and KS4–KS5 ages 16–18.

- KS4–KS5 CVA: This progress measure (for the post compulsory phase of education) covers a very wide range of outcome qualifications and deviates most from the other models. The prior attainment factors are based on average GCSE point score, but include both a quadratic and a cubic term. They also contain terms related specifically to prior attainment in English and mathematics GCSE, the type of qualifications studied in KS5 and other factors linked to number of subjects studied ('volume') at GCSE, and the proportion of A and A* grades obtained. The only contextual variables the model has in common with the other CVA models are gender and mean prior attainment at the school level as a peer effect. In common with some of the other CVA models, there are interaction terms included to account for the fact that prior attainment is correlated with (i.e. is not independent of) some of the other variables in the model, together with a range of interaction terms between the average KS4 points prior attainment terms and the factors for volume of study, type of qualification and gender. Since 2009, adjustments have also been made for ceiling and floor effects, as per the KS2–KS4 CVA model.[12]
- CVA models for special schools: There are corresponding models to evaluate the progress of pupils educated in special schools, and these produce pupil- and school-level CVA scores. The models mirror their counterparts for the same Key Stage transition in mainstream schools, but are somewhat simpler in construction in that they do not include terms for the pupil's SEN level; nor do they include interaction terms between FSM entitlement and ethnicity.

Over time a number of refinements have been made to the models. As will be discussed in greater detail in the next chapter, eligibility to free school meals and ethnicity are not independent of one another, but interact. In 2006, terms were introduced to all the CVA models (except the KS1–KS2 model)[13] in order to capture this interaction/association. Adjustments for ceiling and floor effects were also added to KS2–KS3, KS3–KS4 and KS2–KS4 CVA models, which were further refined in 2008.[14]

---

12 For more details of the KS4–5 CVA model see DCSF (2009), *Guide To Key Stage 4 To 5 Value Added 2009 Model*, www.dcsf.gov.uk/performancetables/16to18_09/VA_Guide_2009v20.doc
13 Presumably the interaction terms were not statistically significant in the KS1–KS2 CVA model and so were not retained.
14 It has already been noted that the floor effect is due (at least in part) to the fact that there is a floor on the lowest points score that can be obtained in National Curriculum tests (see Table 4.1). The ceiling effect is due to the limit imposed on the highest score possible for the outcome variable, either through the maximum level that can be achieved in National Curriculum tests or the capping effect of using the best eight GCSE grades. The methodology introduced in 2006 to correct for these effects overwrote the 'predictions' given at the extremes of the model with the actual values observed for students grouped by

A major refinement in 2009 was the introduction of 'bonus points' to the KS2–KS4 CVA model for attainment in English and mathematics. The purpose of this change was arguably more for accountability purposes than to inform school improvement, and was designed to bring KS2–KS4 CVA into line with a shift (in 2006) in the raw attainment threshold measure, from the percentage of pupils obtaining 5+ A*–C grades to the percentage of pupils obtaining 5+ A*–C grades *including English and mathematics*. In the new KS2–KS4 CVAEM model, the appropriate points are added on, as per Table 4.1, for pupils' English and mathematics scores. Thus the new outcome (dependent variable) for the model has a maximum score equivalent to ten GCSE subjects (a maximum of 580 points) rather than eight (a maximum of 464 points). For the majority of pupils, English and mathematics will be counted twice in the new model since these subjects are likely to be among their 'best eight' and will therefore make up between them 40 per cent of the total GCSE points score.

These refinements, while improving the model by increasing overall explanatory power and by dealing with issues at the extremes, make the comparison of CVA results year-on-year more problematical than they would otherwise be. The full effect of the development of CVAEM is as yet unclear. There is evidence to suggest – from an analysis (ASCL 2009) of the new KS2–KS4 CVAEM scores from the 2008 pilot compared with the published 2008 KS2–KS4 CVA scores using the old methodology – that schools which maintained a similar curriculum model to that used in previous years saw an appreciable *drop* in their CVA scores, even if pupil attainment was in line with that of pupils from previous years. The effect of the new model also appears to be differentially impacting on schools that have pupils with low mean prior attainment at the end of KS2.

Issues around data hierarchy and shrinkage

The standard approach developed by School Effectiveness Research in recent decades acknowledges the hierarchical nature of pupil data and MLM allows for this clustering effect by dividing the variation in the data into a school-level residual and a pupil-level residual. Unlike the OLS method, it offers a more complex set of options to take into account the fact that pupils are grouped by school. One of the advantages of MLM with hierarchical data is that it produces more robust estimates of the standard errors for factors in the model, whereas

---

prediction 'bins'. This was modified in 2008 by applying the mathematical function *arctan* to the predicted student scores generated by the model, which essentially produces the same result as the earlier correction but uses a smooth curve to adjust scores at the extremes rather than the step approach that occurs when student predictions are grouped into discrete bins. For more details see www.dcsf.gov.uk/performancetables/schools_08/documents.shtml, and www.dcsf.gov.uk/performancetables/16to18_09/VA_Guide_2009v20.doc

OLS tends to *underestimate* them.[15] This means that the judgement of whether a factor is statistically significant (at the 95 per cent level, say) is more accurate, and while such judgements of significance are the bread and butter of substantive School Effectiveness Research, it is not clear how such judgements play a role in deciding the method of choice in calculating CVA scores, particularly when other influences play a major role in deciding whether factors are included or excluded from the model, regardless of their statistical significance.

Some recent research on the effect of introducing the class/teacher group as a level in MLM, either as an intermediate level between student and school or as the higher level itself, has generated some important insights into the claim that 'the school' is not the most appropriate level to adjust for clustering in the data. Sharp (2006), for example, researched the progress of pupils during the first year of formal schooling in Edinburgh Primary schools. The study, involving a data set of baseline and end-of-year progress scores in numeracy and literacy, gave Sharp the opportunity to investigate some key methodological issues associated with the statistical models used to calculate value-added progress measures. Sharp constructed a *three-level* MLM with pupils nested within classes nested within schools, but because approximately half the schools had only one class, he conflated the upper two levels (classes and schools) for those schools, and produced two-level multilevel models with pupils nested within schools and pupils nested within classes. Sharp then compared the residuals calculated in these analyses with those produced by an OLS regression model[16] so that issues related to the inclusion of an intermediate level (the class), a potential source of useful information for school improvement purposes, could be explored together with issues surrounding the interpretation of OLS versus MLM residuals.[17] Sharp (2006) produced a multilevel model in which both intercepts and slopes were allowed to vary (a random-slope model which reveals whether schools are differentially effective across the range of prior attainment) and found that the slope residuals *were* significant (at the 95 per cent level) for numeracy, but were *not* significant for literacy. Although statistically

---

15 Since OLS techniques underestimate the standard errors, effects will be judged to be significant when this is not the case; in other words, OLS increases the chance of making 'Type I errors'. [A Type I error is a false positive (i.e. it rejects the null hypothesis when the null hypothesis is true); a Type II error is a false negative (i.e. it accepts the null hypothesis when it is false)]. MLM partitions the variance between the different levels in the data hierarchy allowing inferences to be drawn at the level of analysis (class or school) rather than analysing at the student level and drawing conclusions from aggregated values calculated at student level. However, these benefits need to be weighed up alongside the competing desirables of comprehensibility and interpretability for model outputs.

16 In which class- and school-level residuals are calculated as a mean of the student residuals contained within the level; a form of Residual Gain Analysis.

17 The end-of-year progress scores for literacy demonstrated a pronounced skew towards the upper end of the range so they were adjusted to be normally distributed with a mean of zero and a variance of unity.

significant in the case of numeracy, the differences between the school slopes were small in comparison to the intercept differences in the fixed-slope model, so Sharp decided to restrict the main models so that they had fixed slopes, which, as described earlier, is the current procedure used by the DfE for the calculation of CVA residuals. Essentially, Sharp found that *school* effects were greater than *class* effects; in other words, that the variation *between schools* was greater than the variation between classes *within* schools.[18]

This finding is in contrast to the research summary produced some years earlier by Luyten (2003) who concluded that year-group (teacher/class/grade) effects are *larger* than school effects, though actually Luyten was quite reserved in his conclusions, especially with regard to studies involving parallel classes (where confounders such as age, subject and curriculum content are controlled).[19] Sharp's results also contrast with his own earlier research on literacy progress (Sharp and Croxford 2003) which found that class effects were slightly *greater* than school effects and that some schools had widely differing class-level residuals, suggesting that 'averagely' performing schools are not necessarily made up of 'averagely' performing classes. A one-way analysis of variance (ANOVA) on the class-level residuals grouped at the school level showed the within-school variance to be twice that of the between-school variance, a reverse of the effect shown in the later Sharp (2006) study.

Clearly, there remains more work to be done to gather evidence on the effect of teachers/classes compared to the school effect, and the benefit of adding this intermediate level into models of school effectiveness. With data produced from two-level models, its publication to aid parental choice is undermined by the fact that parents have no control over the allocation of teachers to classes. Three-level models have the power to assist schools in the process of improvement, but there is need for a range of qualitative and quantitative evidence to inform professional judgements. In the early years of primary schooling, it is probably fair to say that classes can be equated with teachers on the assumption that a single class spends a substantial amount of time together as a unified group being taught by a single teacher. Of course, this will not be the case in every school – there may be some two-form entry primary schools (say) where teachers team-teach both classes – but it is *generally* the case. However, in secondary schools, the concept of the class becomes far more fluid as subject teaching is delivered by specialist teachers and children are placed in a variety of ability-groupings for different subjects and rarely stay as a unified group throughout the school day. In this latter case, the value of introducing an intermediate 'class' level to the models is lessened, but ignoring 'third

18 Nearly twice as much for numeracy and almost three times for literacy.
19 It is also interesting to note that Luyten was only able to identify 16 school effectiveness studies (out of hundreds carried out in the period 1987–2001) investigating the differences between school effects and those at an intermediate level between the school and the student (2003: 37).

levels' in MLM is a judgement that needs to be supported by further research, possibly employing more advanced techniques such as multiple-membership and cross-classified multilevel models (cf. Fielding and Goldstein 2006), which allow for the fact that pupils are members of *a number of* classes within a school and can change classes over the period under study.

Another issue is that of the interpretation of MLM school-residuals compared to those generated by taking a mean of OLS student-residuals by residual gain analysis (RGA). Even where schools are found to have more of an effect than classes, the omission of the intermediate level from the model has a significant impact on the size of the variance between schools. There is also an effect, albeit smaller, on the variance between students (e.g. Opdenakker and Van Damme 2000). One of the important knock-on effects of the change in variance values is a change in the number of schools judged to be significantly above or significantly below the mean and therefore judged as high- or low-performing schools.[20] In Sharp's (2006) research, for example, using a two-level MLM (students nested within schools), the number of schools significantly below the mean was 31 (out of 99) with 33 schools above the mean, but when 'class group' was introduced as an intermediate (third) level this reduced to just five schools below the mean and eight schools above. Of course, it is clear that schools are 'responsible' for the variation at class level as well as at the level of the school, but what is striking from Sharp's research (and that of others) is that, for a study in which the school was seen to have a greater effect than the class, when the class was accounted for as a level in the model, it became much harder to differentiate between schools. This certainly calls into question the ability of school-level residuals (of any kind) to inform parental choice. Not only do they fail to capture the differential effectiveness of schools across the prior ability range, between various subgroups of students or across subjects, they also 'hide' the variation between classes/teachers. It may be that schools are more complex than any two-level, random intercept, contextually adjusted value-added model can capture, and any attempt to capture more 'reality' would require even more sophisticated models or (at the very least) multiple measures for each school, which does not serve well the aim of interpretability for public or professional audiences.

We have already seen how (unlike OLS) MLM 'shrinks' the value-added estimates for smaller schools towards the mean; that is to say, the CVA score is reduced to a percentage of its 'raw' size, closer to the mean. OLS also has a problem dealing with small cohorts so that a small school's VA score can only be given with a wide confidence interval. With MLM, the estimate is calculated

20 This is partly due to the fact that the confidence intervals for school VA scores from MLMs are calculated using the variance parameters for the within-school and the between-school variance. The addition of an intermediate level in the model affects the proportion of variance at each level.

from both pupils and the national data, which is then used to modify the estimate when robust information on the school is limited because of its size. The resulting shrunken CVA scores generated by the MLM thus have narrower confidence intervals. Shrinkage also prevents schools at the extremes – those with residuals which suggest that they are very effective or very ineffective – from registering a very high or a very low CVA score. Supporters of MLM say that this is not problematic because the raw residuals for small schools are not known to be good estimates of effectiveness from one year to the next, but Fitz-Gibbon (1991), who advised against the use of MLM, quotes Raudenbush, one of the early developers of MLM in the field of school effectiveness, as saying that shrinkage causes school effectiveness scores to be pulled 'in the socially expected direction, demonstrating a kind of statistical self-fulfilling prophecy' (Fitz-Gibbon 1991: 19).

Fitz-Gibbon (1991) also made an interesting distinction in delineating hierarchy in data sets; namely, that students are nested within departments rather than within schools. In her study, the largest differences were observed between departments with small numbers of students. Fitz-Gibbon attributes this to the effect of shrinkage, which she argues makes benchmarking between departments more difficult with departments having to restrict their comparisons not just to those with similar characteristics but also to those of a similar size; and it makes year-on-year comparisons more difficult due to the fluctuations in uptake from year to year. Supporters of MLM shrinkage argue that this is exactly the benefit; that by borrowing strength from a whole data set, such variations are accounted for in the analysis.

Of course, *variability* in sample size is less of an issue for *longitudinal* studies as school admission numbers tend to remain relatively stable over time, but *small* sample size *is* an issue when making comparisons between schools (due to their large confidence intervals). This affects all types of value-added residual, but shrinkage compounds the issue for CVA scores calculated using MLM, making it possible for schools with the same raw (unshrunken) residual to have different CVA scores, and making it difficult for small schools to achieve significantly high CVA. In England, the issue of sample size is particularly acute for primary schools, a number of which, particularly in rural areas, have very small numbers of students in each year group. Current DfE practice is to exclude from their performance tables any school with ten or fewer students in the cohort under study (and those where less than 50 per cent of students can be matched to the data), but commentators have suggested that this figure (of ten) is too low. Fitz-Gibbon herself (1997) suggests 30 as the minimum cohort size, while others (e.g. Tymms and Dean 2004) have set the minimum at 50. The trade-off, as Ray (2006: 34) put it, is 'between statistical reliability and the desire to include data on as many schools as possible'.

The issue of sample size becomes acute for all schools when CVA scores are 'sliced and diced' down to pupil subgroups, such as those with SEN or those from a specific ethnic background. An example of this is given in Table 4.4 – a sample output from RAISEonline – to illustrate the confusing effect shrinkage

Table 4.4 An extract from a sample RAISEonline output to illustrate the potentially confusing effects of applying shrinkage to multilevel residuals

	Number of pupils	*KS2–KS3 CVA*
All pupils	243	97.9
Gender		
Girls	121	97.9
Boys	122	98.0
Free school meals		
Non-FSM	223	98.0
FSM	20	98.1

Source of data: Thomson 2007.

can have on sub-school level analyses of CVA scores. The KS2–KS3 CVA score for all pupils in the school (n=243) is given as 97.9. When the scores for pupils with FSM entitlement (n=20) and those *without* FSM entitlement (n=223) are examined (98.1 and 98.0 respectively), both scores are above the score *for all* pupils! This is not a 'rounding issue' but rather the differential effect of shrinkage to pupil groups of different sample size: the application of shrinkage has pulled all three residuals closer to the mean, *but it has affected the smaller residuals more*. It is critically important for teachers to be briefed carefully on issues like this – regarding the application of shrinkage – before they use it for self-evaluation and school improvement, because it is counter-intuitive for most, who might have expected the scores to be distributed around the mean (i.e. one value to be above and the other to be below the overall value of 97.9).

Thomson (2007: 76) commented that such models were 'not designed to analyse the performance of pupil groups' because they 'give rise to unreliable scores', and he recommends using Fischer Family Trust (FFT) data instead (the subject of the next chapter). Even in large secondary schools the number of pupils in subgroups can be small. RAISEonline provides the facility to calculate CVA scores for subgroups regardless of sample size, but, not surprisingly, small groups have much larger confidence intervals and the application of the shrinkage factor makes it unlikely that extreme scores will be reported. Therefore, the value of such information for school self-evaluation is limited and needs to be interpreted with caution.

5 The Fischer Family Trust models

Introduction: origins of the Fischer Family Trust and its performance data project

The Fischer Family Trust (FFT) was set up by Mike Fischer, an Oxford graduate and co-founder of Research Machines Ltd, the information and communication technology company. Initially, FFT focused on three projects: one aimed at improving literacy levels in the early years of primary education; one focused on raising the performance of schools in North Islington; and a third related to the provision of (according to Fischer) 'the best possible performance data' to schools and local authorities. Since then the trust has expanded its school improvement focus to include other literacy projects and an analysis of the impact of ICT on learning.[1]

The FFT performance data project began in 2000 and within a year it was supplying analyses to 55 local authorities. By 2004, the project had extended to include all local authorities in England and Wales. The data for all FFT analyses is provided by the DfE (or for Wales, the Welsh Assembly). The project aims to:

> provide analyses and data which help local authorities and schools to make more effective use of pupil performance data. Using a database which now contains performance information on over 10 million pupils in England and Wales we have developed a range of analyses to support the processes of self-evaluation and target-setting.
>
> (FFT 2007a: online)

These twin purposes of self-evaluation and target setting lie at the heart of the metrics developed by FFT, and it is important to hold these in mind when

---

1 Details of which can be found on the company website, www.fischertrust.org. The performance data project has been managed from the start by Mike Treadaway, a former ICT teacher and local authority adviser for South Glamorgan and for the Vale of Glamorgan in Wales. His work for the local authority informed the early development of the measures that lie at the heart of the FFT models.

working through the plethora of training and guidance materials produced by the Trust and in seeking to understand its choice of statistical methods. The measures are *not* designed to be public-consumption indicators of school performance in the same way as the DfE VA and CVA measures. Instead, they are intended to be a tool to inform self-evaluation and school improvement, and as an aid to setting aspirational academic targets at both student and school level. FFT data has always been made available to schools (through local authorities), but is not put into the public domain.

The analyses produced by FFT are held in high regard by schools and its data is widely perceived to be 'versatile, reliable and accurate' (Halsey *et al.* 2005: 17). A survey conducted by the National Foundation for Educational Research on Ofsted's *New Relationship with Schools* found that FFT was the most highly regarded external source of data: 69 per cent gave it the highest rank of 'very helpful' for the purpose of self-evaluation. Only *internally produced* school data – lesson observations and departmental reviews – scored higher. By contrast, the next highest scoring external sources – local authority produced data and PANDA reports – were scored as 'very helpful' by only 38 per cent of respondent schools (Halsey *et al.* 2005).

FFT 'Pupil Estimates' models

FFT produces estimates of pupil attainment for the national tests at the end of KS2 at age 9, for KS3 at age 13 and for KS4 (i.e. GCSE) at age 16. These estimates are calculated for every pupil on roll in local authority schools[2] using two multivariate regression models applied to the attainment of the previous year's pupils.

Targets, predictions and estimates

FFT representatives go to great lengths to explain that the predictive aspect of their models produces *estimates* of pupil attainment, not targets or predictions. These estimates, they say, should always be used in conjunction with the local professional knowledge of teachers to inform the process of predicting pupil potential and moving from that to target setting for individual pupils, departments and schools, and for internal accountability to governors and the local authority. FFT rationalises the differences as follows:

Estimate + Professional Knowledge → Prediction

Prediction + Challenge → Target

---

2 The data is provided for state-maintained schools in England and Wales. It is not available for independent schools in England and Wales, or for schools in Scotland or Northern Ireland.

The FFT approach to target setting is based on the triangulation of FFT estimates with other external sources of data – such as that from Cognitive Ability Tests[3] and MidYIS/Yellis[4] – and with teachers' professional judgement. Delegates at FFT training sessions are urged to use the calculated estimates *as an aid* to inform planning and delivery of lessons, identifying pupils who need extra support, differentiating lesson content for teaching groups, assessing the progress made by individual pupils or teaching groups against expectations, and highlighting potential underachievement while there is time to take remedial action. The language is very much that of development and improvement at all organisational levels of a school, but with a particular focus on pupils and classrooms.

Statistical models used to calculate FFT estimates

Early analysis of pupil attainment data conducted by the Trust revealed a number of pupil- and school-level factors that were associated with pupil attainment in National Curriculum tests and GCSE examinations and these have been incorporated into the FFT predictive statistical models. The conclusions drawn for these analyses hold little surprise for those familiar with the development of VA measures or with school effectiveness literature generally:

- Pupil-level factors: prior attainment based on attainment in NC tests and teacher assessments at the end of the previous Key Stage; gender; and age within the cohort (children born earlier in the school year make better progress than their younger peers).
- School context factors: socio-economic status (pupils from disadvantaged backgrounds generally make less progress than their more advantaged peers); and peer attainment effects (the level and the spread of prior attainment in a particular cohort is associated with level of attainment).

As a result of these findings, FFT developed two models for generating pupil estimates: a *PA model* (Prior Attainment) employing only pupil-level factors

---

3 Cognitive Ability Tests are widely used in UK schools. The most popular, produced by *GL Assessment* (formally *nferNelson*), consist of a battery of assessment items, which are not curriculum-specific but which form tests of verbal, non-verbal and quantitative skills. The results are usually adjusted for age and standardised. (For more details, see: http://shop. gl-assessment.co.uk/home.php?cat=310)

4 The Middle Years Information System (MidYIS) and Year Eleven Information System (Yellis) are predictive tools designed to help set appropriate academic targets for students at the end of KS3 (MidYIS) and GCSE (Yellis). Like ALIS, they are produced by the Curriculum, Evaluation and Management Centre (CEM) at the University of Durham. (For more details see www.cemcentre.org/)

(as above); and an *SE model* (Socio-Economic) incorporating both pupil- and school-level factors (as above). Neither model produces a pure 'prior attainment *only*' estimate of pupil potential: the PA model is contextualised by the addition of the pupil-level factors of gender and age; and the SE model includes the three pupil-level factors of the PA model *plus* the school context factors of mean socio-economic status (SES) and peer attainment.

Tables 5.1 and 5.2 give examples of the data provided in typical FFT estimates reports. Table 5.1 shows KS2 estimates for three pupils ('A', 'B' and 'C') based on the SE model. The estimates include: Average Points Scores[5] for combined attainment in the three core subjects (English, mathematics and science); an estimated National Curriculum level for each subject expressed as a fine-grade decimalised figure; and the percentage probabilities of achieving the national attainment expectation (Levels 4 or above at KS2) and also *above* the national expectation (Level 5 or above at KS2). It is important to reiterate that these estimates are derived from the performance of similar pupils with similar prior attainment and context in the previous year.

Scanning across the row of estimates for pupil A – the top row – it is possible to see that 'A' is estimated to achieve an APS of 25.9, and individual fine-grade estimates for each of the three core subjects ranging from 4.2 to 4.6. The remaining columns [5–12] show the percentage probability of 'A' attaining 'Level 4 or above' and 'Level 5 or above'. The columns entitled 'Core' [5 and 9] relate to the probability of attaining that level threshold *in all three subjects* and so represents a greater challenge than reaching the same level in each single subject. Pupil B has higher estimates across the range of outcomes. This may be due to a higher prior attainment at the end of KS1 or to some other pupil-level contextual factor in the SE model: Pupil B might be *a girl*, for example, as girls achieve higher outcomes than boys, or be *older in the year* since older pupils tend to do better than their younger counterparts. Pupil C has lower estimates than 'A' or 'B', the lowest being for English [column 2; 3.3], due most likely to low prior attainment in that subject at the end of KS1, which is also borne out by the low percentage probability [column 6; 12 per cent] of attaining Level 4 in English.

Table 5.2 shows GCSE estimates for four pupils ('W', 'X', 'Y' and 'Z') based on the SE model. These include: estimates of capped (i.e. best eight subjects)

---

5   As explained in Chapter 2, APS is a system used to quantify attainment in National Curriculum (NC) assessments in the 'core' subjects of reading, writing and mathematics at KS1, and English, mathematics and science at KS2 and KS3. The points score for a subject is calculated from the formula 6L+3 (where L = the NC level in that subject). The average of the three subject scores is then calculated to produce the APS. The national expectation is that it takes more than a year for students to progress from one NC level to the next so the points score system allows progress within a level to be quantified.

Table 5.1 Pupil Estimates for three Year 6 pupils based on their KS test performance and statutory Teacher Assessments in Year 2 (end of KS1)

SE model

Pupil name	KS2 Average Points Score	Estimates → NC (fine) grade			Probability of attaining benchmark Level 4 or above				Probability of attaining benchmark Level 5 or above			
		Eng	*Ma*	*Sc*	*Core*	*Eng*	*Ma*	*Sc*	*Core*	*Eng*	*Ma*	*Sc*
A	25.9	4.4	4.2	4.6	57%	87%	74%	91%	1%	9%	5%	19%
B	27.8	4.8	4.6	4.8	83%	96%	90 %	97%	8%	33%	20%	39%
C	21.4	3.3	3.5	4.0	5%	12%	25%	61%	1%	1%	1%	2%

Source: www.fischertrust.org

Table 5.2 Pupil Estimates for four Year 11 pupils based on their KS test performance and statutory Teacher Assessments in Year 6 (end of KS2) and Year 9 (end of KS3)

SE model

Estimates →

Pupil name	Capped Points		Mean points		Number A*–C pass		Probability 5+A*–C(EM)		Probability 5+A*–C		Probability 5+A*–G		Probability 5+A*–G (EM)	
	Y6	Y9	Y6	Y9	Y6	Y9	Y6	Y9	Y6	Y9	Y6	Y9	Y6	Y9
W	387	394	46.1	46.8	9.4	9.8	96%	99%	98%	99%	99%	99%	99%	99%
X	394	380	47.5	44.7	9.8	9.4	95%	95%	98%	99%	99%	99%	99%	99%
Y	310	240	37.0	29.3	6.4	3.5	54%	7%	79%	35%	99%	97%	98%	96%
Z	366	368	43.3	41.2	8.6	8.2	86%	82%	95%	97%	99%	99%	99%	99%

Source: www.fischertrust.org

scores;[6] an estimate of the number of GCSE passes at grades A* to C [columns 5 and 6]; percentage probabilities of achieving various national attainment benchmarks (five or more A*–C grades, both with [columns 7 and 8] and without [columns 9 and 10] English and mathematics, and five or more A*–G grades with [columns 13 and 14] and without [columns 11 and 12] English and mathematics). Once again, these are based on the performance of similar pupils with similar prior attainment during the previous year. The estimates are listed in pairs based on their KS test performance and Teacher Assessments in Year 6 (end of KS2) and Year 9 (end of KS3) in English, mathematics and science.[7] FFT considers it important to use KS3 data to recalculate the GCSE estimates and urges schools to use both sets of estimates to inform expectations of pupil potential when setting targets at the pupil and school level.

Scanning across the row of estimates for pupil W, it is possible to see that the estimates for this pupil based on Year 9 prior attainment are higher than those based on Year 6 prior attainment. This is because 'W' has made greater than expected progress across KS3 and so boosted his/her outcomes expected by the end of KS4. The estimated capped points score for 'W' of 394 [column 2] is equivalent to approximately four A grades and four B grades in W's best-eight GCSEs (using the points scoring system described in Table 4.1). This matches the estimates for mean points score [columns 3 and 4], which are slightly higher than the B grade score of 46 points. The estimate number of A*–C passes [columns 5 and 6] are well above '5' [9.4 and 9.8] and so it is no surprise to see that the probabilities for gaining 5 + A*–C grades [columns 7–14] are all well over 90 per cent.

Pupil X on the other hand has slightly lower estimates based on his Year 9 prior attainment, since 'X' made slightly lower than expected progress across KS3. Nevertheless, Pupil X still has very high probabilities for gaining the 5 + A*–C grades to cross national expectation thresholds, though if the trends in less-than-expected progress shown by Pupil X *continue into KS4*, these outcomes may not be so secure.

Pupil Y has lower estimates than his/her peers, due predominantly to lower prior attainment. 'Y' also made substantially lower than expected progress

---

6 The GCSE points score system allows a quasi-continuous scale to be produced from the ordinal scale of reported GCSE grades A* to G. The national qualifications framework at age 16 in England and Wales includes many non-GCSE examinations, and these are assigned a GCSE points score equivalence, so that *overall* attainment at age 16 can be quantified. An A* grade is worth 58 points, an A grade worth 52 points and so on down to a G grade worth 16 points. The *capped* points score is the total points derived from a student's best eight GCSE results.

7 Since 'end of KS3' NC Tests at age 14 have been abolished, the Year 9 estimates in future will be based solely on the Teacher Assessments in English, mathematics and science that at present are submitted by all secondary schools in England. FFT is at pains to say that it continues to be committed to the use of Teacher Assessments in its estimate and value-added models.

across KS3 and so his/her estimates based on Year 9 prior attainment are considerably lower than those based on prior attainment in Year 6. This highlights the importance of basing judgements on *all* available information and not just using old data. The capped points score estimate for Pupil Y based on Year 6 (KS2) prior attainment [column 1; 310] would correspond to a mix of (say) C and D grades in pupil Y's best eight GCSEs. The Year 9 (KS3) estimate [column 2; 240] shows this falling to a mix of (say) D and E grades. Based on Year 6 prior attainment, Pupil Y might have been expected to have a reasonable chance [column 7; 54 per cent] of gaining the national expectation of 5+A*–C grades *including English and mathematics*, and an even greater probability [column 9; 79 per cent] of gaining 5+A*–C grades *in any subjects*. The Year 9 estimates, however, show that Pupil Y's chances of reaching these thresholds have reduced to 7 per cent and 35 per cent respectively, which of course is crucial information for structuring the support Pupil Y will need and the effort that he/she will need to put in to realise what Year 6 estimates suggest he/she is capable of achieving.

Pupil Z has very consistent estimates based on Year 6 and Year 9 outcomes, suggesting he/she has made progress across KS3 in line with expectation. Pupil Z's capped points score estimates [columns 1 and 2; 366 and 368] suggest that 'Z' should be able to gain the equivalent of B grades in his/her best eight subjects, although the mean points scores suggests that somewhere between a C and a B grade is likely when considering all subjects. Probabilities for gaining the required grades to cross the national expectation thresholds are high – over 80 per cent for the 5+A*–C including English and mathematics threshold [columns 7 and 8], for example – which information could help 'Z' appreciate that the challenge for him/her is to maintain consistent progress across KS4 in order to reach these goals.

All these estimates are based on FFT's SE model and represent the outcomes that would be in line with the average performance by similar students in similar schools from the previous year's national cohort. This is the basis of what FFT calls 'Type B Estimates'.

Similar estimates of progress in line with the national average, calculated using the less contextualised PA model (prior attainment, gender and age only), are known as 'Type A Estimates'. Type B Estimates allow additionally for the element of school context – mean and spread of cohort prior attainment, and mean socio-economic deprivation – as peer-effect factors, which means that schools in relatively *advantaged* areas and schools with selective pupil intake like grammar schools are likely to find that these estimates present a greater challenge than the *Type A* ones based on the PA model.[8]

An interesting tension develops in the space between considering estimates at the pupil level and considering estimates at the school level. Type A and

8 The converse is true for schools in relatively *dis*advantaged areas.

Type B Estimates focus on sustaining the mean level of progress made by the previous year's cohort. When these are translated into school-level targets, Type A and Type B Estimates can present a considerable challenge for schools currently performing (as adjudged by their VA scores) well *below* the national mean. Conversely, for those schools with a value-added track record well *above* the national mean, achieving the outcomes given by Type A and Type B Estimates can result in reduced performance at school level. In order to assist schools in assessing the level of challenge required to improve pupil performance, two further sets of estimates are provided by FFT:

- 'Type C Estimates', which (like Type B Estimates) are calculated using the SE model, but include the additional challenge of having to meet annual national *DfE improvement targets*. The effect of adding this challenge is averaged for the school and then applied at the pupil level, with the greatest adjustments made for pupils in the middle of the prior attainment range, and smaller adjustments made for those at the low and high extremes of prior attainment (FFT 2006a).
- 'Type D Estimates', which are also based on the SE model, but with the level of challenge increased *to match the top quartile performance* of pupils in the previous year's cohort.

These FFT estimates are for non-specific and aggregate outcomes for pupils at age 16 and therefore have the capacity to inform conversations between teachers, pupils and parents around the general level of effort required to achieve desired attainment outcomes. Subject teachers benefit most from engaging in a focused discussion with pupils and their parents around potential in their own subject area, so to this end FFT also produce *subject-specific* estimates, via their FFTlive[9] online service, in the form of percentage probabilities (known as 'chances') of attaining each grade in each subject.

Lifting the lid on both PA and SE estimates models

Both PA and SE estimates models draw on data that is collected annually in the same National Pupil Database used for the calculation of CVA.

---

9 FFTlive is a web-based resource *available* to all schools in England and Wales to provide access to estimates and value-added data, analogous to RAISEonline. Ninety-eight per cent of secondary schools currently make regular use of FFTlive and the most popular report, the KS4 pupil estimates report, receives an average of 4,000 visits per day (which is approximately one per school). The proportion of primary schools using FFTlive has risen from 10 per cent to 70 per cent in the 12 months to February 2010 (Treadaway 2010). Details are available via the Data Analysis Project section of the FFT website at: www. fischertrust.org/dap_overview.aspx

Pupil-level factors: (a) prior attainment

- *Mean National Curriculum Test Level (the decimalised/fine-grade level, when available).* This is the basic prior attainment measure using the score achieved in the three core National Curriculum (NC) subject tests at each Key Stage. Individual pupil scores, together with 'level' thresholds calculated from the NC tests, are used to generate a fine-grade NC level, which is then used as the primary input variable in a statistical regression model. This is in contrast to earlier VA measures where a national median line was generated using the much broader 'full' NC levels as the input and output measures of attainment. The use of fine levels, as in the calculation of the DfE CVA model, does raise questions about the robustness of the NC assessment framework and the legitimacy of generating fine grades *after* marking individual student examination scripts. The NC tests were not originally designed to produce fine-grade assessments, although schools are familiar with the practice of subdividing levels into finer bands (normally three bands denoting upper, middle and lower [or 'a', 'b' and 'c'] attainment within one NC level). The KS2 estimates, based on prior attainment at KS1, use these broader sub-levels since KS1 test scores are not available in the national data set (because they are *internally* marked). While idiosyncrasies in the marking process may cancel themselves out over the whole national data set, there is clearly a degree of subjectivity associated with the marking process, especially in subjects like English. The current practice of NC marking is that a single marker assesses the scripts *for all pupils in a particular school* so a certain degree of bias is likely to be inherent in the system at both pupil and school level.
- *Differences between National Curriculum test scores and teacher assessments.* The regression model used to calculate estimates includes a term that incorporates the difference (if any) between teacher assessments of NC Level and pupil performance in NC tests. FFT data is unique in utilising the results of statutory Teacher Assessments as a prior attainment measure in their models. Its analysis shows that they *are* statistically significant and their inclusion as inputs produces a better-fitting model for the data;[10] in fact, it may well be one of the reasons why FFT data is held in such high regard by practitioners.
- *Subject differentials.* In its early analyses, FFT found that attainment in some subjects has a greater influence on future attainment than other subjects; for example, prior attainment in English at KS1 is more influential than prior attainment in mathematics at estimating attainment at the end of KS2. This is another significant difference that sets FFT estimates apart from

10 Where a pupil is absent for a National Curriculum test, the Teacher Assessment is used to impute a fine-grade score based on the median of the fine grades awarded for the same Teacher Assessment level.

other predictive metrics, like those generated by the DfE/Ofsted 'Progress Charts',[11] say. (These were once contained in the 'Autumn Package' material sent to schools and are currently available via RAISEonline.) The DfE methodology involves the conversion of NC Levels to APS for the purpose of estimating outcomes at the end of the next Key Stage with no account taken of subject differentials,[12] which misses the subtle but significant differences in outcomes of pupils with a mix of levels in the core subjects but with the same APS.

Figure 5.1, based on a three-year analysis of pupil outcomes carried out by FFT in 2004, illustrates the effect of differential performance in the three core National Curriculum subjects. Using the points scores given in Table 4.1, it is clear that pupils with KS2 Levels (in English, mathematics and science) of 3, 4 and 5 [21 + 27 + 33 points] *in any combination*, or 4, 4, 4 [3 × 27 points], all have an average KS2 points score of 27. The progress charts available in RAISEonline would produce the same range of estimates for each of these children, but analysis has shown that the subject differences at KS2 levels relate to widely differing outcomes at GCSE. As Figure 5.1 shows, 49 per cent of pupils with a score of 3, 4, 5 in English, mathematics and science *respectively* went on to gain five or more A*–C grades at GCSE, whereas 75 per cent of pupils who scored 5, 4, 3 in English, mathematics and science *respectively* went on to gain five or more A*–C passes. This is a significant difference!

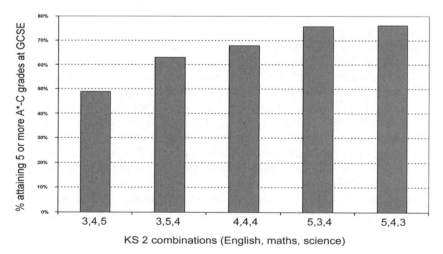

Figure 5.1 The effect of differential performance in the three core National Curriculum subjects at KS2 on GCSE outcomes

11 Also known as 'Chances Charts'.
12 Subject differentials are used in the calculation of CVA as a measure of progress, but not for estimates of pupil attainment.

Pupil-level factors: (b) gender

There has been considerable media interest in the effect of gender on pupil attainment, but despite several waves of policy initiatives in the UK, the school 'gender gap' in achievement, quantified by both raw attainment and value-added measures, has proved stubbornly resistant to change, leading some researchers to suggest that the source of the gender effect might lie outside the realm of school practice (Burgess *et al.* 2004). FFT models, at all levels, include gender as a variable, which explains a statistically significant proportion of the variance in the data. Like many contextual variables used in the two FFT models, its inclusion as a predictor can act as something of a double-edged sword; lowering expectation for some pupils and raising it for others. 'Pure' prior attainment-based models do not have this problem.

Pupil-level factors: (c) month of birth

Students born earlier in the school academic year tend to achieve higher outcomes than their younger peers. This means that if a September-born pupil with an identical prior attainment score to a December-born peer makes better progress than expected during the prior Key Stage, estimates of progress by the end of the next Key Stage will be higher.

School-level factors only present in the SE model: (d) socio-economic status

Originally, the only school-level socio-economic status factor used by FFT was the percentage of pupils entitled to free school meals, but since 2004 school-level socio-economic measures have been based on *both* percentage FSM entitlement *and* a modified form of the Classification of Residential Neighbourhoods (ACORN)[13] deprivation measure which uses a mixture of census data and information derived from the company's Consumer Lifestyle Database. ACORN is predominantly a geo-demographic indicator designed for commercial marketing purposes, but is increasingly being used by public sector bodies. It divides the UK into three levels of deprivation. At the top level there are five overarching categories of deprivation, subdivided into 17 groups and further subdivided into 56 types (see Appendix 1). The measures are linked to postcode and are therefore finer measures of deprivation than the IDACI measure used by the DfE in *its* CVA measures.

FFT has performed some preliminary regression analysis of the association between the 17 ACORN *groups* and mean VA scores (based solely on prior

13 ACORN was developed by CACI International, formally the Consolidated Analysis Centers Inc. For more information on this geo-demographic measure, see www.caci.co.uk/msd.html

attainment) for pupils in each group (FFT 2005a). (The groups are designated by the letters A–Q with 'A' representing the least deprived group and 'Q' the most deprived.) On the basis of the analysis the ACORN groups were gathered into four broader VA bands marking transitions between VA scores (see Table 5.3).

Interestingly, there is a mismatch in the association between deprivation and VA score for one of the ACORN groups, 'Q'. Closer inspection reveals that this 'mismatched' group accounts for a high proportion of pupils from minority ethnic backgrounds who have better VA scores than their ACORN deprivation measure would predict. When percentage FSM entitlement was added to the FFT SE model, both socio-economic factors remained significant, though the ACORN group explains slightly more of the variance in value-added. There is a high correlation (0.82) between the two SES factors (ACORN and FSM entitlement), but for some schools the percentage FSM entitlement and ACORN 'provide significantly *different* pictures' (FFT 2004), so FFT models retain *both* variables as socio-economic measures of school context.

Next, a more detailed analysis by FFT of the association between VA scores and deprivation as measured by the 56 ACORN *types* considered the combined progress of pupils at all Key Stages; between KS1–KS2, KS2–KS3 and KS3–KS4. Again, the association between VA score and deprivation was strong, with any anomalies again due predominantly to the presence of high proportions of minority ethnic pupils in certain ACORN types. As a result of this analysis, FFT re-ordered the ACORN types to match the pattern in VA score and these 56 Modified Types are now used as the postcode-based geo-demographic factor in the FFT contextualised models. To reflect the non-significant effect of living in an area assigned to the *middle* set of Modified ACORN Types – types 20–39 within the 56 – these were all allocated an ACORN score of '30'.[14]

Table 5.3 The 17 ACORN groups gathered into four broader VA bands showing the general link between deprivation and value-added score

ACORN VA band	ACORN group	VA score range
1	A B C D	> 0.3
2	E F G H I J	< 0.2 but > 0.0
3	K L M Q	< 0.0 but > –0.2
4	N O P	< –0.3

Source: Adapted from: FFT 2004 and 2005a.

14 FFT analysts also noted that the majority of these middle types shared a common feature; that is, that school-age pupils made up a relatively *low* proportion of the population (FFT 2005a).

FFT also looked at the moderating effect of ethnicity on the association between capped GCSE scores and school-level FSM entitlement (Figure 5.2). They found that the impact of FSM entitlement on GCSE points score is strongest for those of White British and Caribbean origin. While ethnicity is not included as a factor in the FFT PA and SE models, interaction terms between percentage FSM entitlement and ethnicity *are* included in FFT's fully

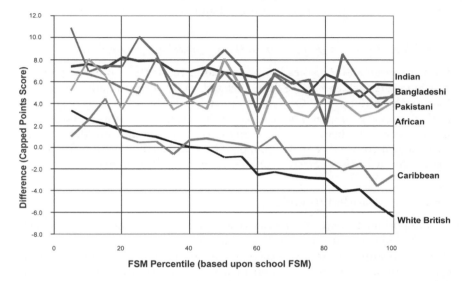

Figure 5.2 The moderating effect of ethnicity on the association between capped GCSE scores and school-level FSM entitlement (source: FFT 2005a)

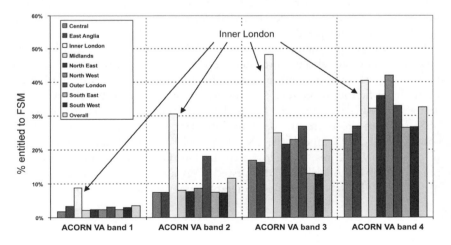

Figure 5.3 Relationship between ACORN VA Group and school FSM (Inner London highlighted [adapted from: FFT 2004])

contextualised model, the SX model[15] (more of which below) as these were found to be statistically significant in the regression analysis.[16]

Another interesting finding from the FFT analysis of ACORN and FSM data was the *regional* variation in the proportion of pupils entitled to FSM in each of the four broad ACORN VA groups (FFT 2004), which was particularly evident for schools in London where inner city schools (see Figure 5.3) have a disproportionately higher proportion of children with FSM entitlement in the ACORN bands with lower deprivation (Bands 1, 2 and 3 in Table 5.3).

School-level factors, only present in the SE model: (e) peer effects

Both the mean and the spread of prior attainment at the end of the previous Key Stage are included in the SE model and both are statistically significant. In common with the DfE/Ofsted CVA model, only the peer effects of students *in the same assessment cohort* are included, rather than *all* students in a school. It is not known whether a *school-wide* peer effect measure was considered at any stage, and if so whether it was found to be statistically non-significant, but there is no such effect currently catered for in any of the models.

FFT valued-added models

It is important to reiterate the key distinction between the *estimates* models described above and the *valued-added* models described now, especially as they are so similar in terms of their statistical procedures. Estimates models calculate pupil- and school-level estimates based on the performance of pupils *from the previous year's cohort*, whereas value-added models produce pupil- and school-level VA scores based on a regression analysis of the outcomes *of the current cohort*. Estimates models are *predictive*, giving an indication of what might be achieved; value-added models are *retrospective*, giving an evaluation of what has been achieved.

In addition to producing estimates for FFT reports, the PA and SE models described above are also used to produce value-added scores. Schools are thus provided with effectiveness measures based on prior attainment plus the pupil-level factors of gender and month of birth (through the PA model) and additionally (through the SE model) the school context factors based on SES and peer-effects (mean and spread of prior attainment). A third, highly contextualised FFT model, the SX (or 'School Extended') model, is also used to calculate VA scores. It is closest to the DfE/Ofsted CVA model, which it predates. Both models (the DfE/Ofsted CVA and the FFT SX) are so close in fact that FFT has devoted considerable time to explaining the subtle but

15 SX stands for 'School eXtended'.
16 Such interaction terms are also included in the DfE KS2–KS4 CVA model (see Chapter 4).

important differences between them. What follows is a summary of the development of the SX model and a discussion of some of the key differences between it and the DfE/Ofsted one, followed by an illustration of how the SX model is used to produce data for school self-evaluation.

In 2003, analysts at FFT investigated a range of school- and pupil-level contextualising factors (FFT 2004). This stemmed from the opportunity to generate highly contextualised models using the wider range of variables made available through the PLASC data-gathering exercise introduced the previous year.[17] The main focus of what follows below is on the statistical model that emerged from the Trust's analysis of KS2–KS4 (GCSE) pupil progress, though similar models are now applied to pupil progress between the other Key Stages, and later research has resulted in modifications to the original model. For the KS2–KS4 SX model, the outcome variable is the capped GCSE points score (DfES 2006b, 2006c, 2006d) and the variables included initially in the model are shown in Table 5.4.

The FFT approach has always been to research the effects of each contextualising variable at both pupil level and school level where possible (though this approach has not been extended as a school-level variable to the percentage of pupils in each ethnic group). The addition of extra contextualising factors improved the model in terms of the percentage of variance explained. The previous (KS2–KS4 SE) model, using the percentage of pupils entitled to FSM as the sole SES factor, explained 55 per cent of the variance, whereas the *revised* SE model, with the modified ACORN types included as a school-level variable *alongside* percentage FSM entitlement, explained 60 per cent. The extra pupil- and school-level factors included in the SX model raised the percentage of variance explained still further, to 65 per cent (FFT 2004).[18]

In common with other value-added models of this type, prior attainment is found to be by far the most important factor in explaining variance in the data, and the association between Mean Test Level (the pupil-level prior attainment factor) and grade or Level obtained at the end of the next Key Stage is found to be non-linear. Whereas the DfE/Ofsted CVA model employs a simple mathematical approach to dealing with the problem of non-linearity – it introduces a quadratic term, the square of the prior attainment score, into the model – the difficulty is addressed by FFT by allocating pupils to one of 96 prior attainment bands prior to the regression analysis, and calculating the Mean GCSE Capped Points score for each of these bands (Thomson and Knight 2006). This Mean Capped Points score is used as the prior attainment

17 The Trust presented its report to the 2004 annual conference (FFT 2004).
18 This figure has since been revised downwards to 60 per cent (FFT 2005b; Thomson and Knight 2006), though it still compares favourably with the percentage explained by the DfE/Ofsted CVA model, which is now quoted at 57 per cent (FFT 2005b).

Table 5.4 The initial variables included by FFT in their KS2–KS4 SX model

Pupil-level variables	School-level variables
Mean GCSE points score for pupil prior attainment band*	Mean of Intake Test Level for cohort
Mean teacher assessment (TA) level	Standard deviation of Intake Test Level for cohort
Individual Subject Test Levels (fine grade)	
Gender	Percentage Girls; Girls School/Boys School
Month of birth	
English as an additional language (EAL)	Percentage of pupils with EAL
Entitlement to free school meals (FSM)	Percentage of pupils entitled to FSM
Special Educational Needs (SEN): 'School Action', 'Action Plus' or 'Statemented'	Percentage SEN: Percentage 'School Action', Percentage 'Action Plus' and Percentage 'Statemented'
Ethnicity	
Time in school	
Joined 'late'	Percentage who joined 'late' in the cohort
FFT modified ACORN group	Mean FFT modified ACORN group
	Mainstream or Special/Unit

* The mean GCSE capped points score for prior attainment band is a prior attainment proxy variable used to overcome issues arising from the non-linearity of the association between KS2 fine-grade test scores and GCSE capped points score.

Source: Modified from FFT 2004.

measure for pupils,[19] who are then allocated to a number of 'broad bands' based on prior attainment at the end of KS2 and separate regressions performed for each broad band. Initially, four such bands were used, though this was later increased to five (FFT 2005b).

The combination of these two techniques is what FFT refers to as 'multilevel modelling'. It is *not* the same statistical procedure as that used in the DfE/Ofsted CVA model, which employs hierarchical regression analysis techniques in which all pupils are considered to be nested within schools. During its early research, FFT considered methodological issues relating to the difference between OLS regression techniques and the hierarchical modelling approaches

---

19 Schagen (2006) has supported this approach to dealing with non-linearity and ceiling effects in value-added analyses.

that were being considered at the time by the DfE in developing its own CVA model. FFT decided to retain OLS techniques largely because of the application of the shrinkage factor in hierarchical modelling, which results in outlying residuals being drawn back towards the mean. Application of the shrinkage factor has the effect of reducing the level of uncertainty associated with outlying residuals and with residuals for small schools, but shrinkage can also mask *true* high or low VA scores and has implications for producing VA scores for groups of pupils *within* a particular school.

Interaction terms between pupils' ethnicity and entitlement to FSM were also included (as described above) and other interaction terms added to the model both at pupil level (e.g. interactions between the differentials in KS2 test scores in different subjects) and at school level (e.g. interactions between mean KS2 prior attainment scores and percentage FSM or ACORN percentile ranks). In essence, interaction terms were retained whenever they improved the model fit or were considered significant.[20]

It is clear from the material presented at FFT conferences that there is a consultative process associated with FFT methodology and practice by which feedback from local authorities and schools is sought, considered and addressed. This may be another contributory factor in the high value placed by schools on FFT data. Many FFT users – 70 per cent according to the NfER survey (Halsey *et al.* 2005) – express a desire to see *more* contextualising factors from PLASC incorporated into FFT models, although typically many of these – half, according to the NfER survey – have reservations about the use of such factors in generating estimates that lower expectations, suggesting that only those factors which raise estimates should be incorporated in predictive models. At the time, as a result of feedback from practitioners, FFT retained its PA and SE models for the production of Type A–D estimates, and only used the new highly contextualised SX model for retrospective measurements of value-added progress. Thus FFT avoided the criticism that the inclusion of some factors – such as SEN, FSM entitlement and ethnicity – lower expectations if used in generating estimates of pupil outcomes or to inform target setting. Schools with a relatively high proportion of pupils in these categories typically find that the standard Type A–D estimates produced by the PA and SE models are *not* a good match for their populations, so FFT published plans in 2006 to allow schools and local authorities to use these contextualised models for generating pupil- and school-level estimates using a web-based tool (FFT 2006b). 'FFTlive', as it became, does not include the facility to base estimates on the SX model, but it does provide the facility to calculate estimates in line with a user-specified percentile (in steps of five from the 50th to the 5th percentile) for both pupil- and school-level estimates.

---

20 A comprehensive list of factors included in the SX model with the values of their coefficients and effect sizes can be found in Appendix 2.

As well as being used to calculate pupil and school VA scores, the SX model is also used in the production of extensive reports for schools entitled *Analyses to Support Self-evaluation*. They were originally known as *Supplements to PANDA* (FFT 2005c, 2005d) as they were pitched alongside Ofsted PANDA reports as tools for school self-evaluation. The reports provide three-year rolling value-added analyses of pupil attainment from KS1–KS2 for primary schools and KS2–KS3, KS2–KS4 and KS3–KS4 for secondary schools (FFT 2007b, 2007c). Primary schools also have analyses produced based on KS1 outcomes, but this is not a value-added exercise as there is no use of prior attainment; it is purely a contextualised comparison of a school's KS1 outcomes with those obtained by pupils in other schools, based on the pupil- and school-level contextual factors included in the SX model. FFT describes the statistical robustness of this type of context-only analysis as '*just* good enough' (FFT 2005e) (emphasis added). It places extensive notes to this effect in the introduction and provides the usual commendably high level of guidance in headers and footers on each page.

The 'Analyses to Support Self-evaluation' reports essentially provide three different analyses of a school's data: 'Value-added Summaries'; 'Significant Areas Grids'; and 'Estimates'.

1 Value-added Summaries

These are three-year retrospective views of school performance across a range of outcomes, such as the percentage of pupils achieving certain benchmarks in National Curriculum or GCSE tests, as well as outcomes involving the attainment of *all* pupils, such as Mean National Curriculum Level or Mean GCSE Capped Point Score (see Table 5.5). The inclusion of percentile ranks in reports enables schools to benchmark their performance against other schools on each of the outcome measures.

Column 1 ['Pupils – Total'] and column 2 ['Pupils – Match'] show the total number of pupils in each of the three yearly cohorts summarised in the report and the number of pupils for whom matching prior attainment data was available at the end of KS2. In the capped points score section [columns 3–6] the actual mean capped points score is shown ['Act'] and then three percentile rank figures ['Raw', 'PA' and 'SX'] associated with the capped points score. The first is the percentile rank for the raw points score, which ranges from 35 to 39, indicating that simply in terms of raw attainment (as measured by the mean capped points score), the school performed above average in the last three years. The second, the PA percentile rank, corresponds to the mean progress pupils have made according to the capped points score outcome, by adjusting for the context factors in the PA model (prior attainment, age and gender at the pupil level). For this school, the PA percentile rank was the same as for the raw unadjusted analysis in 2003/4 [column 5; 38], but in the next two years the PA percentile ranks [column 5; 14 and 24] show that the school performed in the top quartile of schools nationally (after adjusting for the factors in the PA model). Assuming that the mix of boys and girls, and ages, did not change

Table 5.5 A three-year FFT Value-added Summary

KS234
Value Added (3 Year Summary)
Version 2.1

SCH ID

Example School

Example LEA

The purpose of this analysis is to support review and evaluation within schools and local authorities. Publication or use outside of this context is NOT permitted.

KS2 -> KS4	Pupils		Capped Points Score				5 + A*–C				5 + A*–G			
					Percentile Rank				Percentile Rank				Percentile Rank	
	Total	Match	Act	Raw	PA	SX	Act	Raw	PA	SX	Act	Raw	PA	SX
2003/4	220	215	298.8	38	38	13	61%	32	27	14	94%	42	35	23
2004/5	231	228	305.6	35	14	4	65%	30	9	7	94%	46	18	14
2005/6	217	216	306.3	39	24	7	67%	30	12	9	94%	50	34	24
3 Years Combined			303.6	37	23	6	64%	30	12	8	94%	44	25	17
3 Year Trend			–	–	↑	↑	–	–	↑	↑	–	–	–	–

21	Significantly higher than 'expected'
89	Significantly lower than 'expected'

↑ Improving (relative to schools nationally)

→ Declining (relative to schools nationally)

- - - No trend calculated

Cases where the PA or SX value-added score is significant (to 95% confidence limits) are highlighted

↕ Improving both years

↕ Declining both years

↕ Varying over three years

Indicators are shown as a Percentile Rank where
1 = Highest value-added,
100 = Lowest value-added.

The percentile rank and significance for the three years combined are based on the total number of matched pupils, and their overall value-added. It's possible that in each separate year value-added is not significant, but over the three years it is due to the number of pupils.

Source: Adapted from: FFT 2007b, 2007c.

appreciably from year to year, this suggests that pupils have below-average prior attainment on entry to the school, and when adjustment is made for this, the pupils are shown to have made substantial progress, especially in the most recent two years of the analysis. Thirdly and finally, the percentile ranks for the SX model are shown [column 6], ranging from 4 to 13, which shows that after adjusting for the additional factors in the SX model, the school is performing around or within the top 10 per cent of schools nationally. (This might suggest that the school is located in an area of above-average deprivation or has an above-average number of pupils with Special Educational Needs.) The shaded boxes show where the progress made by pupils is significantly above the average progress made by all pupils nationally. It would also show significantly below-average progress (as per the legend on the left-hand side, beneath the table), but there is no underperformance in this school.

A similar analysis is shown for the two threshold outcome measures of 5 + A*–C grades [columns 7–10] and 5 + A*–G grades at GCSE [columns 11–14]. Based on these two outcomes, especially the former, the progress of pupils is shown to be almost consistently significantly above average in all three years [most of the boxes are shaded]. An equivalent analysis for the three-year mean of each outcome is shown with trend markers [bottom row] showing a rising trend in progress over the three-year period.

2 Significant Areas Grid

This gives a breakdown of value-added measures of progress by gender, prior ability band (upper, middle and lower), SEN, entitlement to FSM and ethnicity. Only those groups for whom value-added progress (as measured by the SX model) has changed significantly over the three years are included.

Table 5.6 shows the Significant Areas Grid for progress across KS2 in a primary school. In this example, only trends in English are shown, suggesting that there are no *significant* trends in pupil progress in mathematics and science, which may in turn suggest evidence of differential effectiveness in the teaching of English compared to the other two core subjects. For the 'Level 4 and above' threshold outcome, the report shows that *boys* in the *middle* band of prior attainment at KS1 [main row in upper half of table] have a falling trend from 16.3 per cent more boys in the middle PA band attaining Level 4 than estimated by the SX model [significantly *above* the national average progress, as indicated by the shading] in 2004, down to 2.8 per cent more than the SX estimate in 2006 [broadly in line with the national average progress, as indicated by the absence of shading]. This, while still showing mean progress for this group of pupils above the national average, might be a point of focus for future school improvement.

Similarly, the progress of all pupils [upper row; lower half of table] to attain Level 4 and above in English has shown some variation over the three-year period, from 4.5 per cent *more* than estimated by the SX model in 2004, to 6.9 per cent *less* in 2005 and then 3.3 per cent *more* than estimated in 2006. While

Table 5.6 A three-year FFT Significant Areas Grid

Example School
SCH ID Example LEA

The purpose of this analysis is to support review and evaluation within schools and local authorities. Publication or use outside of this context is NOT permitted.

Indicator: English – Level 4+

Significance – Over 3 Years Combined: Significantly above

Value-added – Trend	Category	Pup (3 Yr)	Significance			Difference		
			2004	2005	2006	2004	2005	2006
Declining	Boys – Middle	34	O			16.3%	7.1%	2.8%

Indicator: English – Level 4+

Significance – Over 3 Years Combined: In expected range

Value-added – Trend	Category	Pup (3 Yr)	Significance			Difference		
			2004	2005	2006	2004	2005	2006
Declining	All Pupils	257		■		4.5%	−6.9%	3.3%
Declining	SEN – N	196	O	■		6.7%	−6.9%	1.1%

In this analysis the term SIGNIFICANT is used to mean those aspects where we can be 95% confident that the difference is larger than would be expected. The report shows, for a range of indicators and for a range of pupil categories, areas where performance (over the last 3 years) was significantly high or low or where value-added has changed to a significant degree. In the data shown for individual years:

6.7%	*Significantly higher than 'expected'*	■ / −6.9%	*Significantly lower than 'expected'*	**Uses FFT SX Model**
O / 6.7%				

Source: FFT 2007b.

the progress to reach the 'Level 4 or above' threshold is broadly in line with the national average in 2004 and 2006 [no shading], the significantly below-average progress based on this measure in 2005 [dark shaded box in penultimate column] has triggered this group to appear in the report. The progress of children *not* on the SEN code of practice ['SEN-N'] also shows wide variation from significantly more-than-average progress [light shaded box] to attain Level 4 or above in 2004 [lower row; 6.7 per cent] to a significantly below-average percentage [–6.9 per cent] making progress to Level 4 or above in 2005.

3 *Three-year Estimates Reports*

These contain school-level *Estimates* for a range of outcomes based on the progress trend over the previous three years (see Table 5.7). These use the same terminology as pupil-level estimates, namely Type A (average progress based on the PA model), Type B (average progress based on the SE model) and Type D (top-quartile progress based on the SE model). Type C estimates are not included.

Table 5.7 is a school-level Estimates Report for a secondary school. The figures in boxes represent the percentage of pupils likely to gain the grades to cross the national attainment thresholds of 5 + A*–C grades [after 3rd column; 67 per cent] and 5 + A*–C grades including English and mathematics [after 2nd column; 43 per cent]. [Two sets of Type A, B and D estimates are given for each outcome: one set based on the current cohort's prior attainment in Year 6 (end of KS2) and one based on Year 9 (end of KS3) prior attainment.] These percentage estimates assume that next year's cohort will continue the trend in progress made by the previous three cohorts of pupils in the school. The Type A [PA], Type B [SE] and Type D [TQ = 'top quartile'] school-level estimates for the current cohort of pupils are shown. The report suggests that the recent trend in progress means that if the estimates are achieved, the percentage of pupils gaining 5 + A*–C grades will represent performance in the top quartile of schools based on the SE model and between the mean and the top quartile on the SE model (for 5 + A*–C grades including English and mathematics).

Table 5.7 A three-year FFT Estimates Report

Academic Year 2007/08	Estimate Range							
	Estimates are based on Y6 (KS2) and, where available, Y9 (K3S)							246 pupils
5 or more A*–C (Y6)	55%	(SE)	56%	(PA)		66%	(TQ)	67%
5 or more A*–C (*Y9*)	57%	(SE)	58%	(PA)		64%	(TQ)	67%
5+ A*–C (incl En & Ma) (Y6)	41%	(SE)	42%	(PA)	43%	49%	(TQ)	
5+ A*–C (incl En & Ma) (*Y9*)	43%	(SE)	43%	(PA)	43%	47%	(TQ)	

Source: FFT 2007b, 2007c.

The Type A estimates [PA] for this school are very similar to the Type B estimates [SE], suggesting that the mean deprivation of the cohort is similar to (or slightly higher than) the national average, and has a mean and spread of prior attainment on entry that is broadly similar to the national average. The fact that the estimates based on Year 9 prior attainment are higher than those for Year 6 suggests that this cohort made better-than-average progress from KS2 to KS3, but also emphasises the importance of basing estimates on the most recently available data.

The advantage of the three-year rolling model is that it presents a measure of school progress *over time*, providing a richer and 'smoother' picture of school value-added. The merging of three years of pupil data also produces larger sample sizes in subgroups such as pupils with SEN or pupils from ethnic backgrounds, and therefore smaller confidence intervals and more accurate measures. For small rural schools, the model provides benefits when working with data at the 'whole pupil cohort' level and avoids the need to resort to hierarchical modelling techniques that use shrinkage to achieve the same improvement in the calculation of estimates.

When the launch of RAISEonline was delayed from its planned summer 2006 date, FFT was commissioned by Ofsted and the DfES to produce *Analyses to Support Self-Evaluation* reports for every maintained school in England and Wales. RAISEonline eventually launched in a reduced format in January 2007, but with no paper PANDAs issued by Ofsted during the autumn term, the FFT reports were for some schools the only detailed source of external data available to assist them in completing/updating their Self-Evaluation Forms (SEF) and in informing conversations with School Improvement Partners and Ofsted inspectors, both of which were and are crucial aspects of Ofsted's New Relationship with Schools inspection regime. Although no detailed PANDA analysis was subsequently made available, overall CVA scores for schools were published by the DfES, based on pupil attainment in the 2006 examinations. Thus schools were faced with two measures of overall school performance in the form of SX and government CVA school-level scores, but only one set of finer analyses giving value-added progress measures for groups of students and by subject, which schools had been utilising for self-evaluation and improvement purposes. This situation served to highlight issues related to multiple measures of value-added, particularly for those schools whose analyses from the FFT SX model and the CVA model differed. Thomson and Knight's (2006) work for FFT comparing SX measures with CVA scores concluded that 21 per cent of schools had a *different significance state* for KS2–KS4 CVA (for example, a statistically significant above-average CVA score, but an SX score broadly in line with the national average), but only 4 per cent had a *significantly different result* (comparing the two measures together to find that the 95 per cent confidence intervals for the two measures did not overlap). The difference between these two 'significances' is a subtle but important one. As measures of significance compared to national means are included in PANDA/RAISEonline data, they are clearly important to school leaders and inspectors. It would require a detailed working knowledge of the two statistical models to unpick why (say) a school's CVA score would be significantly above the national average but its SX score only broadly in line; not an easy job for a school head at any time, but especially when under the scrutiny of inspection. This has clearly brought FFT data more sharply into the arena of accountability measurement – a departure from its stated primary purpose of supporting school *self-evaluation* – though school leaders continue to argue for the greater use of FFT data in Ofsted inspections.

6 Slopes, intercepts and differential effectiveness

Introduction

Value-added is a *retrospective* measure of school effectiveness based on the progress of students who have already moved on to a new Key Stage or who have left the school. It can never reflect the *current* impact of practice. It is also a *relative* measure of effectiveness since school-level CVA scores – the residuals from the model – and average performance are generated or redefined each year. It is not uncommon to hear all manner of stakeholders, from teachers to politicians, suggest that it is possible for *all* schools to be in the upper quartile performance band, or to question why such a high percentage of schools are below average! Value-added as a measure of school effectiveness is limited to 'scholastic achievement' (Mortimore 1998), but even within that it is limited to measuring school effectiveness by aggregating the value added for each student to a single score for the whole cohort. School-level scores therefore represent the value that the school adds *for the average student*, after adjusting for context. They are cross-sectional snapshots of the school since they only consider the progress made by a *single cohort* of students *over a particular phase* of their education,[1] so that schools are only as good as their last set of data. This chapter addresses the issues raised by the aggregate nature of school-level scores and the restrictive snapshot view that value-added data provides.

Background

Ever since the landmark study *Fifteen Thousand Hours* by Rutter *et al.* (1979) demonstrated that schools *do* make a significant difference to student outcomes, thereby launching the modern field of School Effectiveness Research, the focus of research has been mainly on variation in outcomes and differential

---

1 It *would* be possible to produce VA scores based on combined data sets of several cohorts, but this is rarely done, although FFT does produce comparison reports that combine data from the previous three cohorts of students (as described in the previous chapter).

effectiveness *between schools*. The use of value-added data for this purpose places a strong focus on the calculation and interpretation of school-level scores, which provide an opportunity to benchmark the average progress of students in a cohort with that of similar students in similar schools (depending on the level of contextualisation). Such an analysis allows a school to consider how its educational interventions impact on the average academic progress of students relative to the progress of the national cohort. The addition of percentile ranks to school VA scores also gives the impression of accuracy and fine detail within the analysis, but they must be interpreted with caution, as we have seen. Over-reliance on the 'one-number-describes-all' approach leaves itself open to falling prey to an 'ecological inference' fallacy, whereby the results of aggregated analyses at the school level are assumed to hold for all the individuals located therein, although we know that cohorts of students are not homogeneous and there is evidence from a range of studies that schools are differentially effective with different groups of students. Mortimore *et al.* (1988: 210), for example, found evidence that Inner London junior schools were differentially effective in their ability to promote reading for boys and girls. Sammons *et al.* (1993) later re-analysed this data and found additional differential effectiveness across the range of prior attainment in mathematics also. While they found no evidence of differential effectiveness for other factors such as gender, social class and ethnicity, in an earlier study of 31,000 students from 140 London schools, Nuttall *et al.* (1989) *did*, leading them to conclude that:

> To attempt to summarise school differences, even after adjusting for intake, sex and ethnic background . . . in a single quantity is misleading. . . . It is more meaningful to describe differences between schools for different subgroups: the concept of overall effectiveness is not useful.
>
> (776)

Jesson and Gray (1991) re-analysed the Nuttall *et al.* data together with data from three other local authorities and found that when prior attainment scores from verbal reasoning tests were grouped in three broad bands, significant evidence of differential effectiveness was found. The evidence may have been an artefact of the banding, but Jesson and Gray nevertheless conceded that: 'it [did] not make sense to answer questions about schools' effectiveness without simultaneously *providing evidence about their effects on the full range of their pupils'* (p. 246).

Thomas *et al.* (1997b) also found evidence of differential school effectiveness for subgroups of students by gender, eligibility for free school meals, ethnicity and prior attainment. Their value-added models adjusted for prior attainment, gender, age in year, ethnicity and level of parental income, but the greatest differential effectiveness within schools was found to be for prior attainment and ethnicity, and across subjects.

Kyriakides (2004) refers to the importance of *consistency* in value-added estimates, suggesting that there is little difference in the results even when a wide range of outcome variables is used. He points to the work of Fitz-Gibbon (1990), which demonstrated that there is considerable variation in the effectiveness of different subject departments within schools, when he suggests that: 'the unidimensionality of the school effect in secondary schools is very questionable and [that] departmental differences in effectiveness may be a more relevant concept than overall school differences in effectiveness' (Kyriakides 2004: 143).

Using the metrics

Figures 6.1 and 6.2 represent a random-intercept, *fixed*-slope multilevel VA analysis of the GCSE outcomes of approximately 4,000 students from a single cohort; the same approach as that used for calculating school-level VA scores using RAISEonline. This model, with the slope value fixed, assumes that the value added by a school (the school effect) is constant across the full range of prior attainment. In this model the intercept residual becomes the measure of the school VA score. However, it is possible to produce a *random*-slope model for the same student data which allows the school-level slope residual to vary across the range of prior attainment. The results of such an analysis for a KS2–KS4 VA multilevel model (adjusted for prior attainment only) is shown in Figure 6.1.

The 20 individual school lines are no longer parallel as they were in the fixed-slope model. Towards the lower end of KS2 prior attainment APS, the school lines fan out, which is evidence of differential effectiveness across the prior attainment range. Such a result is to be expected given the greater variance in individual student data points in this region seen on the right-hand side of

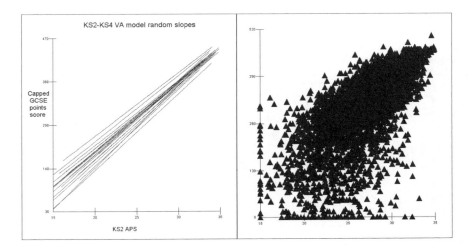

Figure 6.1 A random-slopes KS2–KS4 VA multilevel model for a cohort of approximately 4,000 students

Figure 6.1. At the higher end of KS2 APS, it is much more difficult to distinguish individual schools – the lines are closer together – suggesting that for the most able students among the 4,000, the progress made is similar regardless of school attended. This will be, at least in part, due to ceiling effects in the model, which are not adjusted for in any way here. The proportion of the variance in student outcomes at school level – the *between*-school variance – is plotted against KS2 prior attainment in Figure 6.2, which confirms the conclusion drawn from the visual inspection of Figure 6.1 that the variation between schools [Level 2 variance] is much greater at lower levels of KS2 prior attainment.

It is possible to plot a graph of the slope versus the intercept residuals for each of the 20 schools in the analysis. One such plot is shown on Figure 6.3 and the schools with the lowest and highest slope residuals are highlighted as School X and Y respectively. Schools with low slope residuals have less variation in student outcomes across the range of prior attainment. These are the schools represented by the lines with the shallowest slopes in Figure 6.1. In such schools those students entering at the lower end of the prior attainment range make greater progress than their peers *in other schools* and possibly even greater than their higher prior attainment peers *in the same school*. Such schools could be termed 'high-equity schools' as they help to address the imbalance in student attainment that existed upon entry.

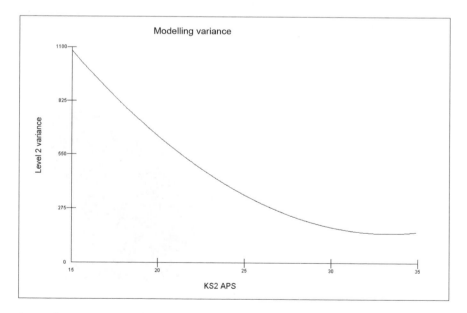

Figure 6.2 Proportion of variance in student outcomes at school level plotted against KS2 prior attainment (KS2 APS)

Schools with the highest value slope residuals (represented by the steepest school lines in Figure 6.1) are those in which there is the greatest variation in the progress made by students across the range of prior attainment. By contrast with schools with low slope residuals, the imbalance in student attainment that existed when students entered these schools is sustained and even compounded by the time students leave. However, a note of caution: as with the residuals of fixed-slope models, the residuals produced by random-slope models are *relative*. There will always be 50 per cent of schools with slope residuals higher than the mean slope value, and 50 per cent below, so the distinction between high- and low-equity schools in this context is a relative one.

The difference between the school lines is emphasised in the following figures. In Figure 6.4 the school line with the shallowest slope (lowest slope residual) is highlighted ('X'). It represents the school in which students with low prior attainment made the most progress from KS2 to KS4. Coincidentally, students in this school make the most progress *across the full range of prior attainment* – i.e. at the high prior attainment end too – so it is not surprising

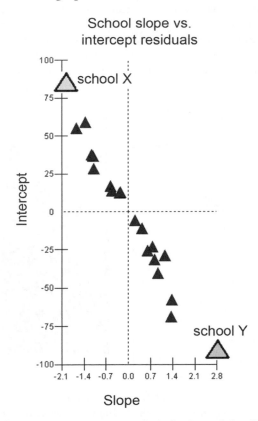

Figure 6.3 Plot of slopes versus intercept residuals for the multilevel VA model (schools with the highest and lowest slope residuals highlighted)

that in the simpler fixed-slope model, this school has the highest VA score (see Figure 6.6) and could therefore be called a 'high-effectiveness, high-equity school'.

The individual data points for students attending 'School X' are highlighted on the right-hand side of Figure 6.4, to make it clear how the distribution of the individual student outcomes compares with that of the entire cohort. From an inspection of these data points, it is clear that (even in this school) some individual students fail to make the progress made by the majority of their peers. As this value-added model is adjusted for prior attainment *only*, a number of contextual factors *might* account for at least some of that variation. Of course, it may be *because of the school* that some students fail to make good progress while others do so well; for example, there may be a strong 'hothouse' culture in the school that promotes academic excellence for some at the expense of others. Such are the complexities of the culture of learning and student engagement in schools, and such is the disadvantage of using *aggregated* effectiveness data to inform school improvement and self-evaluation.

In Figure 6.5, the line with the steepest slope is highlighted ('Y'), representing the school with the greatest differential effectiveness across the prior attainment range. The individual data points for its students are also highlighted (on the right-hand side). From an inspection of the school line, it can be seen that the students entering the school with high prior attainment make progress (on

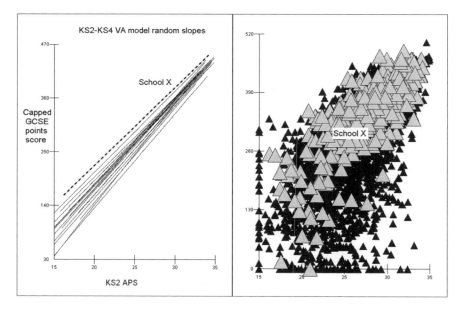

Figure 6.4 A random-slopes MLM, with the school with lowest slope residual high-lighted (School X also has the highest intercept, but the interpretation of intercept is really only meaningful for students with the lowest prior attainment, whereas the slope speaks across the whole range)

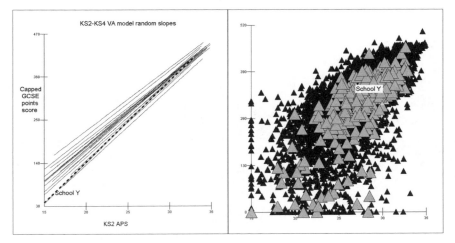

Figure 6.5 A random-slopes MLM with the school with the highest slope residual (the steepest line) highlighted

average) broadly in line with their high prior attainment peers at the other schools clustered around the average for the set. The school regression line then comes down to cross the lines of a number of other schools until, at the lowest KS2 APS prior attainment score of 15, it becomes the school where students (on average) make the *least* progress. Interestingly, when a *fixed*-slope model is used to calculate a VA score for each school, School Y is significantly below average, as the snake plot (Figure 6.6) for the fixed-slope model shows (there are only three worse performing schools in this set). Thus, the 'one-number-for-all' approach derived from simple fixed-slope models masks, to some extent, the poorer progress *of students with low prior attainment* in this school.

It is possible to see evidence of differential effectiveness in MLM outputs, but the key question is whether these differences are *significant*, either practically or statistically. For the random-slope KS2–KS4 VA data modelled above, the random component of the intercept was statistically significant (p<0.05), as was the corresponding random component of the slope (p<0.05).[2] While this provides evidence that there is significant differential effectiveness within the whole set of schools, it does not get at the core of the issue for any individual

2 The estimate of the school-level random component for the intercept variance (u_{0j}) was 3230.353 with a standard error of 1512.707 and for the slope variance (u_{1j}) the estimate was −92.376 (SE 46.410). As the comparison set was made up of only 20 schools, these results need to be treated with caution as this is below the number of Level 2 units required for the efficient estimation of multilevel models (Maas and Hox 2005). The estimates were calculated using Markov Chain Monte Carlo (MCMC) estimation, which is available in MLwiN (Rasbash *et al.* 2009).

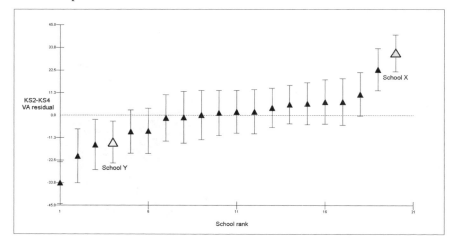

Figure 6.6 Snake (or caterpillar) plot of school residuals from a simpler fixed-slopes
multilevel VA model, with the two focus schools again highlighted

school. To illustrate this using an example drawn from the primary school
sector, we take a model for KS1–KS2 value-added.

The fixed-slope model shown in Figure 6.7 produces a regression line for
each school. Once again it is clear that there is greater variation in outcomes at
the lower end of prior attainment, but this is not captured in the school-level
lines which are forced to be parallel by the assumption of fixed slopes. (Again,
both ceiling and floor effects have not been 'adjusted for'.) The school residuals
(i.e. the VA scores) are shown in the snake plot in Figure 6.8. Four schools have
been highlighted: a high-ranked school with a significantly high VA score;[3]
two middle-ranked schools with average VA scores; the lowest-ranked school
with a significantly low VA score. Importantly, there are statistically significant
differences between the high-ranked, the two middle-ranked and the lowest-
ranked schools, demonstrated by the fact that the confidence intervals for the
high- and lowest-ranked schools do not overlap with those for either of the two
middle-ranked schools. It is also worth noting how the number of students
in each school can influence the size of the confidence interval. Some schools
have high *non-significant* value-added while other lower-ranked schools have
significantly high value-added by virtue of their shorter confidence interval.[4]
This situation is paralleled for schools with low residuals.

3 The second rank school was selected as it has a much larger number of pupils in the cohort
   than the highest ranked school.
4 Strictly speaking, the size of the confidence interval also depends on the spread of student
   value-added scores in the school: the higher the spread of scores, the wider the confidence
   interval.

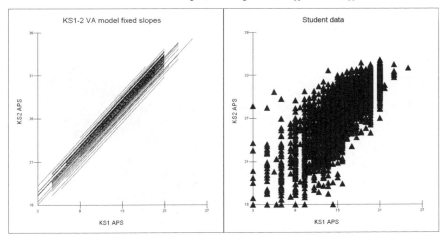

Figure 6.7 A fixed-slopes model for KS1–KS2 VA for a cohort of approximately 4,000 students

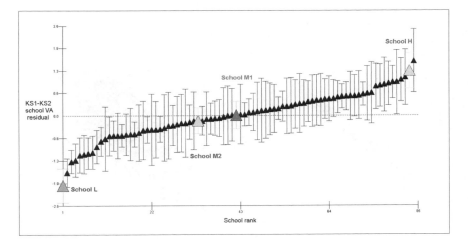

Figure 6.8 A snake plot of KS1–KS2 VA school residuals (VA scores) plus 95 per cent confidence intervals, with four specific schools highlighted

Figure 6.9 shows the regression lines for each of the four highlighted schools in Figure 6.8 together with their student data points highlighted amongst the data for the whole cohort. The four highlighted student data points on the horizontal axis (corresponding to a KS2 APS = 15, the lowest possible KS2 score as per Table 4.1) are all students at one of the two 'average' schools; a fact masked by other students whose high VA raised the school's residual to 'average'.

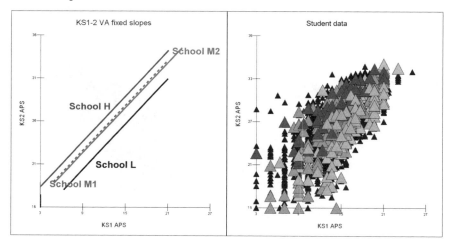

Figure 6.9 A fixed-slopes model showing regression lines and student data points for the four highlighted schools in Figure 6.8

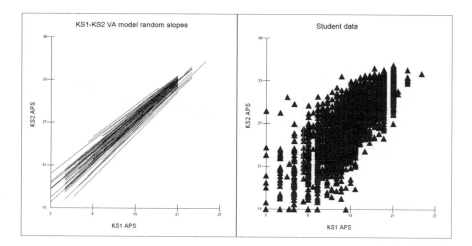

Figure 6.10 A random-slopes model for the data set as Figures 6.8 and 6.9

The random-slope model for the same KS1–KS2 data set is shown in Figure 6.10. Once again, the school lines fan out towards the lower range of prior attainment: visual evidence of differential school effectiveness across the prior attainment range. KS1–KS2 CVA models demonstrate greater between-school variance than KS2–KS4 CVA models (see Table 4.3), so it is no surprise that the estimates for the random components of both (school-level) intercept and slope are significant ($p<0.05$). There is statistically significant evidence of differential school effectiveness across the KS1 prior attainment range.

The regression lines for the four highlighted schools are shown on Figure 6.11. At the very highest levels of prior attainment there is little to distinguish between the average progress made by students in the schools with the three highest VA scores. Again, this is due at least in part to ceiling effects produced

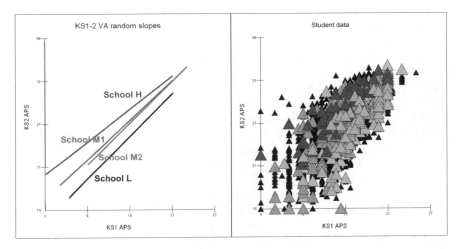

Figure 6.11 A random-slopes model showing regression lines and student points data for the four highlighted schools

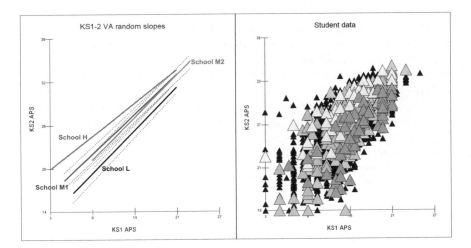

Figure 6.12 Regression lines for the four highlighted schools from the random-slopes model, with 95 per cent confidence intervals added

at the maximum level of attainment in the KS2 National Curriculum tests.[5] At the lower end of the prior attainment range, the differential effectiveness of the schools becomes more apparent: the gap in average progress made by students in the high-ranked school compared with the two middle-ranked schools becomes wider as we move across to lower levels of prior attainment, and one of the middle-ranked schools clearly has a steeper slope than the other.

The limits for 95 per cent confidence intervals can be calculated for each of the four school regression lines, and these have been plotted in Figure 6.12. Close inspection reveals that they are wider at the extremes (particularly at the low end of prior attainment) as there are fewer data points there. At the high end of prior attainment, the confidence intervals for the high- and middle-ranked schools all overlap substantially, and in fact the confidence interval for the lowest-ranked school just overlaps with those for the two middle-ranked schools (but not for the high-ranked school). We can conclude that students with the very highest levels of KS1 prior attainment make significantly greater progress in School H than in School L, but the progress of similarly high-attaining students in School M1 and School M2 is *not* significantly different from their peers in School H and School L.

Moving down to lower levels of prior attainment, the effects of differential attainment become more apparent. Students with a KS1 APS of 12 or lower in School H make significantly greater progress on average than their peers in either of the middle-ranked schools. At the same prior attainment level, there is no longer any significant difference in the progress made by students in School M2 (the middle-ranked school with the steeper slope) compared with their peers in the School L, the lowest-ranked school. On the other hand, students in School M1 (the middle-ranked school with the shallower slope) make significantly higher progress than those in School L right across the prior attainment range.

While the results of random-slope multilevel analyses like these are not normally given to schools, they *do* have access to data that can help them uncover evidence of differential effectiveness for themselves, via RAISEonline or using data from the Fischer Family Trust (either in FFT reports or via the FFTlive website).

Table 6.1 is an example of a report from RAISEonline of KS1–KS2 CVA scores for a typical primary school. It is important to remember that differences in gender, prior attainment (including subject differences in prior attainment) and FSM entitlement have all been adjusted for in the model and therefore these CVA scores compare students in each of these groups with similar pupil

---

5 In reality the highest KS2 APS possible is greater than 33 (see Table 4.1) since fine-grade KS2 APS is used here, as it is in DfE KS1–KS2 VA and CVA models. Fine-grade scores take into account the fact that some students exceed the threshold score for Level 5 (the maximum KS2 test level) by a greater margin than other students.

Table 6.1 Typical data from a RAISEonline output for KS1–KS2 CVA scores

	No. of pupils	Overall CVA	CVA by subject		
			English	Maths	Science
All pupils	243	99.6	100.1	99.6	99.2
Gender					
Girls	121	99.5	100.0	99.4	99.1
Boys	122	99.7	100.2	99.8	99.3
Prior Attainment					
Below level 2b	30	98.4	99.5	98.1	98.2
At level 2b	130	99.5	99.8	99.4	98.9
Above level 2b	83	100.4	100.8	100.5	100.1
Free School Meals					
Non-FSM	223	99.7	100.2	99.7	99.3
FSM	20	98.9	99.2	98.9	98.6

Note: Dark shaded boxes mark significantly low CVA scores (normally dark blue on reports). Pale shaded boxes mark significantly high CVA scores (normally green in reports).

groups after adjusting for other contextual factors in the CVA model. The overall CVA score for the school represented here is 99.6 [top row, second column], which is significantly *lower* than the national average CVA score of 100. Scanning across the top row, we see that students make progress in English broadly in line with the national average [no shading], while in mathematics and science their progress is significantly lower than the national average [dark shading]. If this were KS2–KS4 CVA data, it might be considered evidence of differential *departmental* effectiveness, but this is unlikely to be the case in a primary school where the teaching of English, mathematics and science is unlikely to be undertaken by different teachers. Nevertheless there is some evidence of differential effectiveness by subject and by gender (but only in mathematics) as the overall CVA score for girls [99.4] is significantly below the national average while the score for boys [99.8] is broadly in line with the national average.

The strongest evidence for differential effectiveness in this school is by prior attainment. Students with KS1 prior attainment 'above Level 2b' have consistently different significance markers (shading on the table) compared to the other two rows in the prior attainment section [row 4 ('Below Level 2b') and row 5 ('At Level 2b')]. Even in English, although students in the lower two prior attainment bands make progress broadly in line with the national average [no shading in row 4 and row 5, column 3], students with prior attainment 'above Level 2b' make significantly higher-than-average progress [pale shading in row 6, column 3]. Both the overall CVA scores as well as the subject-specific CVA scores therefore demonstrate clear associations with level of prior attainment.

There is also evidence of differential effectiveness by FSM entitlement, but this is harder to determine from the significance flags, as the low number of students entitled to FSM [20] means that confidence intervals for this group are wide. In this case, it would be necessary to look at *actual* CVA scores to find out more.

Table 6.2 shows an example of output from an FFT report for KS2–KS3 value-added data for 'School A'. The picture is somewhat mixed in terms of the statistical significance flags and is therefore challenging to interpret. The first three columns show the attainment outcomes in terms of the percentage of students attaining Level 5 or above, [90 per cent] Level 6 or above, [77 per cent] and the mean National Curriculum level attained by students in that cohort [6.3]. The middle columns [5–7] display *the percentile ranks* for the school outcomes after adjusting for pupil-level context (in the PA model, only for prior attainment, gender and age in year; the SX model is fully contextualised) The final set of columns [8–13] divides the students by gender and by broad KS2 prior attainment bands (Lower, Middle and Upper). The figures in these boxes are *numbers of students*.

Using the partially contextualised PA value-added model,[6] it is clear that in terms of the percentage of students achieving 'Level 5 and above' and 'Level 6 and above' in mathematics [pale shading of boxes in column 5 and column 6, upper row], the students have made significantly higher-than-average progress when compared with similar students nationally. This places the school comfortably in the upper quartile of schools [16th and 11th percentile ranks respectively]. However, when the fine-grade National Curriculum level attained is the outcome measure, according to the PA model, the school is only broadly in line with average progress [52]. This suggests that while students

Table 6.2 KS2–KS3 value-added data for outcomes in mathematics from an FFT report for 'School A'

Subject	Lev 5+	Lev 6+	NC Lev	Model	Lev 5+	Lev 6+	NC Lev	Number Boys			Number Girls		
								L	M	U	L	M	U
Maths	90%	77%	6.3	PA	16	11	52	15	28	38	19	27	42
				SX	42	40	95	15	28	38	19	27	42

Note: Dark shaded boxes mark significantly low CVA scores (normally dark blue on reports). Pale shaded boxes mark significantly high CVA scores (normally green in reports).

6 As we have seen, the FFT PA model adjusts for gender and age-in-year, as well as prior attainment.

have demonstrated significant progress in terms of their ability to cross the raw attainment thresholds of Level 5 and Level 6, they have *not* made such strong progress in terms of fine-grade National Curriculum levels.[7]

Scanning across the boxes that divide by gender and prior attainment bands [final six columns], the data suggests that it is the fine-grade progress *of girls* in the *upper* prior attainment band ['U'] that is significantly low [42 students in final column, shaded dark], which is *suggestive* of differential effectiveness both by prior attainment and by gender.

When the fully contextualised SX model is used, the picture becomes less positive. The addition of contextual variables (such as ethnicity, eligibility to free school meals, mobility, special educational need, school-level mean prior attainment and socio-economic status) results in the same student outcomes at KS3 representing less progress when compared to the national average. The data suggests that the percentage of students crossing the Level 5 and Level 6 thresholds was just above the national average when compared with similar students in similar schools [42nd and 40th percentile ranks respectively in column 5 and column 6], which is broadly in line with the national average progress [no shading] after adjusting for context. The overall progress in terms of fine-grade National Curriculum levels is significantly below the national average [dark shading in column 7], and in fact places the school on the cusp of the bottom 5 per cent of schools [95th percentile rank]. Once again, scanning across the boxes that divide by gender and prior attainment bands, the data reveals that it is the fine-grade progress of students in the higher prior attainment bands that is significantly low after adjusting for context; this time for *both* boys and girls [columns 10, 12 and 13, shaded dark], which provides further evidence of differential effectiveness by prior attainment and gender.

The data in this example is *actual* data from a *real* school, and it is worth dwelling a little longer on it. Like a small but not insignificant number of schools at the time, this school was engaged in an innovative curriculum project that involved teaching the KS3 programme in *two* years rather than the normal three. The relatively high prior attainment of pupils at the end of KS2 meant that many students *did* cross the Level 5 and Level 6 thresholds, but the fact that they made less progress in terms of fine-grade National Curriculum levels suggests that there may have been a cost to the 'fast track programme' for students with high prior attainment. At the time, this mixed data picture caused considerable concern for staff at the school who called the results (and therefore the FFT model underpinning them) into question.

---

7 This analysis suggests that the two-level progress measure used by the DfE can be misleading. Student A with a KS2 fine grade of 3.9 is deemed to have made two *whole levels* progress by reaching a fine-grade level of 5.0 by the end of KS3 (i.e. from Level 3 to Level 5). Student B, with a KS2 fine grade of 3.0, by reaching 4.9 at the end of KS3, is only deemed to have made one *whole level* progress (Level 3 to Level 4) despite having made more progress than Student A in terms of fine-grade levels.

When it was pointed out that, after taking context into account, their most able students *had* made significantly *less* progress than similar students in similar schools, the school was highly critical, suggesting that it was counter-intuitive to expect that 42 per cent of schools had achieved a higher percentage of students attaining Level 5 [column 5, using the SX model] than their own very healthy looking 90 per cent [column 1]; and there was great suspicion over the assertion that 95 per cent of schools had achieved a mean National Curriculum level greater than 6.3 [column 7 using the SX model]. This is a misinterpretation of the data. Percentile ranks and significance flags are based on progress *after adjusting for context*, which can be illustrated by comparing the data in Table 6.2 with that for a different school, 'School B', in a more deprived area (Table 6.3).

The data in Table 6.3 shows that students in 'School B' have lower raw attainment measures in terms of the percentage of its students crossing the Level 5 and Level 6 thresholds and in terms of mean National Curriculum level attained [columns 1–3]. The lightly contextualised PA model places the school around the national average [columns 5–7 using the PA model], much lower than School A which was well inside the upper quartile, and an inspection of the *numbers of students* in the three prior attainment bands shows that School B has a much lower prior attainment profile than School A [fewer pupils in the 'U' columns 10 and 13]. However, when the additional student- and school-level contextual variables in the SX model are taken into account, the progress of students in School B is much stronger than for School A, placing the school on the cusp of the upper quartile for all three measures [columns 5–7 using the SX model; 20th, 26th and 23rd percentile ranks respectively]. The mean fine-grade National Curriculum level is significantly higher than the national average, as is the progress for boys in the lower prior attainment band [shaded boxes in columns 7 and 8].

Faced with such data, School A could have considered the evidence that their KS3 curriculum innovation might have come at something of a cost in terms of fine-grade progress for students, particularly for those with high levels of prior attainment at the end of KS2. It is possible that a focus on ensuring that high proportions of students still crossed the Level 5 and Level 6 attainment thresholds, despite the reduced time frame for teaching, meant that there was

Table 6.3 A comparative set of KS2–KS3 value-added data for outcomes in mathematics from an FFT report for 'School B'

Subject	Lev 5+	Lev 6+	NC Lev	Model	Lev 5+	Lev 6+	NC Lev	Number Boys			Number Girls		
								L	M	U	L	M	U
Maths	78%	55%	5.9	PA	46	55	50	30	25	21	22	32	17
				SX	20	26	23	30	25	21	22	32	17

Note: Pale shaded boxes mark significantly high CVA scores (normally green in reports).

less emphasis on supporting the most able to make as much overall progress as they had in the past. As KS3 tests were not considered to be particularly high-stakes tests by schools, School A might have felt justified in its decision to change the curriculum to provide greater opportunities for development across an extended KS4. The appropriate action might have been to monitor more carefully the progress of students with high prior attainment – especially the girls – across KS4.

Extending the analysis to look for trends: some caveats

Care must be taken in translating an analysis of slopes and intercepts for a school to a trend over time. Most school effectiveness studies are cross-sectional in nature, as we have seen; that is, they look at the relative performance of students in a particular cohort or schools in a particular year. Longitudinal studies are rare as the data needed is only recently available and the changing nature of the measures makes comparison difficult. As we saw in Chapter 3, Gray and Thomas have been particularly active in this area over the last two decades (e.g. Gray *et al.* 1996; Thomas *et al.* 1997a), though some of their studies were conducted over relatively short (e.g. three-year) time spans. Other studies (e.g. Mangan *et al.* 2005), which made use of raw threshold (rather than value-added) measures, found that although some schools exhibit improvement over time, it is typically an 'aggregate phenomenon that does not survive disaggregation' (Mangan *et al.* 2005: 47), and a large amount of year-on-year variation is usual. The main criticism of longitudinal raw attainment research is that no adjustment is made for intake in terms of prior attainment or context, and this is where studies like Thomas *et al.* (2007) have the advantage. In a ten-year study (1993–2002) of data from secondary schools in one large English local authority, Thomas *et al.* found that raw-model residuals were more stable over time than value-added residuals, which suggests that schools have the capacity to transform their relative positions based on VA scores in a way that is more difficult when using raw attainment measures. Some of the key findings of the Thomas *et al.* study[8] can be summarised as follows:

8 A multilevel model was used which assumed a linear trend over the period and this was compared with a corresponding multilevel model that did *not* impose a linear trend (by assigning dummy variables to each year). Nonlinearity was explored using quadratic and cubic terms, but these were not found to be statistically significant. The prior attainment measure used was score in Cognitive Ability Tests at age 11, rather than the KS2 SAT APS used in KS2–KS4 CVA scores. CATs were chosen as they were not considered to be high-stakes tests for which students were specifically prepared (in contrast to KS2 NC tests). The contextualising factors included in the model were month of birth, gender, FSM entitlement, ethnicity, SEN and mobility.

- Although some schools can demonstrate significant improvement trends based on raw attainment, judging trends using value-added measures can lead to different conclusions.
- Schools with a low baseline value-added are more likely to demonstrate high levels of improvement over time, but it is harder to demonstrate high levels of improvement using raw scores.
- A substantial period of time – more than five years – is normally required to establish above-average improvement. Year-on-year improvement, even using VA scores, is difficult to sustain beyond two- or three-year bursts.

Finally, it should be noted that comparisons of schools such as those generated in the Thomas *et al.* study always result in 'losers' as well as 'winners'. Schools that show strong and sustained improvement trajectories force other schools to show negative trajectories with respect to the mean. As much as it is laudable for *all* schools to aim to be higher performing schools at some point in the future, when school residuals are re-ordered at the next 'time point', by definition only a limited number of schools will achieve the desired designation.

7 Getting more value from value-added

Blending data from different sources

Introduction

One of the major hurdles for schools using value-added data for school improvement purposes, at whatever level of contextualisation, is the time lag between the publication of results in the summer and the issuing of validated[1] value-added data by the DfE the following January (typically) when it is uploaded onto RAISEonline (though the Fischer Family Trust uploads its unamended value-added data late in October). One way around this time-lag is to calculate a kind of 'quasi VA score' for each student by subtracting the estimate[2] for the student at the end of the Key Stage from the actual outcome scores achieved in National Curriculum tests or GCSE examinations. For individual subjects, progress can be calculated by converting each grade to a points score and again subtracting the estimate for that subject from the actual attainment. For National Curriculum tests at KS2, this would be a little more complex as it would require calculating a fine-grade level from a knowledge of the raw scores that correspond with each of the level thresholds, which information is normally published and available to schools shortly after the close of the marking process. And the results of optional National Curriculum tests for students in Year 9 could be treated in the same way. 'Actual-minus-estimate' scores are *quasi* scores because they are not based on an analysis of the progress of students within a specific cohort, but rather the progress made by each student compared with his/her estimate, and these estimates are based on the progress made by students in the previous year's national cohort. It is important to recognise that actual-minus-estimate scores may therefore vary from *true* VA scores published later in the year, but that notwithstanding they allow teachers in schools to produce measures of progress at the student level

---

1 Validated data released in RAISEonline incorporates any approved changes to the data that was requested as part of a data-checking exercise.
2 These estimates can be obtained from the Fischer Family Trust database 'FFTlive', from RAISEonline or from any other source of estimates data that the school uses to inform the process of student- and school-level target setting.

fairly quickly after results are published and thereby seize the initiative of using data to inform improvement and development plans for the coming academic year. Group-level scores (for example by gender, FSM entitlement, ethnicity or social class) can be produced by simply calculating the mean score for all students in that particular group.

An example: using value-added data as a predictor of fixed-term exclusion

The proportion of students receiving either permanent or fixed-term exclusions in England is much greater in secondary than in primary schools. In the period 2003–08, 85 per cent of fixed-term exclusions occurred in secondary schools, 11 per cent in primary schools and the remainder in special schools. The figures for permanent exclusions were very similar (DCSF 2009a). From Figure 7.1, it is clear that there is a strong *age* trend in the data with the proportion of students receiving fixed-term exclusions rising year on year until the final year of secondary school, when it drops slightly. There is a clear jump at age 11, at the transition from primary to secondary school for the majority of pupils in England.

While exclusion during KS1 or KS2 may be a significant indicator of risk of exclusion at KS3 or KS4, it is clear that a number of students who have no record of exclusion at primary school go on to receive them at secondary school. Research using data from 35,000 students over a five-year period (Downey and Kelly 2007b) found that lower-than-expected academic progress across KS2 is an indicator of risk of fixed-term exclusion later on, in secondary school.[3] If the aim is *pre*vention rather than *inter*vention, a cut-off value for lower-than-expected progress needs to be selected in order to determine whether a student has a low enough progress across KS2, and in order to decide the cut-off to identify those students at risk, we can plot the proportion of 'true positives' from the model versus the proportion of 'false positives' that would result at each possible cut-off value; what is known as a ROC[4] curve (see Figure 7.2).

'Sensitivity' represents the proportion of *true positives* (e.g. the percentage who received a 6+ day period of fixed-term exclusion that was correctly predicted by the model). 'Specificity' represents the proportion of *true negatives* (e.g. the percentage who did *not* receive a 6+ day period of fixed-term exclusion correctly

---

3 Part of the rationale for the research was a change in policy from September 2007 that required schools to be responsible for ensuring appropriate educational provision from Day 6 of any period of fixed-term exclusion. Previously, the requirement was from Day 16 (Ofsted 2009). The analysis was carried out using actual-minus-estimate scores calculated using SE estimates from the FFT database and a binary logistic regression analysis conducted.

4 ROC is an acronym for Receiver Operating Characteristic developed in the 1950s to help radio operators determine true signals from noise. They are now widely used in medicine to determine appropriate cut-off thresholds for diagnostic tests.

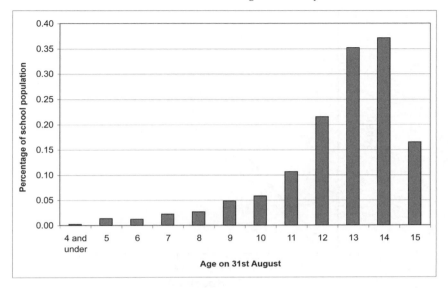

Figure 7.1 Proportion of students receiving at least one fixed-term exclusion during the 2007–08 academic year in English primary and secondary schools (source: www.dcsf.gov.uk/)

identified as *not* being at risk).[5] Perfect prediction can achieve 100 per cent sensitivity (i.e. predict all people from the 'likely to be excluded' group as being likely to be excluded) and 100 per cent specificity (i.e. not predict anyone from the *not* likely to be excluded group as being 'likely to be excluded'). Unity-minus-specificity ('1 − Specificity') therefore represents the corresponding proportion of *false* positives (e.g. '*not* likely to be excluded' students *incorrectly* identified as 'likely to be excluded') present.[6] The straight line on Figure 7.2 marks where the proportion of true positives and false positives are equal (and therefore represents a model which provides the same predictive power as a simple coin toss). Since the curve in our example is only slightly above this line, it provides a little more predictive power than random.

Table 7.1 shows the mean and standard deviations for three groups of students in the Downey and Kelly (2007b) research: all students; students receiving at least one fixed-term exclusion *of any duration*; students receiving at least one fixed-term exclusion *of six days or longer*. The table shows that all students receiving at least one fixed-term exclusion of any duration make just

5 The two measures are closely related to the concepts of Type I and Type II errors. Type I error: the null hypothesis is rejected when it is true. Type II error: the null hypothesis is not rejected when it is false. A test with a high specificity has a low Type I error rate; a test with a high sensitivity has a low Type II error rate.
6 The false negative rate = 1 − sensitivity.

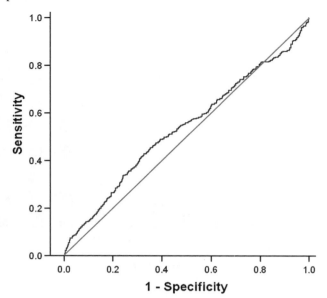

Figure 7.2 Sample ROC curve for a predictive model for (say) 6+ day fixed-term
exclusion based on (say) KS2 actual-minus-estimate score

Table 7.1 Descriptive KS2 progress data for three sets of students in a fixed-term
exclusion analysis

Students	Mean KS2 actual-minus-estimate score	Standard deviation	KS1–KS2 percentile rank*
All students	−0.0078	0.38012	53
All Fixed-Term Exclusion (of any duration) students	−0.1252	0.46035	81
All 6+days Fixed-Term Exclusion students	−0.0666	0.4668	69

* Using FFT SE percentile rank thresholds.

over 0.1 of a National Curriculum level *less* progress on average from KS1
to KS2 than the mean for all students. Those receiving 6+ day fixed-term
exclusions make on average 0.06 of a National Curriculum level less progress.
The practical significance of such small differences in mean scores is hard to
interpret, but one way is to assign percentile ranks to the mean 'actual-minus-
estimate' progress measures. This is a commonly used approach by FFT and
DfE in their value-added reports to help schools benchmark their progress
against that of similar students in similar schools (after adjusting for level of
contextualisation). These percentile ranks can be visualised using a caterpillar

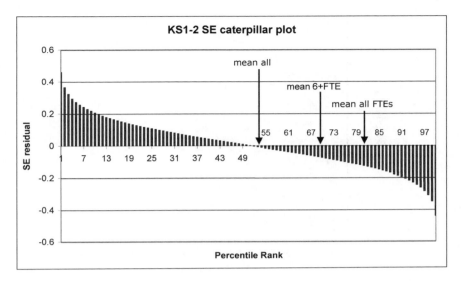

Figure 7.3 Caterpillar plot of actual-minus-estimate residual thresholds for each percentile rank (FTE = fixed-term exclusions)

plot to show the size of the actual-minus-estimate residual threshold for each percentile rank (see Figure 7.3).

Recalling the analogy used in Chapter 4 of the spread of runners in a long distance race, each of these groups could be considered to be 'in the main pack' in terms of comparative progress. The analogy suggests that for the majority of groups around the mean, small differences in residuals (VA scores) produce quite large changes in rank.[7] With a percentile rank of 53, the mean for 'all students' is in the middle of the pack. Those who have received at least one period of fixed-term exclusion *of any length*, with a percentile rank of 81, can be considered to be at the back of the main pack. Those who received at least one period *of six-day (or longer)* fixed-term exclusion made better progress (on average) and (with a percentile rank of 69) are well within the main pack.

A new, more predictive model can be generated following an analysis of other factors — gender, level of SEN in primary school and entitlement to FSM — associated with incidence of exclusion. These factors, together with the KS2 attainment[8] and the KS2 actual-minus-estimate score can be entered stepwise into the logistic regression and a ROC curve produced as on Figure 7.4.

---

7 Those between the 20th and 80th percentiles might be considered to be analogous to the main pack of runners in a long-distance race. Those with ranks above 20 are spread out at the head of the race and those with ranks below 80 are spread out in the tail.

8 Mean fine-grade KS2 test level attained.

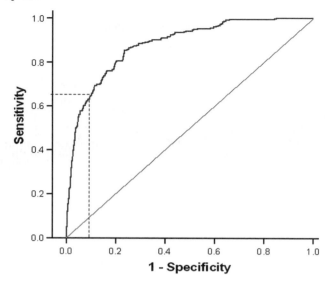

Figure 7.4 Sample ROC curve for a predictive model for (say) 6+ day fixed-term exclusion based on (say) a range of predictive factors

Clearly, from Figure 7.4, this model has greater predictive power than the model in which KS2 progress was the sole independent predictor variable. It remains an issue, of course, to decide how many false positives are acceptable. If a false positive rate of 10 per cent (say) were accepted, this would result in an ability to predict a true positive of 65 per cent (see Figure 7.4). This is a big improvement over the KS2 progress score alone, but if fixed-term exclusion is a relatively rare event, 10 per cent false positives may represent a greater number than the number who actually go on to receive them. For example, in a school in which only 2 per cent of students go on to receive a 6+ day fixed-term exclusion, for a cohort of 300 students we would expect the predictive test correctly to identify four of the six students [65 per cent] who go on to receive a six-day (or longer) fixed-term exclusion, but the test would additionally *falsely* identify 30 students [10 per cent] as likely to receive them. Selecting a cut-off value that reduces the false positives to (say) 4 per cent would reduce the predictive power of the test to 50 per cent in this model, so for our cohort of 300 now, only three of the six students [still 2 per cent of cohort] are likely to be identified together with 12 false positives [4 per cent]. This might be considered a better trade-off as the 12 false-positive students would in any case benefit from additional support (even if received in error).[9]

---

9 In other words, doing preventative work with 34 students, only four of whom are likely to go on to 'offend', may be considered *less* appropriate than working with 15 from whom three are likely to go on to 'offend'.

A predictive model like this is crude, of course – it should certainly be used in conjunction with other data, especially transfer reports from primary schools – but it serves to highlight some students who otherwise might fall 'beneath the radar'.

Another example

Combining value-added and attendance data

Great care needs to be taken with predictive modelling so that inferences/ generalisations *from cohorts* are not thoughtlessly applied to *individuals*. This is as true of value-added estimates generated in RAISEonline and FFT to inform target setting, as it is of the example above to predict fixed-term exclusions. Care needs to be taken (when using predictive data) to consider and triangulate all sources of data and use the professional judgement of teachers to inform the processes of target setting and prevention support.

It is not only predictive models which make the assumption that the characteristics of individuals are similar to those of a group at large. We have already seen in the previous chapter that a single value-added progress score for a school can mask differential effectiveness across the prior attainment range or between students belonging to various subgroups. The assumption that group-level aggregated data is indicative of the characteristics of all the individuals within the group is, as we have seen in the previous chapter, an 'ecological inference fallacy'.[10] The fallacy – a stereotyping fallacy – is that individual members of a group have the average characteristics of the group at large. An example in the field of school effectiveness would be to say that 'poor school attendance results in poor progress': while the statement carries a strong internal logic, the reality is that there is an association between attendance and academic progress *for some* – possibly even for *most* – but definitely *not* for *all* students. Notwithstanding, Figure 7.5 shows an example of a strong and significant association between school-level threshold attainment at KS4 and the mean attendance rate for a school.

There may be common underlying (or moderating) factors to explain the relationship between fixed-term exclusions or absence rate and academic progress, but sometimes the association is not strong, as shown in Figure 7.6 for that between KS1–KS2 CVA and mean attendance rate at school level. Yet despite the weak and non-significant association as shown, it would be wrong to assume that there was therefore *no effect* of absence on academic progress for *any* of students in the school. It is important to avoid a fallacy in that direction too.

---

10 So called because it was a common error in the interpretation of statistical data in ecological research.

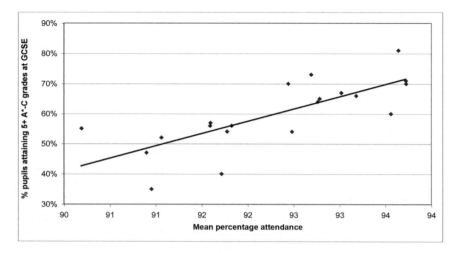

Figure 7.5 Association between KS4 school-level threshold attainment and mean attendance rate for each school (Pearson correlation r = 0.758 [p<0.001])

Working with data – attendance and progress data in this example – *at the student level* provides a means to avoid falling foul of ecological fallacies. The next three sample figures show an analysis of KS4 attainment, progress and attendance for a typical cohort of students, which could provide some useful evidence to inform discussions with students about to embark on post-16 programmes of study/training.[11] Figure 7.7 shows the association between the number of GCSE passes at A*–C and the attendance residual for each student. This is calculated by taking the mean attendance across the Key Stage for each student and subtracting the 'whole cohort average'. The Key Stage attendance residual therefore facilitates comparisons at student level with the mean attendance for the whole cohort.

The figure shows a fairly weak association between mean attendance and number of GCSE passes. It divides up into four uneven-sized quadrants: those students who achieved five or more A*–C passes despite lower-than-average attendance; those with five or more A*–C passes and *higher*-than-average attendance; those who did *not* achieve five A*–C passes but nevertheless had higher-than-average attendance; and those who did *not* achieve five A*–C passes and had lower-than-average attendance. The *school-level* conclusion that attainment and attendance are linked does not hold so well for students in the bottom-right quadrant or the top-left quadrant. The former had good attendance but poor GCSE results; the latter had poor attendance but good

11 It is possible to conduct similar analyses for attainment and progress at the end of other Key Stages.

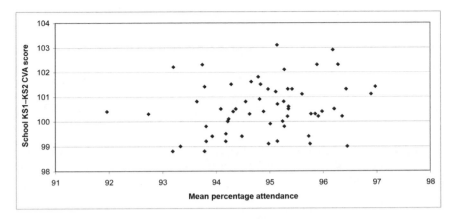

Figure 7.6 Association between school-level KS1–KS2 CVA and mean attendance rate for each school (Pearson correlation r = 0.220 [p>0.09])

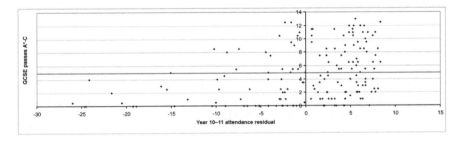

Figure 7.7 Association between number of GCSE passes at A*–C (level 2) and the attendance residual for each student (Pearson correlation r = 0.360 [p<0.001])

GCSE results. Similarly, the bottom-left and top-right quadrants may contain students for whom low attendance *did* impact on attainment, but even here this result would need to be considered against other possible explanations.

Figure 7.8 shows a similar analysis for attainment at the Level 1 threshold of five or more passes at grades A*–G. Here the association between attainment and attendance is stronger, but the lower attainment threshold means that the analysis does not discriminate so well.

And Figure 7.9 shows the results of an analysis of KS3–KS4 'actual-minus-estimate' progress measures for each student with their attendance residual. This association is the strongest of the three and discriminates much better between students with low attendance rates for KS4. In practice, by highlighting the point for an individual student, it might be possible to discuss with that student (and his/her parents) the impact that low attendance might have had on progress across the Key Stage. Using the 'actual-minus-estimate'

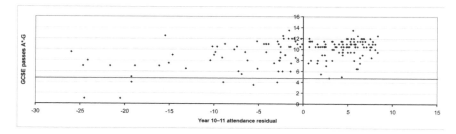

Figure 7.8 Association between number of GCSE passes at A*–C (level 1) and the attendance residual for each student (Pearson correlation r = 0.498 [p<0.001])

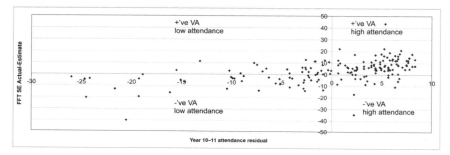

Figure 7.9 Association between progress (FFT SE actual-minus-estimate for GCSE capped point score) and attendance residual at student level (Pearson correlation r = 0.530 [p<0.001])

measure allows such a discussion to occur *at the start of the autumn term* rather than waiting for value-added data to be published halfway through the year.

It is possible to use other measures of attendance in analyses like these; one useful metric is the total number of 'broken weeks' during the Key Stage, which would help to discriminate between those students with low attendance as a result of 'serial absenteeism' and those who (say) had a single extended period of illness or unauthorised leave.

A third example: combining attainment and progress data with student attitudes and self-concept data

An increasing number of student attitude and self-concept measures are available to schools to gather 'student voice' data. Some of these are commercial services such as the 'Pupil Attitudes to Self and School' (PASS) survey produced by W3insights,[12] which assesses the attitudes of students across nine

12 See www.w3insights.pass-survey.com/pass.htm

dimensions: feelings about school, perceived learning capacity, self-regard, preparedness for learning, attitudes to teachers, general work ethic, learner confidence, attendance attitudes, and response to the curriculum. Other sources include CEM's MidYIS, Yellis and Alis services,[13] and freely available survey instruments from various School Effectiveness Research projects (e.g. Van Damme *et al.* 2002).

When PASS data is analysed and returned to schools, student responses to the questions related to each dimension are shown as percentile scores based on responses from *all* students in *all* subscribing schools. The percentile scores are colour-coded: scores in the range 0–5 (incl.) – i.e. in the lowest 5 per cent of responses – are flagged red; 5–20 are flagged amber; and scores greater than 20 are flagged green. Teachers familiar with PASS are accustomed to working with the red/amber/green 'traffic light' colour scheme, so a similar colour-coding can be applied to data such as (say) actual-minus-estimate progress scores or attendance rates: a red flag for an actual-minus-estimate score of half a level or worse below estimate (<-0.5); amber for equal-to-estimate or below-estimate progress no worse than half a level (-0.5 to 0.0); and green for any scores above the estimate (>0.0). However, care needs to be taken not to overstate the link between student perception of own self-concept and attitude, and attainment and progress, because School Effectiveness Research suggests only a modest association (Van Landeghem *et al.* 2002). For example, Downey and Kelly (2007b, 2008) found that the associations between actual-minus-estimate *progress* and the nine PASS self-concept and attitude scores were *not* significant, but that there *were* significant positive associations between *attainment* (using NC fine-grade levels) and some of the PASS dimensions. This may be indicative of the high-stakes nature of raw *attainment* outcomes for students and a lower emphasis on *progress* per se. It may also suggest (causally) that a legacy of low attainment is low self-concept. In any case, using these low associations as grounds for rejecting the use of self-concept and attitudes data would be another example of an ecological fallacy – for some students, there *will* be direct links between their attainment/progress and their attitudes and self-concept, even if that is not the case for the entire group – and bringing the two sets of data together can help identify those students and inform teachers' own professional judgement.

If an attitude survey is repeated each year or at the beginning and end of a Key Stage say, *changes* in attitude and self-concept across a Key Stage can be mapped against progress (across the same Key Stage). Table 7.2 is an example of one such survey. It shows PASS-type 'attitude and self-concept' data [columns 3–11], 'attainment' and 'progress' data [columns 12–14], and 'attendance' data [column 15] for five students. An analysis of the data might run something like this:

13 See www.cemcentre.org

- Students A, B and C are all attaining around the national expectation for students at age 14 (i.e. between NC Levels 5 and 6) [columns 12–14; rows A, B and C; top line], but their progress patterns are contrasting. Student A [row A; lower line] has made *greater* than estimated progress [green] in all three subjects [columns 12–14], more than a half a level more than estimated in mathematics and science [0.51 and 0.60]. The 'self-concept attitude' data [columns 3–11] for Student A shows a fairly low baseline in Year 7 [columns 3–11] with movement to a more positive set of responses in Year 9, although it should be borne in mind that students are more self-critical at some times than at other times. Attendance Attitudes [column 10] have improved and attendance [column 15; 3.09] is well above the cohort average for the Key Stage.

- Student B on the other hand made *less* progress than estimated [red] from KS2 prior attainment levels in all three subjects [columns 12–14; row B; lower line]: over half a level less progress in science [–0.68] and at least one level less in mathematics and English [–1.27 and –1.00]. For this student, low attendance in Year 7 was an issue that resulted in below-average attendance for the three years of KS3 [column 15; amber; –1.6]. The attitude and self-concept responses [columns 3–11] all show a downward trend [columns 3–11; Year 9 lower than Year 7] from a high baseline in Year 7. If such a trend were to continue into KS4, there would be implications for likely attainment at GCSE.

- Student C shows mixed progress: mathematics is in line with the estimate [0.00], English is slightly below [–0.16] and science slightly above [0.23]. The attitude and self-concept responses [columns 3–11] also show a mixed pattern with most of the domains associated with attainment (Perceived Learning Capacity, Self-regard, Preparedness for Learning, General Work Ethic and Response to the Curriculum) showing an upward trend, but feelings about school and attitudes to teachers showing a marked decline [columns 3 and 7; Year 9 line lower than Year 7 line]. This may be due to a disagreement with a teacher around the time the Year 9 survey was carried out and so may not reflect a trend, but discussion with the student might get to the bottom of this and ascertain whether there are implications for progress (at KS4). Importantly, the disaffection expressed in the attitudes and self-concept data appears not (yet) to have manifested itself in poor attendance,[14] which is well above the cohort average for the Key Stage [6.21].

- Students D and E have attainment below national expectations for students at age 14 [columns 12–14; top line; numbers are less that 5 and 6]. Again,

---

14 Of course, there may well be no association for this student between attendance and disaffection, but a conversation around the data would at a minimum help to establish that fact and/or uncover other factors.

Table 7.2 Bringing together attitude, self-concept, attainment/progress and attendance data for five students

Student	Year	Feelings about School	Perceived Learning Capability	Self-regard	Preparedness for Learning	Attitudes to Teachers	General Work Ethic	Learner Confidence	Attendance Attitudes	Response to the Curriculum	KS2–3 maths fine grade attainment (top) & act.-minus-est. progress (below)	KS2–3 English fine grade (top) attainment (top) & act.-minus-est. progress (below)	KS2–3 science fine grade (top) attainment (top) & act.-minus-est. progress (below)	KS3 attendance residual and Yr7–8 & Yr 8–9 trend
A	7	1.5	30.3	0.4	14.9	5.5	18.2	6.0	6.5	2.4	7.1	5.6	6.8	3.09
	9	10.6	67.4	17.5	16.6	29.9	18.4	18.5	47.5	34.9	0.51	0.17	0.60	↗ ↘
B	7	95.3	63.5	60.5	92.3	70.8	89.7	80.4	69.9	61.2	6.1	5.3	5.7	−1.6
	9	52.2	48.6	39.5	41.0	29.9	84.2	59.7	47.5	34.9	−1.27	−1.00	−0.68	↑ ↘
C	7	38.5	54.2	36.0	46.0	37.7	77.6	14.4	46.6	32.7	5.3	5.0	5.6	6.21
	9	4.4	95.2	88.2	51.9	1.4	38.3	78.8	25.1	84.6	0.00	−0.16	0.23	↗ ↗
D	7	22.9	20.5	15.2	18.6	24.2	77.6	27.5	26.8	20.0	4.4	4.3	4.4	5.96
	9	27.7	17.7	26.6	12.0	17.7	7.9	49.4	47.5	11.6	0.12	0.11	0.40	↗ ↗
E	7	62.4	67.4	69.1	67.4	45.1	77.6	85.8	61.9	52.5	4.4	4.7	4.7	−2.35
	9	13.2	38.8	10.4	41.0	9.9	38.3	59.7	35.1	11.6	−0.83	−0.71	−0.51	↘ ↘

Notes: Columns 3–11: red (dark shade) for 0–5; amber (mid shade) for 5–20; green (light shade) >20. Columns 12–15: red flag for <−0.5 to 0.0; and green for >0.0. Numbers in columns 3–11 are percentiles; numbers in columns 12–14 are (top line) fine-grade NC levels and (lower line) KS2–3 actual minus estimate progress scores; numbers in column 15 are percentages. In column 15, a 'straight-down' arrow means a sharp (>3.0%) decline, an 'inclined-down' arrow means a smaller decrease, etc.

there are contrasting patterns of progress. Student D has made progress broadly in line with estimates in each subject [0.12, 0.11 and 0.40]. The attitude and self-concept responses [columns 3–11] show mixed changes from Year 7 to Year 9, but some of the domains most closely associated with attainment are still fairly low scoring. This student would benefit from specific encouragement and support in order to continue making progress during KS4 in line with (or above) expectation.

- Student E has a similar pattern of attainment to Student D, but has made more than half a level less progress across all three subjects [–0.83, –0.71 and –0.51]. The attitude and self-concept responses are less positive for Year 9 than for the Year 7 baseline [columns 3–11; Year 9 line lower than Year 7 line] and mean KS3 attendance is over 2 per cent lower than average [–2.35], with a big drop in attendance in Year 9 [column 15; straight down arrow]. This may be a reason for the lower-than-expected attainment in Year 9 assessments, but the change in attitude and self-concept responses also raises concerns which may be worth exploring with the student as KS4 study begins.

Of course this type of data is 'pupil voice' and as such does not provide answers per se, but it does provide a platform for further personal discussion with students, which process is likely to be more informative and beneficial in terms of revealing the link between attitudes and progress than the data itself.

A fourth example: using attainment and progress data to monitor transitions to post-16 education and training[15]

In the UK, many local authorities have data-sharing arrangements with other agencies; for example, with the Connexions service which manages data on the destinations of young people after reaching the end of compulsory schooling. By merging attainment and progress data with destination data from Connexions (say), it is possible to compare the pre-16 academic trajectories of young people with post-16 destinations (Downey and Kelly 2010).

Figure 7.10 shows an example from one local authority in England of the mean GCSE attainment of young people (in two cohorts) arranged according to post-16 destination (in seven categories plus 'not known'):

- *FT training* – young people engaged in full-time training programmes at GCSE or pre-GCSE level.

---

15 The school-leaving age in the UK is being raised from its traditional 16. The terms 'post-16' and 'post-compulsory', which used to be synonymous, now refer to different stages. We use 'post-16' to mean the phase immediately after GCSE/KS4, and 'post-compulsory' to mean a later phase when schooling is optional.

- *NEET* – young people 'not in employment, education or training'. *Unavailable* and *available* denotes whether or not the young person was able to take up an offer of employment, education or training.
- *JWT* – young people in jobs without a national recognised training component.
- *WBL* – young people in work-based learning settings such as apprenticeships.
- *FT Educn (FE)* – young people in full-time education in Further Education colleges.
- *FT Educn (school)* – young people in full-time education in school and sixth-form colleges.

Figure 7.10 shows a marked difference in the mean number of GCSE grades A*–C achieved by young people who went on to full-time education in school settings compared to any of the other destinations. The lower mean number of A*–C grades for those in full-time education in Further Education (FE) settings might be indicative of the wider ability range going into the varied mix of full-time programmes there.

A similar analysis can be carried out using measures of *progress* (rather than of *attainment*). Figure 7.11 shows a similar presentation of the KS2–KS4 CVA progress scores for the same two cohorts as in Figure 7.10. The pattern is similar. Only those groups in school-based or FE-based full-time education made progress

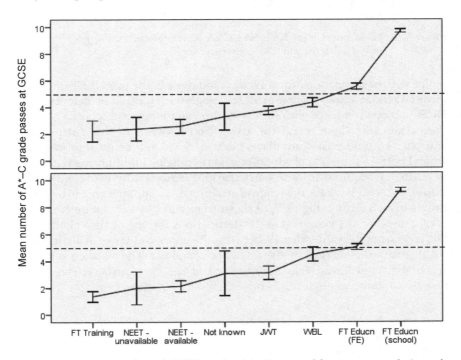

Figure 7.10 Mean number of GCSE grades A*–C attained by young people in each post-16 destination (two consecutive cohorts)

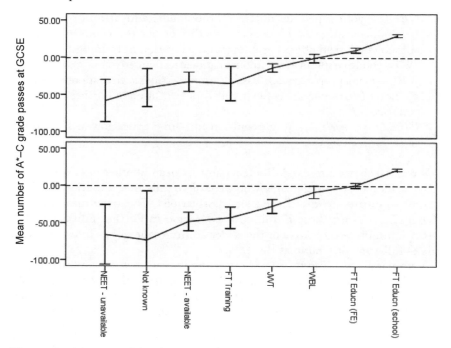

Figure 7.11 Mean pupil-level KS2–KS4 CVA scores for the young people in each post-16 destination (two consecutive cohorts)

in line with or above the national average, and those in the two NEET categories made on average at least a whole grade less progress in every one of their best eight GCSE subjects compared with similar students in the national cohort.

Analyses like these reveal the association between attainment/progress and post-16 (and post-compulsory) destinations, and could inform policy around post-16 provision of education and training by highlighting the degree of challenge required to raise participation. However, by using only mean values, the analyses mask the range of attainment and progress made by young people in each setting. Figure 7.12 shows a box and whisker plot for KS2–KS4 CVA scores for the various post-16 destinations for one of the cohorts. The box represents the values that lie between the upper and lower quartiles, with the median value marked by the small horizontal bar. The whiskers represent the highest and lowest values for the rest of the data, with extreme values ('outliers') shown as circles and crosses.[16]

16 Circles are used to represent outliers that are between 1.5 and 3 times the box length (i.e. the inter-quartile range). The crosses represent scores that are more than 3 box lengths from the edge of the box.

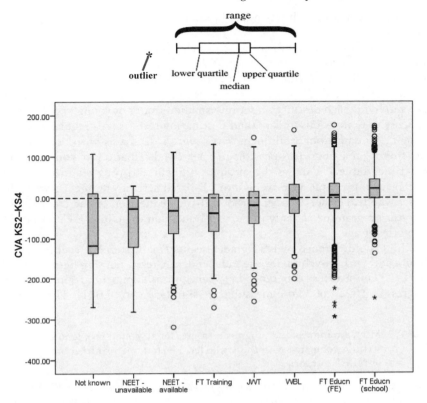

Figure 7.12 Box and whisker plots of KS2–KS4 CVA scores for each post-16 destination (for one cohort)

The box and whisker plots very clearly display the wide spread of KS2–KS4 CVA scores for each post-16 destination. Approximately three-quarters of the young people in school-based settings had positive KS2–KS4 CVA scores and had therefore made progress in line with or above that made by all students in their cohort nationally (after adjusting for all the factors in the CVA model). It is also possible to see just how wide was the range of progress for those who went into full-time FE settings: almost half made *less-than-average* progress compared to their peers in the national cohort and there is a 'tail' of outliers extending down to extremely low (i.e. very negative) CVA scores. The young people represented in these tails are students who made very low progress and failed to complete eight GCSEs (thereby compromising their best-eight GCSE points score), as well as those who obtained low grades across the whole range of their best eight GCSEs. Improving post-16 participation rates requires all providers of post-16 education and training to move more young people out of non-participation categories into full-time education and training settings, which obviously has implications for the academic attainment and progress made by students in each setting and requires an appropriate mix of post-16 provision.

A simple focus on overall mean scores also masks evidence of differential effectiveness *in terms of the support and guidance given to students* to make appropriate transitions from pre-16 to post-16 education and training. One of the ways to reveal differential effectiveness in the post-16 progression setting is to subdivide each destination set into smaller groups of young people. Local branches of Connexions update their destination records on a regular basis, so by merging data from attainment and progress databases with destinations data from Connexions, it is possible to track the destinations of young people over time. Table 7.3 shows the mean attainment and progress measures for a set of young people who went into FE-based settings at age 16 with the subset who had either dropped out of full-time education or had completed a one-year programme of study in Further Education to go into JWT or NEET categories at age 17.

While the difference in KS2 grades seems small, some of them are still significant, with 'p-values' for the independent t-test[17] ranging between 0.02 and 0.1. The greatest difference between groups comes in attainment and progress at 16, all of whose measures are significant (p<0.001). The clearest

Table 7.3 Mean attainment and progress measures for all young people in FE settings compared with those who left FE after one year to go into JWT or NEET categories

Attainment/progress measure (mean)	*Value for all young people in FE settings*	*Value for those leaving FE after one year to go into JWT or NEET*
KS2 Reading	4.4	4.3
KS2 Writing	4.0	3.9
KS2 Maths	4.2	4.0
Passes A*–G at GCSE	9.4 (93% attain Level 1)	8.6 (93% attain Level 1)
Passes A*–C at GCSE	5.5 (53% attain Level 2)	3.4 (31% attain Level 2)
KS2–KS4 CVA	11.0	−16.3
KS3–KS4 CVA	6.5	−14.0
5+A*–C inc EM at GCSE	33%	14%

17 A t-test is any statistical hypothesis test in which the test statistic follows a Student's t distribution if the null hypothesis is true. (A 'Student's t' distribution – or simply a 't-distribution' – is a probability distribution that arises in estimating the mean of a normally distributed population when the sample size is small.)

gap can be observed at the higher attainment thresholds – number of A*–C passes [row 5; 53 per cent vs. 31 per cent] and the proportion achieving this Level 2 threshold including English and mathematics [bottom row; 33 per cent vs. 14 per cent] – and in the mean KS2–KS4 CVA progress scores [row 6; 11.0 and –16.3].

In Table 7.4, the pre-16 academic trajectories for students who made transition from Further Education to JWT and NEET (non-participation) categories are compared with all those who went directly into JWT settings at age 16. It can be seen that they are very similar in profile.

A similar analysis can be conducted for those students who left school after one year of post-16 study. Table 7.5 shows the mean attainment and progress measures for those who went into school-based settings at age 16 with the subset who had either dropped out or completed their programmes of study in school to go into one of the non-participation categories of JWT or NEET.

The differences in KS2 mean grades are greater than those in Further Education (cf. Table 7.4), but as with the FE comparison, the greatest difference comes at the higher attainment thresholds: number of A*–C passes [row 5; 87 per cent vs. 55 per cent] and the proportion achieving that threshold including English and mathematics [bottom row; 76 per cent vs. 38 per cent]. The differences in the mean CVA progress scores are also significant (p<0.001 for the KS2–KS4 and p<0.01 for the KS3–KS4 CVA) [rows 6 and 7]. If the group who left school after one year to go into the JWT or NEET categories is compared to those who went straight into Further Education at 16+ (Table 7.4), it can be seen that these students were more akin to their peers

Table 7.4 Mean attainment and progress measures for young people who left FE after one year to go into JWT or NEET categories compared with those who went straight into JWT settings at age 16

Attainment/progress measure (mean)	Value for those leaving FE after one year to go into 'JWT' or 'NEET'	Value for all young people in 'JWT' or 'NEET'
KS2 Reading	4.3	4.2
KS2 Writing	3.9	3.8
KS2 Maths	4.0	4.0
Passes A*–G at GCSE	8.6 (93% attain Level 1)	8.5 (87% attain Level 1)
Passes A*–C at GCSE	3.4 (31% attain Level 2)	2.9 (25% attain Level 2)
KS2–KS4 CVA	–16.3	–19.8
KS3–KS4 CVA	–14.0	–13.7
5+A*–C inc EM at GCSE	14%	13%

Table 7.5 Mean attainment and progress measures for all young people in school
settings and sixth-form colleges compared with those who left schools and
sixth-form colleges after one year to go into JWT or NEET categories

Attainment/progress measure (mean)	Value for all young people in school settings	Value for those leaving school after one year to go into JWT or NEET
KS2 Reading	5.0	4.6
KS2 Writing	4.5	4.1
KS2 Maths	4.7	4.4
Passes A*–G at GCSE	10.9 (99% attain Level 1)	10.1 (99% attain Level 1)
Passes A*–C at GCSE	9.3 (87% attain Level 2)	5.5 (55% attain Level 2)
KS2–KS4 CVA	27.2	6.7
KS3–KS4 CVA	15.8	7.2
5+A*–C inc EM at GCSE	76%	38%

who were in Further Education (in terms of their academic trajectory to age 16)
than their fellow students in schools.

One of the issues raised by progression data and its analysis, like that
given above, is that the process of giving advice to young people to inform
their decision making regarding transitions – what is known in the UK as
'Independent Information, Advice and Guidance' (IIAG) – may itself be
differentially effective across the prior attainment range, just like teaching
in classrooms! While the system may be working well for the majority of
students, those who are on the cusp of suitability for school-based study would
benefit from a more *targeted* approach to IIAG. Since it is possible to identify
these students *from their pre-16 attainment and progress measures*, as above, it
should be possible to implement focused monitoring and support strategies
to help them cope better with the challenges.

Part III

The future

Why data is important

8 Managing effectiveness data for school improvement

Introduction

Data and data-informed research generates value in schools, and managing it is an increasingly important function since it used to hold schools and teachers accountable for their performance and to drive improvement. The most successful organisations in the commercial sector are the ones that have the capacity to act on data even when circumstances and metrics change, and there is no reason to suppose that schools are any different in this respect. The belief that effectiveness data can be used to leverage improvement depends on having it shared and used in the right places. It requires:

- good systems, well managed;
- the ability to retain, analyse and interpret some data centrally and other data 'at the chalkface';
- the capability everywhere to use data *reflectively*.

Data management as a set of complementary processes

Data management can be represented as a set of complementary orthogonal processes (see Figure 8.1): data analysed, interpreted and transferred between managers; data transferred in pre-digested form from senior management, via 'data managers' as gatekeepers, to classroom teachers and subject leaders; and data transferred as 'folk knowledge'[1] between classroom teachers. If there is a tendency to skew the way data is managed, it is in respect of the relative importance given to these processes, and the role played by data managers as 'opening' or 'closing' gatekeepers.

Traditionally, the transfer of data from management to teachers has dominated the agenda, but the potential loss (and cost of remediation) to the school when this malfunctions has been largely ignored. The obvious consequences of a data system like this is that individual teachers and subject departments do not

---

1 The term is *not* used here in a pejorative sense.

feel (or accept) ownership of the data – they can only wonder and worry at the analysis and interpretation of others – and therefore do not optimise its use to inform teaching and learning *in the classroom*. If the term 'high leverage' is used to describe processes whereby a disproportionately high effect is generated by a relatively low effort, the deficit generated by data *not* getting to teachers, in a form that enables them to own it and use it, can be said to create a culture of 'low leverage' within schools. Good data analysis and interpretation is 'normalised' in schools by the intelligent, repeated and refined use of experience. It must have value added to it to morph it into useful practitioner-focused information and this is ideally done by practitioners who are best placed to dictate the most appropriate analytical technique (assuming they are statistically literate) and validate from experience (and other data) the emerging interpretations. When a school cannot do that, it is the poorer for it.

Good data management is about growing in-house expertise in handling data, managing its transfer between individuals, retaining and maintaining it as a school resource, managing its analysis and interpretation, and facilitating its dissemination. However, value is not added everywhere. There is no value added to data in merely collecting and storing it, or in transferring it in pre-interpreted form from one colleague to another. The value is added *through interpretation and use*, and feeding back that experience to the school as an organisation, where it can be stored. In terms of statistical literacy, which is more often than not the practical barrier in school data systems, a starting point may be a 'directory of expertise', which might typically emerge from an internal

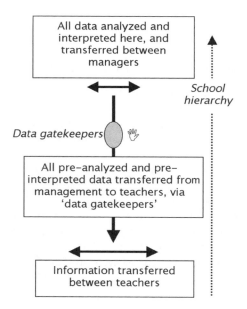

Figure 8.1 Data management system as a pair of complementary processes

audit of statistical expertise and experience among staff. In large commercial companies, this can be posted on an intranet; in smaller organisations like schools, it is more likely to be located in the memory of senior and curriculum leadership teams. Updating details of individual expertise should be the responsibility of individual teachers, but the updating should be regular and it should be a contractual obligation or a basis for promotion, rather than merely a professional desire.

The need for data management in schools is driven by recent changes in the way schools are managed, problems of recruitment and retention of teachers and heads, and the need for schools to account for their performance in pupil attainment terms. The higher turnover of teachers and the increasing importance of teaching assistants in the delivery of education have created a greater need for teachers to be able to access, analyse and interpret data for themselves, and spread good practice in respect of data. New funding imperatives have brought performance to the top of the agenda and greater competition between schools has kept it there, but as human resources become scarce in the sector and as operational conditions become more difficult, tensions grow between the need to nourish the ability of individuals to handle and exploit data, and the need to lock that expertise into schools.

Challenges to data management

How data can be collected, analysed, interpreted and utilised resides in the professional capital of teachers and school managers, and in the systemic processes, routines, relationships, infrastructure, culture and symbolism of the school as an organisation. However, to safeguard its use for the benefit of the school, it should reside in more than the person of the data manager. Concentration of expertise, which can sometimes tip over into 'hoarding', can come about as a result of management ineptitude or (as is frequently the case in bureaucracies because of their nature) because colleagues refuse to share their expertise. The 'know-how dependency' created by the hoarding of expertise is very damaging to organisations like schools, particularly in relation to attainment and progress data. Apart from the more obvious ways of dealing with the problem – convincing the incumbent or making it a contractual obligation to share – there are other ways of avoiding the situation: rotation of responsibilities among senior post-holders or obviating the need for a data gatekeeper altogether. It is also disconcerting when data expertise exists in a school, but no one is sure where it is; or when some expertise is located and codified (i.e. rendered capable of being shared), but is incomplete. It is a 'half-knowledge': enough to keep colleagues frantic in their search for the missing pieces, but not enough to enable them to complete any useful analysis. Analysis and interpretation *are* done, of course, but not well enough that teachers could stand over their results with any great authority, and some run scared that flawed interpretations will come back to haunt them (Kelly 2004).

The worst offenders in terms of passing on half-knowledge are those who themselves were victims of the same disadvantage, and it is all too easy for this kind of situation to perpetuate itself in schools, where work is so person-centred and success depends to such a large extent on imponderables like confidence and trust. Consequently, the problem of half-knowledge can and does occur in schools even when there is good will on all sides, which makes the need for a properly structured data management system even more important. Schools need data, but teachers can suffer from overload when they are swamped with it without the experience or expertise to utilise it effectively and efficiently. Either the data is poorly organised or it is transferred from colleague to colleague without adequate explanation of how it fits together in a whole-school way or how it can be used for school improvement. Data is not information, and information is not knowledge.

Unfortunately, when expertise *is* properly classified and transferred in education settings, it can quickly become obsolete. The shelf life for pupil attainment and progress data and the models that make it useful, for example, is very short and the situation changes according to a political (rather than an educational) timetable. The struggle to disentangle current from obsolete information is part and parcel of everyday life for schools, which is why as much as possible of a school's work with data should be done *at the practitioner interface*. Failure to disregard obsolete data leads to myth and ignorance, and is guaranteed only to undermine good practice and reduce school improvement to a 'paint-by-numbers' process. Success in encouraging a culture where data is sought after, and its analysis and interpretation valued, is best achieved through formal forums and critical reviews of understanding among staff.

Data management is about using data to promote improvement, not generating more of it for its own sake, so it must involve training teachers to develop new skills and adapt to new procedures as and when they emerge or are needed. Schools, like commercial companies, should have 'futures forums' where likely change is recognised in advance, and analysis and interpretation techniques are discussed and planned. At present that happens too infrequently, with teachers perceiving themselves only as the passive recipients of someone else's interpretation (Kelly *et al.* 2010). Training is needed and it should be tailored to individual teacher and subject need as this results in a 'longer burn' for acquired skills. Training ties know-how to the school through the individual, not to the individual through the school, preventing knowledge-hoarding and encouraging networking within the organisation.

In addition to being a good staff retention strategy, good data management can be an effective *recruitment* tool, offering fast-track employees a fast-track start. The best teachers want to get into their careers quickly and surely, meeting and (hopefully) exceeding expectations. Good data management, because of its predicative dimension, is a manifestation of a school's commitment to its own future, and for the welfare and success of its staff. Data generates new value and expertise every time it is operationalised or transferred to a colleague; old insights are preserved and new ones generated. Good data management is the antidote to organisational entropy and the 'coasting' malaise (characterised by a lack of challenge to established ways-of-doing) that seems to affect some successful schools. After a while, participation in (and commitment to) data becomes part of the culture of a school, so there must be some systemic facility for storage. What data managers must do is ensure that there is no obstacle to engagement and that associated bureaucratic chores are minimised. Belief in the school's data systems is also critical. The only way to convince cynical teachers of the benefits of data to them (as well as to the school) is to demonstrate in concrete terms how it would otherwise be worse: engagement with data avoids duplication of effort, it reinforces professional judgement and it codifies experience.

Data management as a networked system

The traditional arrangement whereby a deputy head, assistant head or a head of department assumes responsibility for coordinating the overall management of data in a school usually reflects its historical nature and extent of use. However, the most important thing is for a system to be set up within a school so that pupil attainment data eventually becomes part of everyone's modus operandi, and expectations as to its use become part of the culture. The wider use of data – by which we mean its access, analysis, interpretation and utilisation – cannot be imposed by diktat. It requires the cooperation and participation of teachers, so an essential ingredient to success is the extent to which effective teams can be built around the issues it throws up. This necessarily involves the coming together of teachers and groups of teachers, and the manner in which they form a network is of obvious importance.

A data network can be thought of as an intermeshed system of information conduits involving teachers (including school managers and curriculum leaders) or groups of teachers working together, around a hub, towards a common goal. The networked system links together 'factions' that have common (albeit transitory) interests, enabling them to share resources, ideas, expertise and experience in an efficient manner. The complexity of networks will vary from school to school of course, but they all aspire to add value to, and learn from, the data they use. From an organisational point of view, networks are about 'data intelligence': the ability of a school to learn from its data and be quick in taking meaning from its data experience.

There are two features of data intelligence in particular that make networked systems different from non-networked ones, and that have a bearing on the management of data: where the data intelligence of the network resides; and how the *fluidity* of its members' efforts affects the network's effectiveness. Networked data intelligence is the ability of a network to accumulate, share, adapt and distribute information gained from the experience of engaging with and utilising data. It imparts value to the actions a school takes on the basis of its data, and to its attempt to manage implications for practice. Some writers (e.g. Sawhney and Parikh 2001) have differentiated between 'back-end' and 'front-end' organisational intelligence. The former is intelligence that becomes embedded in the shared infrastructure at the network core; it is centralised, robust and standardised. The latter, on the other hand, fragments into different forms at the periphery of the network; it is *de*centralised, flexible and contextualised. Both types of intelligence are needed by a school managing its data: back-end intelligence to store and process institutional memory and professional expertise; front-end intelligence to make use of data in the classroom and in the school's dealings with students and parents at the stakeholder interface (Kelly 2001). The two intelligences may occasionally need to be coupled together, but generally a school network needs to partition them so that the core can efficiently store, process, analyse and interpret whole-school data, and the periphery (the interface with pupils and parents) can be customised by analysing and interpreting data to meet the requirements of individual teachers, pupils and subjects.

The 'partition of intelligence' – not unlike the 'partition of variance' in multilevel modelling – is one determinant of a network's efficiency. In an efficient network, back-end intelligence is *not* replicated at the periphery. It is pushed back to the core, where it is embedded in the infrastructure. Meanwhile, front-end intelligence is (deliberately) fragmented at the periphery of the network, and the conduits between the periphery and the core are 'hollowed out' to become passive; in other words, with little or no capacity for

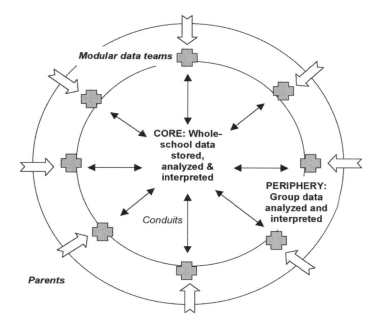

Figure 8.2 Data management as a networked system

generating value *themselves*. Only the peripheral ends (classroom practitioners) and the core become significant sources of value-creation (see Figure 8.2).

The total effort of a data network is the sum of all the individual attempts to interpret and utilise data. The fluidity of this effort – how easily it can respond to new demands made of the data – is another determinant of the network's effectiveness, reflecting the way the school organises its staff and the way it serves the local community. In terms of data, in traditional schools individual teachers are tightly grouped in large units of effort, isolated from each other in departments. In contrast, a data-networked school has smaller free-floating units of effort and data expertise coalesces in temporary coalitions as and when the data demands it. This notion of 'fluidity of effort' has implications for schools seeking to manage their engagement with pupil attainment and progress data. Different teachers or groups of teachers can combine their capabilities and experiences in temporary and flexible alliances to capitalise on particular opportunities or to address particular issues thrown up by the data. Management then becomes associated with *orchestrating the flow of intelligence* and *coordinating the effort*, rather than with instructional leadership, but a protocol or system is required for this. Without it, individual coalitions cannot communicate effectively with each other, never mind collaborate, and this has clear implications for staff development.

Schools preparing for data management and consolidating their data expertise must take account of the influence of 'partition' and 'fluidity' on their structures, which need to be highly connected. For schools and colleges, the ability to respond to the demands of pupil (and external) data is now more important than the ability simply to collect it. The notion of adding and retaining value has altered too. In a network, everyone and everything is connected and value behaves differently than in a (traditional) hierarchical organisation (Kelly 2004):

- *Value is added at the periphery and retained in the core*: Most value is added at the periphery, near pupils and parents, where highly customised connections are made. However, as far as managing data is concerned, the important thing is that the value generated in interactions at the periphery is retained at the core, where generic data-processing functions consolidate know-how and expertise.
- *Value lies in the shared infrastructure and in modularity*: A shared infrastructure typically takes the form of basic experiential storage-type functions as well as common functions like administration. In a network, organisational capabilities and processes are restructured as well-defined, self-contained modules that can quickly and seamlessly connect together in different ways. If a value-adding/value-retaining process is defined as a series of modules operating sequentially to create a process by which some piece of intelligence has value added to it and is retained by the school, success in managing it lies in creating modules that can be plugged into as many

different value-adding processes as possible so that capability can be distributed as broadly as possible.

• *Value is added through orchestration*: As modularisation becomes more prevalent, the ability to coordinate independent modules becomes a valuable new leadership skill.

Reshaping a school as a network of data teams

The shrinking of middle management in schools is a consequence of intelligence getting pushed one way to the core *and* the other way to the periphery. Networked organisations have less need for *middle* managers because communication is faster and easier, and collaboration is almost unwitting. In old style organisations, there was a need for middle management to package and distribute data on its way up or down the hierarchical structure between the core and the periphery. However, this gate-keeping function is redundant in schools committed to 'democratising' data, and the role of middle management, where it exists at all, is just to direct (or facilitate) communication between the core and the periphery.

Just as value-adding intelligence is concentrated at the periphery of a network (where data is interpreted and used to improve practice), value-retention (the storing of whole-school data and the collective experience of analysing it) is located primarily at the core. Leadership and strategic functions are also concentrated at the core, but day-to-day decision making is of necessity pushed to the teaching periphery, creating the need for a new professionalism among teachers with regard to data and how to use it. Fluidity of effort has its effect too. Organisational capability becomes more distributed and modular and passive conduits allow dispersed individuals and groups to connect together to solve problems and respond to opportunities without restructuring cost to the school. Cooperation between previously unconnected departments is no longer problematic or unusual; in fact, it becomes an expectation.

The fundamental data restructuring of a school and the roles within it is threatening, but it does offer certain opportunities: staff, parents and students can become better informed and therefore (potentially) more supportive; and competing departments can come together more freely to provide a better service. The greatest obstacle to restructuring data systems in schools is the preconception of what the result should look like. Schools reconfigured as 'data-aware' need properly trained managers who have the confidence to overcome these preconceptions. The need to understand the nature of networks means that senior managers must dedicate resources to both the core and the periphery, and they must support the value-storage and value-adding processes that takes place (respectively) in both places. Data managers must change their role from *filtration* (sorting information as it passes up and down the organisation) to *facilitation* (orchestrating the interaction between the periphery and the core). Organisational elements at the periphery, where the school interfaces with students and parents, must accept more responsibility and greater self-direction. Action must be dictated by independent professional judgement, but informed by institutional strategy (see Figure 8.3).

A failing school is characterised by an inability to adapt, an unwillingness to learn and unreliable communications. Whereas networked schools are structured to encourage effective communications, poor schools build barriers to it and the cyclical flow of data and feedback suffers thrombosis as boundaries grow between hierarchical levels and between subject departments on the same hierarchical level. However, networked organisations are not maintenance- or barrier-free. Horizontal (hierarchical/seniority) barriers to vertical commun-

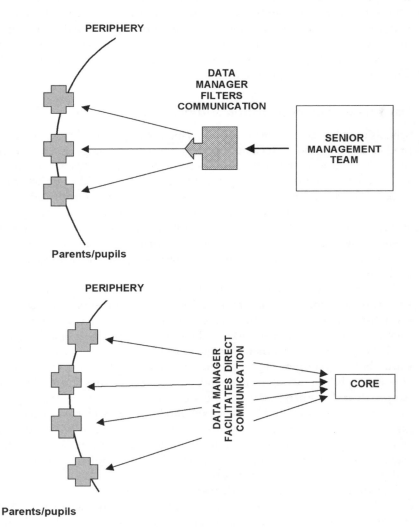

Figure 8.3 Filter and facilitator styles of middle management

ication may have been removed, but vertical (data expertise-driven) barriers to effective team working may remain.

To equip schools to survive and thrive in a data-rich world, internal relationships should make and break around issues and opportunities, rather than around competencies or status. Schools should be characterised by data-*inter*dependence and reciprocity, with responsibility devolved to autonomous modular groups and individuals who are expected to exercise what could be termed 'informed discretion'.

Networked organisations typically adopt a multifaceted approach to problem solving, achieving outcomes by assembling, disassembling and reassembling data teams. They set unambiguous goals and have a shared sense of ownership. Performance appraisal is then done in a transparent manner and teams appraise their own performance relative to other teams in the network. Improvement is achieved through the pursuit of exacting standards, supported by a shared sense of responsibility and mission.

Barriers to data networking and data management

Schools need teachers to create, refine, adapt and implement change to practice predicated on a good understanding of attainment and progress data. Teachers in a data-aware school need autonomy more than teachers in traditional schools. They need the freedom to make decisions, the will to do what needs to be done and the ability to improve own performance. On the other hand, data-aware schools also need teachers to share information and good practice, and to be able to work constructively with others. This creates a tension that is not always easy to resolve, with the result that the confidence necessary for autonomous endeavour to flourish is not always supported by the organisation's leadership.

Teachers as knowledge workers are driven by the need for recognition. In the past, this has come from the status conferred on incumbents by virtue of their specialism and place in the hierarchy. So when status barriers are removed, as they must be in a data-networked school, one of the traditional rewards for teachers disappears with them, and a sense of insecurity replaces it. '*Network status*' becomes the new motivation; a cross-weave in the fabric of the school as an organisation. It derives from an individual's connections and his/her ability to open doors for others and to collaborate over a wide spectrum of activities. In a data-networked school, individuals and modular teams are rewarded by being asked to undertake important projects, by being asked for technical advice and assistance, by having interpretations acknowledged in front of peers, by being asked to represent the organisation externally, and by getting more resources and greater remuneration (see Chapter 11).

Experts identify strongly with their areas of expertise and they gain recognition by visibly demonstrating that expertise to others. Typically, they either hide their technical know-how from outsiders, creating a myth of private knowledge, or they frame the world in terms of what others want to know. Either way, an ethos of arrogance, though it removes any obligation 'experts' might feel to explain what they know, is a barrier to effective data management and is the antithesis of what data networking is all about – sharing intelligence. It provides a cultural barrier to change, which many organisations find difficult to overcome.

Another barrier to data networking and its management lies in the 'cult of the maverick outsider'; the teacher as hero achieving the impossible as a lone agent. Seeking assistance is seen as an admission of failure, of disempowerment even, despite the fact that the myth of the hero innovator is just that . . . a myth. Actually, most successful innovators in science and industry rely on their ability *to mobilise other people* in pursuit of their objectives, rather than rely solely on their own efforts (Kanter 1983), and that is their great 'heroic' skill.

Data teams in schools

Data networks provide an integrated team approach to solving problems. Teams built around tasks are constantly evolving and dissolving as old problems are solved and new ones present themselves. Although such multi-functional teams are the result of a networking culture, a network is in many ways the product of the belief that improvement itself is an infinite series of incremental steps. These steps will sometimes be visible and formally instituted; at other times, they will be invisible and have a very short shelf life. Which it is depends largely on the nature of the issue around which the data group is gathered, and the extent of its success depends on how much its members share an understanding of the fundamental nature of the problem.

A team's mix of expertise and experience, rather than the status of its members, is also crucial to success. Teachers should belong to it because they can contribute to its success, not because they enhance its status. Quality moderation within the team is not a hierarchical function, but a peer-imposed one. Members are driven by the status of success and the need for achievement and their reward is the status they get out of it rather than the status they bring to it. Teams have the privilege of autonomy, but they also carry the burden of accountability and the pressure to perform for the common good.

Some significant problems associated with data-team working have arisen in data-centred schools: data-teams fail because management does not support them to the necessary extent; they find it difficult to agree priorities; individual expectation is not matched by that of the collective; teams find it difficult to meet in person in which case they fail to build cohesiveness or a shared sense of purpose; badly managed and unproductive meetings are problematic; teachers are untrained in data skills; and data teams become self-justifying and cliquish and neglect their duty to relate to colleagues.

A school with an ever-changing mix of issue-centred data groups, involving different combinations of people at different times, presents senior managers with new challenges in tracking, prioritisation and monitoring. They must, for example, keep track of all the data projects in progress at any one time; what Hastings (1993) has called the 'portfolio of organisational work'. A portfolio of data projects can best be managed by ensuring that data utilisation in the classroom is linked to strategy, and that defunct projects are shut down and staffing reconfigured as early as possible. However, putting people together in the right mix in a school is something that comes not just from management, but from participating teachers as well. Staff must take responsibility and not merely accept instruction.

9 Understanding teacher attitudes to data use

Introduction and background

Since their introduction, both raw attainment and value-added measures have been used to focus school improvement on self-evaluation and pupil target setting, as well as being part of the public accountability agenda. In the UK, data now flows to schools from a variety of sources: the DfE, Ofsted, FFT and various collaborations such as the London Families and the Lancashire Schools projects, and the ability to use performance data is written into England's Teacher Performance Standards: from trainees seeking Qualified Teacher Status providing evidence that they can use it 'to evaluate the effectiveness of their teaching' (TDA 2007a: 9), to the recently introduced category of 'Excellent Teacher' being able to use it to 'analyse and evaluate the effectiveness of teaching and learning across the school' (TDA 2007b, 2007c, 2007d: 7, 2007e). The assumption is that the availability and use of attainment data can improve performance at school, teacher and pupil levels, but this presupposes that school culture around its use can facilitate high-level professional inquiry and that adequate networked management structures (as described in the previous chapter) exist in schools to facilitate its utilisation. Yet good management structures alone are not sufficient: there are other obstacles to the development of data-friendly cultures in schools.

- The tension inherent in the fact that the same data is used for both improvement-evaluation and accountability-monitoring purposes; in other words, the same (yard)stick used by teachers to improve their own performance can also be used to 'beat' them.
- Data literacy; in other words, as was mentioned in Chapter 1, the terminology used to facilitate the professional dialogue needed when schools engage with data is based on complex statistical models that use a specific lexicon whose terms and cognates have different meanings in everyday life.

Previous research on developing a positive school culture around the use of data, drawing as it does almost exclusively on the practice and views of school *leaders* rather than school *teachers*, has not properly represented data culture as it affects classroom practice. There are many recognised 'top-down' issues regarding data usage (e.g. Day *et al.* 2008), but such a perspective must be balanced by the equally important 'bottom-up' perspective of teachers (Kelly *et al.* 2010). CVA metrics, for example, are little understood among teachers, who express frustration that their ('good') work is not always reflected in measures of school performance (Bush *et al.* 2005), and research suggests that some of the other challenges associated with data usage relate to perceptions of trust, to the fact that the data is sometimes (perceived as) unreliable or untimely, to inherent difficulties in interpreting it for use in classrooms, and to the fact that schools need to be 'ready' (in terms of their maturity) to derive benefit from it.

Alongside teachers themselves, data managers (where they exist) are important to the development of statistical literacy in schools. The role is viewed by some as valuable in providing tailored outputs that obviate the need to learn complex systems, and by others as adding yet another layer to hierarchy in schools (Kirkup *et al.* 2005). Views and perceptions have also been found to vary among subject leaders; an important finding since the DfE CVA model uses prior attainment only *in the core subjects of mathematics, science and English* as its main independent (predictor) variable.[1] Teacher attitude is thought to depend on the way data is presented and managed (Dudley 1997, 1999a, 1999b) – from an action-orientated view aimed at improvement, through passive acceptance/rejection, to active denial – and studies of teacher

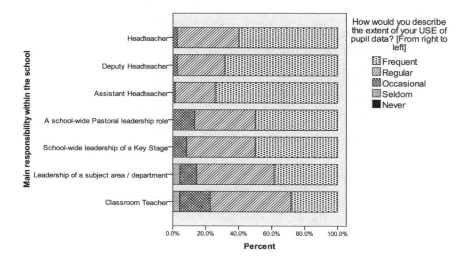

Figure 9.1 Use of pupil attainment and progress data across the teaching profession

---

1　Unlike the DfE/Ofsted CVA models, which exclusively use the results from national tests in English, mathematics and science for their KS2–KS4 progress indicators, the various value-added measures provided by FFT incorporate teacher assessment data from both core *and non-core* subjects.

attitudes to sharing performance data in and between schools (e.g. Saunders 2000) suggests a range of emotional and intellectual responses as teachers vary in their enthusiasm for the potential of the data to inform their teaching.

The extent of use of pupil data

A recent national survey in England by Kelly, Downey and Rietdijk (2010) suggests that the use of pupil attainment and progress data is widespread across the profession – approximately 85 per cent report using it 'regularly' or 'frequently' (see Figure 9.1) – but it is least in use among classroom teachers, especially Newly Qualified Teachers. Further analysis shows a significant association (p<0.001) between level of responsibility and frequency of use, with heads delegating the role of 'data manager' within the senior leadership team so that deputies and assistant heads report a higher usage.

Overall, schools with significantly positive CVA have higher levels of data use, and coasting schools (and schools with high raw attainment but negative CVA) the lowest levels of use. When exploring school type as a moderator of the association between usage and level of responsibility, it becomes clear that *within* high-use schools, it is the assistant heads and those with school-wide pastoral responsibilities that report the highest levels of use, which may suggest greater delegation (but not down to the level of classroom teacher). Assistant and deputy heads also report the highest *levels of satisfaction* with use and classroom teachers the lowest levels. The correlation between satisfaction and reported extent of use[2] suggests a significant positive association between usage and satisfaction, and analysis adjusting for the moderating effect of level of responsibility supports this finding. Kelly *et al.* further suggest that any tension in the relationship between usage and satisfaction stems from the perception that time spent on data detracts from other (perceived) crucial elements of teaching.

Confidence in skills to access, utilise and interpret data

A large proportion of school staff in the UK are confident with their skills to access, utilise and interpret pupil performance data (Kelly *et al.* 2010), but there is a significant difference in skills confidence depending on length of service and age: younger and newly qualified staff are significantly less confident. Issues relating to lack of confidence include:

- technical/software aspects of processing and interpretation;
- the need for more and better refresher/in-service training;

2 0.539, p<0.001.

- the lack of training in the interpretation of data, particularly regarding CVA;
- the lack of time to develop better skills;
- concerns that data lacks application to *individual* pupils and problems regarding aggregation;
- the jargon and acronyms associated with the field;
- lack of help for those using official sources of data, like RAISEonline;
- problems linking data with aptitude, intervention and classroom practice;
- lack of familiarity with what is available so that informed choices can be made as to the utility value of the various data sources;
- the tension between the metrics being too crude on the one hand and too complex on the other;
- concerns about school size and subject-specific factors.

Kelly *et al.* report that there is little resistance to data use among teachers, but there is a widespread perception that teachers lack opportunities to avail of training. Teachers could have (and would like) their skills developed and improved via the provision of:

- after-school/twilight sessions;
- one-to-one help;
- school-specific, in-school and subject-specific training, using if necessary local training centres for generic aspects of data utilisation;
- better preparation as part of initial teacher training courses and for newly qualified teachers;
- regular in-school forums to establish priorities and update staff once skills are acquired;
- regular opportunities to dry-run/practise data techniques, with proper checks that interpretations are correct through the use of worked examples in training;
- policy-makers not 'moving the goalposts'.

Using pupil performance data to inform practice

Figure 9.2 shows what staff in UK schools *actually do* with pupil performance data (Kelly *et al.* 2010). The most popular uses are pupil-focused, rather than teacher-focused or accountability-focused: principally *to evaluate pupil performance* and *to set targets for pupils*.

Staff in schools with both low raw and low CVA scores use pupil performance data *to evaluate pupil learning* and *to set targets for own teaching* more often than staff in more successful schools; staff in schools with low raw but high CVA scores use it less *to evaluate own teaching* (in most other schools this is around 60 per cent); staff in schools with high raw and high CVA scores use it mostly *to evaluate own subject area*. Coasting schools use pupil data least *for*

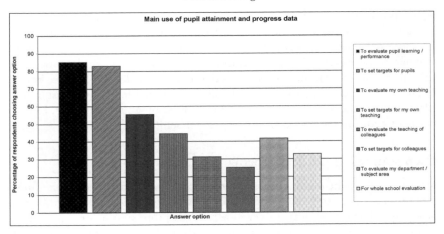

Figure 9.2 Main use of pupil attainment and progress data

whole school evaluation. Those who use pupil data to inform their practice also use it to:

- share targets and current working levels *with pupils and parents*;
- motivate pupils;
- identify and evaluate groups for interventions;
- track pupils (especially re attendance and punctuality) and write student references;
- select mixed ability groups and/or make 'strategic' seating arrangements within teaching groups;
- differentiate within lessons;
- identify aspects of courses with which pupils struggle (or find easy).

School staff have been found to rate their understanding of pupil attainment data as good, but staff in more successful schools rate their understanding higher. Staff *satisfaction with* level of understanding follows the same pattern as level of understanding itself: schools and staff that report higher/lower levels of understanding also report higher/lower levels *of satisfaction with* understanding.

Training and continuing professional development

Kelly *et al.* (2010) found that more than half of all school staff have received training/continuing professional development (CPD) less frequently than annually or (in the case of nearly one-fifth) not at all. Given the high volume of CPD in schools generally, this is not a positive picture! There is a significant association between frequency of training and confidence in accessing, utilising and interpreting data, with a very clear drop in confidence among those who report not having received training any time during the last five years. The impact of recent training, however infrequent, is appreciable, and is greater for those who are at an earlier stage in their teaching careers. The significant association between training and improved understanding (of data) has clear CPD implications. The positive news is that training makes a difference both to teachers' understanding *and* their satisfaction with that level of understanding. Classroom teachers need to have training at least on an annual basis, but less frequent training has a significant impact for senior leaders.

Own sources of pupil performance data

Most teachers make regular use of their *own* pupil performance data *and* find it more useful than external 'official' data. Viewing own sources of data as more or equally useful is almost universal across the profession in England. It is a significant verdict on how teachers perceive the utility value of official data and is a clear challenge for policy-makers: to raise perception and levels of use for official data and to create a 'mixed economy' of data sources. Senior managers, especially deputy heads, report a higher level of use of own data; head teachers and school-wide pastoral personnel report the least frequent use. The longer teachers have been in the profession, the more frequently and regularly they use their own data, but curiously the less they find it 'more useful', which may suggest that more experienced teachers use own data, but see it as only part of the picture as they get more familiar with alternative sources.

Own data is used in a variety of ways and for a variety of reasons:

- It is more specific to subject and topics within subjects.
- It better takes into account student motivation and effort, and personal factors affecting performance.
- External data is about targets whereas own pupil data is about where students are *with regard to* targets, making it easier to track progress and spot trends.
- Staff trust own data more than computer-generated data, believing it to be more accurate, more realistic and more consistent.
- It is more immediate, up to date, user-friendly, accessible, and easier to adapt and interpret.
- External data does not take account of the *level of effort* pupils put in to their work.
- External data cannot tell teachers what areas to concentrate on, and does not take into account cultural experience, behaviour or attitude to learning.
- Own data is more useful for tracking purposes; external data is more useful for standardisation, wider comparisons and setting expectations.

The management, analysis and interpretation of data: who does what and who should do what in schools

In England, data *management* is mostly done by one member of senior staff. It is less often delegated than data *analysis* and data *interpretation*, hence the suggested structure for data-network systems described in the previous chapter. The preferred approach among teachers is for heads of department or for a team of senior colleagues to *analyse and interpret* the data (Kelly *et al.* 2010), but there is an expectation that all teachers should be responsible for data *interpretation*. Pupil performance data is widely and readily available in schools, but is least widely available in coasting schools and schools with negative CVA. In schools with high CVA scores, more teachers can access data *and* carry out their own analysis and interpretation, but generally schools give pre-interpreted data to teachers in a top-down way, which is a cause of frustration among teachers. The more senior the role, the greater the access to data and the greater the facility to carry out own analysis and interpretation. Classroom teachers and heads of department are less likely to be able to access anything *other than* own subject data, which is important in light of a range of international School Effectiveness Research studies which show that even after adjusting for prior attainment and other contextual factors, most of the variation in pupil outcomes lies *within* (rather than *between*) schools.[3] However, in England, only about a quarter of all staff – and only about 5 per cent of classroom teachers – have personal access to pupil data via RAISEonline, the government's official school-data portal described in Chapter 4.

Reasons for collecting pupil performance data: what it is and what it should be

Figure 9.3 shows what teachers feel are the reasons why pupil performance data is collected (Kelly *et al.* 2010). The first three [on the left of Figure 9.3] and the last [on the right of Figure 9.3] are reasons *internal* to the school; the second set of four [in the 'middle' of Figure 9.3] are reasons *external* to the school. It is noticeable that internal (evaluation) reasons are slightly more often chosen than external (accountability) reasons.

Many teachers have negative feelings around the reasons for collecting pupil performance data: that it is just to tick a box or to satisfy statisticians; that it is designed to set ever-increasing (and unrealistic) targets for schools and teachers; and that it is used to encourage competition between schools. Others think that it is collected because governments do not trust teachers to act professionally, that parents do not understand data well enough to be able

---

3 For an overview of insights gained from school effectiveness research, see for example Sammons (2007).

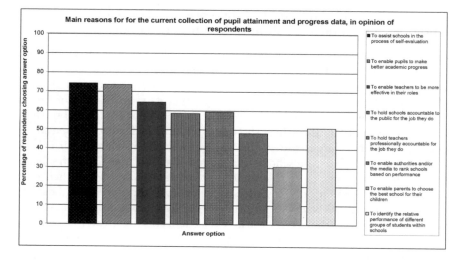

Figure 9.3 Main reasons for the current collection of pupil attainment and progress data, in opinion of respondents

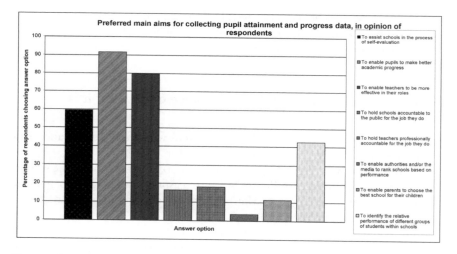

Figure 9.4 Preferred main aims for collecting pupil attainment and progress data, in opinion of respondents

use it to choose schools, and that over-reliance on it detracts from other more important issues.

Figure 9.4 shows what teachers feel are the reasons why pupil performance data *should be* collected, and they are markedly different to those on Figure 9.3. What is clear is that teachers think that the current reasons for collecting pupil data are significantly 'external' (i.e. for accountability and public use) [the middle bars on Figure 9.3], but that it *should be* collected overwhelmingly for 'internal' reasons (i.e. for self-evaluation, and pupil and teacher improvement) [the first three bars and the last bar on Figure 9.3].

Of course, not everyone views external pressures as negative. A key question is where the balance lies in terms of the accountability-improvement tension and its effect on the professionalism of teachers. Generally, teachers are positive about using data to enable pupils to make better academic progress and to enable teachers to be more effective, but are negative about data being used to hold them to account, even in schools that have the most positive data pictures.

10 Developing and utilising non-cognitive metrics

Validity and reliability issues for the measurement of social and emotional aspects of learning

Introduction to the Social and Emotional Aspects of Learning programme

The UK's Social and Emotional Aspects of Learning (SEAL) programme (DfES 2005) was launched for use in English primary schools (for children aged 4–11) in 2005 after a two-year pilot. The purpose of the SEAL programme is to support the development of a range of affective skills conducive to positive learning. It focuses on the development of five 'aspects' of social and emotional competence – self-awareness, managing feelings, empathy, motivation and social skills – which is very similar to the five-dimensional model of emotional intelligence popularised by Goleman in 1996, although SEAL draws from a much wider base (Weare and Gray 2003). In 2007, a version of the programme for use in the early years of secondary school (for students aged 11–14) was launched as Secondary SEAL (DfES 2007a) based on the same five-aspect model.

From the outset, SEAL was designed to be part of both a *universal* and a *whole-school* approach to emotional health and well-being, through which the needs of all students and staff were considered (Weare 2004). To this end, SEAL materials include a broad range of resources for use with children in whole-class teaching and school assemblies, small-group resources for more targeted skills development, training resources for teachers and other school staff, and guidance on developing policies to support the development (and raise the profile) of social and emotional skills in the school community. Both Primary and Secondary SEAL programmes were launched as part of the National Strategies, a collection of UK government initiatives to support school development and raise standards. SEAL found a home within the 'Behaviour and Attendance' strand of the National Strategy and schools were encouraged to use it to support classic school improvement aims such as better attendance, reduced exclusion on behavioural grounds and as a significant contributor to improved academic attainment (DfES 2005; 2007b). SEAL is not a statutory element of the National Strategy – schools subscribe to the programme *voluntarily* – but its popularity is demonstrated by the fact that SEAL resources are currently used in approximately 80 per cent of English primary schools (Humphrey *et al.* 2008: 5).

Over time, the association between SEAL and the promotion of emotional health and well-being in schools became more explicit in policy documents (Ofsted 2005; NICE 2007, 2008) to the point where it is now an integral part of the national Targeted Mental Health in Schools (TaMHS) project, due to run in a large sample of English schools between 2008 and 2011 (DCSF 2008a).

The challenge of evaluating the impact of SEAL on academic outcomes

Evaluating the efficacy of SEAL in schools presents an enormous challenge due to its scope, the breadth of its aims and its modus operandi. One of the desired outcomes is its impact on capacity for learning in schools, the metrics for which focus on academic outcomes. The DfE is not averse to this; indeed, on its Standards website it presents details of a SEAL case study which describes SEAL as forming a central part of the school's efforts to raise pupil attainment (DCSF 2007a). A key element of the case study lies in evidence of impact and the report provides a summary of KS2 attainment threshold data for the years 2004–2006, represented here in Figure 10.1.[1] It shows that levels of attainment have generally been rising, especially in terms of the percentage of pupils attaining the national expected standard for KS2 (Level 4 and above) during the period in which SEAL was implemented in the school.

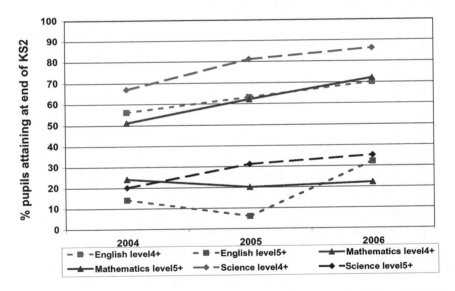

Figure 10.1 KS2 attainment data for SEAL case study school, 2004–06 (source: DCSF 2007a)

1 The case study only makes use of raw attainment data and not value-added.

The improvement in the percentage of KS2 passes at Level 5+ (the Level *above* the national expectation at age 11) was not so marked, though the three-year trend for science (and possibly English) showed an increase and the percentage reaching Level 5+ in mathematics (the highest of the three core subjects in 2004) remained stable.

The Raising Attainment Plan – commonly referred to as the School Development Plan or School Improvement Plan – for the school is included as an attachment to the case study (though it was drawn up prior to the implementation of SEAL) and a cursory glance at it makes it clear that a veritable raft of school improvement initiatives was planned for implementation *during the same period* (DCSF 2007b). These included an in-depth analysis of pupil attainment data, tracking of pupil progress against targets combined with intensive monitoring and support for targeted groups, the implementation of Assessment for Learning (AfL) practices into teaching focused on formative-, peer- and self-assessment, the development of teaching using visual, auditory and kinaesthetic (VAK) approaches, peer coaching by teachers and measures to enhance home-school relationships. These interventions, alongside those drawn from the SEAL programme, were all linked to expected improvements in academic outcomes, so it is enormously challenging to evaluate the unique causal contribution made by SEAL to student outcomes.

One could argue that firmer evidence of the impact of SEAL on academic outcomes should come from the results of *later* cohorts of students, since the KS2 2005 and KS2 2006 cohorts had only one or two years of SEAL experience. In fact, more recent KS2 assessments (for 2007–2009) paint a rather different picture (Figure 10.2). In 2007, there was a marked *decrease* in the percentage

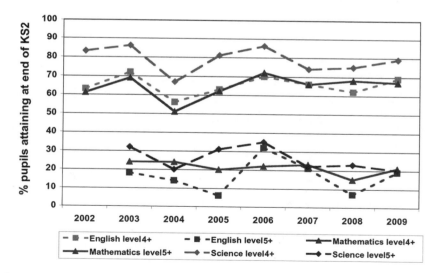

Figure 10.2 KS2 attainment data for SEAL case study school, 2002–09 (data source: DfE school and college achievement and attainment tables)

attaining Level 4+ and Level 5+ in all outcomes except mathematics at Level 5+. Since then the percentage of students attaining Level 4+ in the three core subjects has remained below the percentages in 2006, but with some consolidation of 2004–2006 gains. At Level 5+, the 2004–2006 gains in English and science appear to have been lost, while the percentage attaining Level 5 in mathematics took a dip in 2008 but returned to an otherwise consistent level in 2009. This is in line with the findings of longitudinal analyses of raw attainment and progress data discussed in Chapter 6, which suggest that schools find it hard to sustain year-on-year improvement beyond two- or three-year bursts.

The slopes[2] for the trend graphs for each core subject for a three-year *pre*-SEAL baseline period[3] plus the *post*-SEAL periods 2004–06 and 2004–09 are shown in Table 10.1. At first glance, the data suggests that the gains accrued after the implementation of SEAL have not been easy to sustain, and in some areas may even have been lost. However, to be fair, for the same reason that one would find it hard to argue that SEAL was responsible for the 2004–2006 *gains*, it would be simplistic to blame it for subsequent *falls* in attainment, especially when so many other school improvement initiatives were being implemented at the same time.

Thus, overall, the evidence for the impact of SEAL on academic attainment and progress is fairly equivocal, though in the 2008 Ofsted report for the case study school, inspectors suggest that SEAL was 'having a positive impact on learning and behaviour' (Ofsted 2008: 6). Conversely, academic attainment and progress measures – what Mortimore (1998) calls 'scholastic' measures – can only have a partial role to play in evaluating the impact of something as broad as SEAL. Of course they have a place within the evidence framework, but alongside non-cognitive (or 'non-scholastic') measures of effectiveness. These might include improved attendance rates, the number of fixed-term

Table 10.1 Trends (per year) in KS2 threshold measures for the SEAL case study school, 2002–09

Subject	02–04 gradient	04–06 gradient	04–09 gradient	Subject	04–06 gradient	04–09 gradient
English level 4+	−3.5%/yr	9.5%/yr	1.7%/yr	English level 5+	9.0%/yr	0.5%/yr
Maths level 4+	−5.0%/yr	10.5%/yr	2.6%/yr	Maths level 5+	−1.0%/yr	−0.8%/yr
Science level 4+	−8.0%/yr	7.0%/yr	1.7%/yr	Science level 5+	7.5%/yr	−1.1%/yr

Source: DCSF 2007a.

2 Generated by OLS regression.
3 Level 4+ outcomes only.

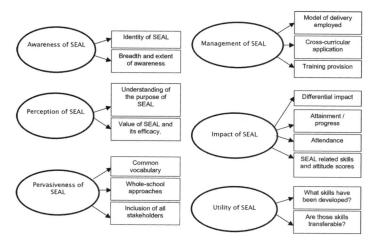

Figure 10.3 A suggested framework for assessing the impact of SEAL (and, with some adjustment, similar programmes)

and permanent exclusions (cf. Chapter 7), the number of 'serious incidents' recorded, the extent to which children are better able to sustain independent learning, evidence of improvement in self-esteem, resilience, understanding of others' points of view and self-control, and the extent to which children can talk about their emotions and behaviour. There is little firm evidence in school inspection reports as to the usefulness, accuracy or validity of these measures, though this may be influenced by the fact that since the implementation of the 'New Relationship with Schools', inspection reports have become much shorter so there is less space to explore SEAL-related issues beyond the most basic metrics.

In Figure 10.3 we propose a possible evidence framework for evaluating the impact of SEAL (and with some adjustment, similar programmes), with an emphasis on a broad range of data to reflect the breadth of the programme.

Gathering qualitative evidence of SEAL impact

In gathering evidence for impact, it is important to seek the views of a wide range of stakeholders to reflect the whole-school nature of initiatives like SEAL: a random sample of students, stratified from the full range of year groups and by gender; the parents of sampled children; all staff at the school (school leaders, teachers, teaching assistants, support staff, lunchtime supervisors, caretaking and cleaning staff); and school governors. Although each group should receive a questionnaire tailored to its own particular perspective, in order to triangulate the evidence provided by each group, each questionnaire should contain a common core, the nature of which will vary depending on the particular focus, but a useful starting point might include:

- The respondent's awareness of the nature and purpose of SEAL.
- The breadth of coverage of SEAL themes and identifying those with the greatest impact.
- The profile of SEAL at the school.
- The impact of SEAL on the learning and skills of children in lessons across the range of curriculum areas, in the playground and around the school, and at home and in outside-school activities with friends.
- The impact of SEAL on the learning environment for the wider school community.

Other questions should be specific to each respondent group. For example, in the staff survey, it would be appropriate to include some items on the mode of implementation of SEAL (e.g. whether *discrete* SEAL lessons are taught or whether lessons are blended with other whole-school curricular components), the management of SEAL, and the breadth and impact of training.

Student self-rating scales for SEAL skills and attitudes

Prior to the introduction of Primary SEAL, the DfES commissioned a wide-ranging study of instruments designed to measure the social and emotional competence of young people. In their report (Edmunds and Stewart-Brown 2003) the authors describe 58 such instruments and the opinions of a wide range of school and local authority practitioners about their value and use. The report identifies four contexts for measurement:

- Screening – the identification of children with poor social and emotional skills.
- Profiling – mapping the range and contexts in which social and emotional competence is displayed.
- Improving practice – enabling teachers to identify appropriate ways to support the development of social and emotional competence.
- Monitoring progress – measuring the development of children's levels of competence over time.

In the Edmunds and Stewart-Brown report (p. 32), many practitioners expressed the view that it is essential to gather *self-assessment pupil voice* in assessing SEAL, so we propose an alternative analytical approach, validated by factor analysis, to the existing About Me and My School questionnaire produced as part of the Social, Emotional and Behavioural Skills pilot evaluation (Hallam *et al.* 2006), the forerunner of Primary SEAL. The KS2 version of the survey consists of 40 statements rated on a five-point Likert scale from 'strongly agree' to 'strongly disagree'. (A KS1 version consists of a subset of 25 statements from the 40 above, some of them simplified, to which students respond simply with 'Yes', 'No' or 'Don't Know'.)

Individual school-level analysis for each of the 40 statements from the questionnaire can be produced showing the distribution of responses given by students. It can be broken down by gender, year group and teaching group so that each school can use the data to inform and plan implementation. Since the 'About Me and My School' questionnaire was designed to evaluate the forerunner of Primary SEAL, it is somewhat broader in scope. As a result, using confirmatory factor analysis (CFA),[4] we identified seven dimensions (Downey *et al.* 2008), a number of which align directly with the five-aspect SEAL programme. The resulting model simplifies the interpretation of survey data, assists teachers seeking to use the data to inform implementation, and provides an opportunity for monitoring the progress of SEAL in schools. A student self-rating 'score' for each of the seven dimensions provides a tool for student self-assessment of their SEAL-related skills and competencies. The final model contains only half of the 40 items in the 'About Me and My School' questionnaire (Table 10.2), but this is not to imply that the 20 other items are of no value: on the contrary, there are some potentially enlightening items among them, including the two items on bullying. Rather it is the case that these items stand on their own and as such could be analysed and interpreted separately.

Producing scores for the student self-ratings for each of the seven dimensions

The standardised regression weights in Table 10.2 suggest that it would be inappropriate to weight equally the student responses to the survey items when calculating a score for each of the seven dimensions. The standardised weights can instead be used as factor loadings in calculating scores, processed as follows:

- Convert the response from the five-point Likert scale to an ordinal numerical scale (1 = 'strongly disagree' through to 5 = 'strongly agree', reversing this scale for negatively worded items).
- Multiply the resulting ordinal response to each survey item by the corresponding standardised regression weight for that item.
- Add item scores together to give an overall score for each dimension.
- Determine the range of possible scores for each of the seven dimensions using the most and least positive responses.
- Express each score as a percentage based on the position along the range of possible scores.

4 The fundamental nature of CFA is that it is hypothesis-driven and the data is approached from an *a priori* framework based on evidence and theory, in contrast to Exploratory Factor Analysis (EFA) where the data is approached with no theoretical structure in mind. The strength of CFA over EFA is that a theoretical framework is confirmed through data analysis rather than relying on serendipitous discoveries from a sample, which may or may not be representative of the population. CFA is also able to assess robustly the construct validity of instruments because of its facility to adjust for measurement error in the data.

Table 10.2 The 20 items distributed across seven dimensions of the CFA model, with standardised regression weights and scale reliability values

SEAL dimension	Survey items associated in the model	Standardised regression weights	Raykov's* reliability rho for the dimension
Self-image	Q28 I am happy being me.	0.608	0.744
	Q29 I am good at some things.	0.553	
Managing Feelings	Q12 I calm down quickly after I have got angry or upset.	0.593	0.679
	Q15 I am usually calm.	0.689	
	Q24 I sulk or argue when I am told off.	−0.406	
Managing Behaviour	Q17 I find it easy to pay attention in class.	0.752	0.797
	Q20 I work quietly in my class.	0.642	
	Q22 I sometimes leave the room without permission.	−0.400	
	Q27 I listen well in class.	0.808	
Independence	Q10 If I find something difficult I still try to do it.	0.547	0.677
	Q30 I can work without my teacher's help.	0.355	
Resilience	Q7 I get upset if I don't do something well.	−0.497	0.751
	Q11 I'm easily hurt by what others say about me.	−0.603	
	Q18 I worry about the things I can't do well.	−0.527	
Friendships	Q13 Other children let me play with them.	0.689	0.841
	Q16 I have lots of friends at school.	0.764	
Attitudes to Teachers and School	Q23 I get on well with my teachers.	0.729	0.824
	Q33 Our teachers are fair in the way they treat us.	0.711	
	Q35 I can talk to my teacher about anything.	0.518	
	Q39 I like coming to school.	0.608	

* See Raykov 2004.

Figure 10.4 A radar plot from a SEAL skills and attitudes student self-rating survey data. (The shaded area represents how positively students have responded to the questionnaire items associated with each of the seven dimensions.)

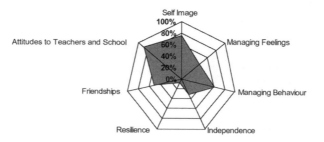

Figure 10.5 A more extreme example of radar plots from a SEAL skills survey (The shaded area represents how positively students have responded to the questionnaire items associated with each of the seven dimensions.)

The final percentage scores then represent how positively students have responded to the items compared to the *most positive possible* outcome. These percentages can be mapped onto a 'radar plot', examples of which are shown on Figure 10.4 and Figure 10.5.

Some might argue that measuring attitude and social and emotional competency in this way opens up some important reliability and validity issues beyond those already accounted for in testing construct validity and scale reliability (Downey *et al.* 2008), especially when using individual student data. An important validity check can be carried out by allowing students to reflect on their own radar plots. Since it is 'student voice' data, it is important that students have ownership of it and are able to confirm its veracity. In many ways, these discussions with individual students about their radar plots, representing as they do their responses to the variables summarised in the model, are the most beneficial part of the exercise.

Radar plots also raise other formative and developmental questions:

- What kind of learner do the plots represent?

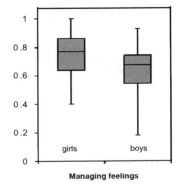

Figure 10.6 A box and whisker plot comparing the percentage scores for the 'managing feelings' scale, by gender

- How do students get on in whole-class sessions and group work?
- How can the SEAL programme be used to help develop social and emotional competence in the learning context?

Similarly, group-level data produced for various student groupings (class, gender, year group, etc.) can be presented in the form of mean percentage scores, but these mask so much of the richness in the overall data set that a better approach is to use box and whisker plots to show both the spread of the data and the location of the quartiles. An example of a box and whisker plot for group data is shown in Figure 10.6.

Figure 10.7 shows a group-level analysis of the responses to the items associated with the dimension 'independence' ('If I find something difficult I still try to do it' and 'I can work without my teacher's help' [Row 4 of Figure 10.2]) for students from Years 3–6 in a single school. The box and whisker plots reveal an age-related trend with an increase in the median 'independence' score for students in Years 3–5. The overall distribution of scores also shifts to higher percentages across the age range from Year 3 to Year 5, which suggests that students are feeling they can work more independently the greater their school experience. The distribution and median scores for Year 6 students run counter to this trend and there is a pronounced tail in their scores suggesting a number of students do not feel they are able to work as independently as their peers. Data like this (and its analysis) has implications for how the primary-secondary transition is managed.

Using teacher and parent measures of students' social and emotional competence to evaluate Family SEAL

The 'Family SEAL' programme (DfES 2006e) seeks to engage parents as partners in developing children's social and emotional competence through a

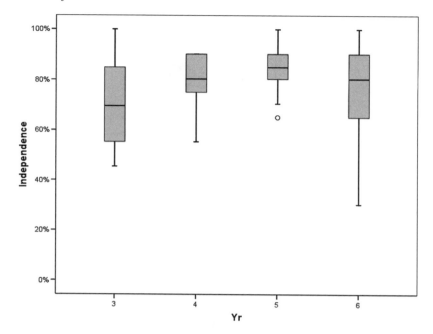

Figure 10.7 Box and whisker plots showing a group-level analysis of the percentage score produced by the responses to the items associated with the 'independence' dimension for pupils in Year 3–6 in a single school (The lack of the upper whisker for Year 4 is due to fact that all students in the upper quartile have the same score for 'independence'. An outlier is shown below the plot for Year 5.)

series of seven two-hour sessions, led by teacher-facilitators, which (broadly) tackle each of the seven themes in Table 10.3.[5]

Each session has a parent workshop in which the range of Primary SEAL approaches used by schools is described, and parents are encouraged (through discussion and role-play) to consider how such approaches might be applied in family and home situations, and how they compare with parents' own childhood experiences. Children join the workshops after the first hour to engage in a further hour of structured activity with their parents, designed to provide opportunities to consolidate some of the strategies for social and emotional development covered in the first half of the workshop.

When evaluating initiatives as broad as SEAL, it is important to have an appropriate focus. Humphrey (2008) makes the distinction between

5 The 'Say No to Bullying' theme, which is part of Primary SEAL, is not covered in Family SEAL.

Table 10.3 The outline of the Family SEAL programme and its relationship to the
five aspects of SEAL

Family SEAL session	SEAL theme	Key SEAL addressed*
Week 1	New beginnings	• **Empathy** • Self-awareness • Motivation • Social skills
Week 2	Getting on and falling out	• **Managing feelings** • Empathy • Social skills
Week 3	Going for goals! − 1	• **Motivation** • Self-awareness
Week 4	Going for goals! − 2	• **Motivation** • Self-awareness
Week 5	Good to be me	• **Self-awareness** • **Managing feelings** • Empathy
Week 6	Relationships	• **Self-awareness** • **Managing feelings** • Empathy
Week 7	Changes	• **Motivation** • **Social skills** • Managing feelings

* The main aspect(s) addressed by each theme are given in bold.

'proximal'[6] and 'distal'[7] variables in the evaluation of school-based social
and emotional learning programmes. He lists typical proximal variables as
measures of pupil or staff social and emotional skills and measures of school
climate, and contrasts these with distal variables such as improved behaviour,
reduced exclusions, improved pupil attendance and attainment. Clearly, teacher
and parent ratings of the social and emotional skills of their children (collected
before and after engaging with Family SEAL, say) are proximal, but contrary
to general opinion, evaluations of programmes like SEAL are not based solely
on qualitative tactile measures; they can and should be supplemented by distal,
quantitative evidence.

Parent and Teacher Emotional Literacy Checklists (Faupel 2003) have also
been used to evaluate the social and emotional skills of children in Family

6 Meaning next to or nearest a central point or point of view.
7 Meaning situated away from a central point or point of view.

SEAL pilots (Downey and Williams 2010).[8] The Checklists were issued to parents attending SEAL workshops and to class teachers, and consist of a series of items linked to five dimensions: self-awareness, self-regulation, motivation, empathy and social skills (Figure 10.8). As the model draws on the work of Goleman (1996), the dimensions are very closely allied to the five aspects of learning that form the basis of SEAL, so the instrument has proved a useful tool for reporting evidence of impact.[9]

Each of the five dimensions in the emotional literacy model is measured by four items in the case of the *teacher* Checklist, and five items in the case of the *parent* Checklist. Participants respond using a four-point Likert scale. For the purpose of analysis these are converted to a numerical score in the usual manner ('4' for the most positive response; '1' for the least positive response) and the item scores totalled to give an overall score for each of the five dimensions. The score is then converted to a percentage of the maximum possible score to allow a direct comparison of parent and teacher ratings.

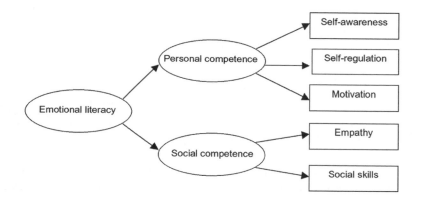

Figure 10.8 Faupel's five-dimensional model of emotional literacy

8 Scale reliability testing was conducted for the Checklists using Cronbach's alpha and the content validity of the subscales confirmed by principal components analysis. Cronbach's alpha coefficient is a widely used measure of the reliability or 'internal consistency' of a scale. It measures how well a set of items/variables measures a latent construct. It equals zero when the true score is not measured at all and there is only an error component; it equals unity when all items measure only the true score and there is no error component. By convention, a Cronbach's alpha of 0.6 is acceptable as a lenient cut-off for exploratory research, but it should be at least 0.7 for an 'adequate' scale (and 0.8 for a 'good' scale). However, Brown (2006) suggests an alternative reliability measure specifically for CFA measurement, 'Raykov's Reliability rho' (Raykov 2001; 2004), which is why we used it on Table 10.2.
9 The Checklists have also been used in an evaluation of *small-group* SEAL (Humphrey *et al.* 2008) where a small proportion of participating children were younger than the specified age range for the instrument (ages 7–11). This fact was found not to skew the data significantly (2008: 34).

Prior to commencing Family SEAL, class teachers and coordinators identify children who are considered to be causing concern in their social or emotional development. The information allows comparisons between changes in emotional literacy levels for 'concern' and 'non-concern' children to determine the impact of Family SEAL as both a 'universal' and a 'targeted' intervention. The classification of children as giving 'cause for concern' (or not) is left solely to teachers' professional judgement, but is informed by 'criteria for assessing emotional and behavioural development' issued by the QCA (see Table 10.4).[10] For children identified in the 'concern' group, Downey and Williams (2010) found evidence of significant (p<0.01) post-Family SEAL gains in their Emotional Literacy scores (as rated by teachers).

At the end of the series of Family SEAL workshops, parents are asked to complete a simple semi-structured evaluation questionnaire, allowing them to express what (they feel) they and their children have gained from the programme. Specific responses referring *solely* to gains for children are fairly rare; instead, they usually offer evidence that both parents and children value the opportunities provided by SEAL to network with others. Most parents value the opportunity to get to know teachers and find comfort in the knowledge that they are not alone in their problems, and pilot studies have shown that parents also value spending quality one-to-one time with their children away from siblings and family 'distractions' (Downey and Williams 2010).

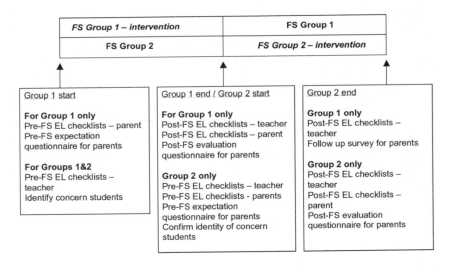

Figure 10.9 'Crossover' design for evaluating Family SEAL in schools running two groups in the same school year

10 The QCA is a public body charged by the UK government with oversight of the development of the National Curriculum and the administration of national assessment procedures.

Table 10.4 QCA criteria for assessing emotional and behavioural development

Learning behaviour		*Conduct behaviour*		*Emotional behaviour*
1	Is attentive and has an interest in schoolwork	6	Behaves respectfully towards staff	11	Has empathy
2	Has good learning organization	7	Shows respect to other pupils	12	Is socially aware
3	Is an effective communicator	8	Only interrupts and seeks attention appropriately	13	Is happy
4	Works efficiently in a group	9	Is physically peaceable	14	Is confident
5	Seeks help where necessary	10	Respects property	15	Is emotionally stable and shows good self-control

Source: QCA 2001.

Of course, the lack of an experimental design in SEAL programmes makes it impossible to draw causal conclusions as to whether gains in social and emotional literacy (as reported by parents and teachers) are due to Family SEAL or to other parallel interventions. Randomised control trials are both controversial and difficult to implement in educational settings, although Tymms *et al.* (2008) have recently argued to the contrary when an intervention is implemented *for the first time*. An alternative approach for schools that run two or more Family SEAL groups during each year is to use a 'crossover design' (e.g. Humphrey *et al.* 2008). In this approach, evidence is gathered at three time points during the year to allow for comparison between the two groups which will eventually both engage in Family SEAL (Figure 10.9). During the initial phase, the crossover design treats the first group to engage as the intervention group while the second group, which will engage in SEAL later, acts as a control. At the midway point, Group 1 has completed the series of workshops and Group 2 is about to commence. During the second phase, Group 2 is the intervention group and Group 1 acts a measure of the lasting impact of Family SEAL over the short term.

11 Developing and utilising non-cognitive metrics

Moving beyond the pupil to assess staff responsibility and reward for engagement with data

Introduction

For reasons described in the previous chapter, schools that are data-driven – in other words, schools where its collection, analysis, interpretation, use and storage are not exceptional, but are accepted parts of daily practice – should have extensive and fair *responsibility* structures, which in today's performance-related environment has implications for how teachers and managers are compensated for (and what they think about) doing their jobs. How onerous a task is the analysis (say) of whole-school value-added data, who should do it and what time-in-lieu or financial allowance should be made as a result? To answers questions like these, we need to define some common terms in new ways.

A 'job' is a set of recognisable, recurring, non-exceptional tasks, duties and responsibilities[1] assigned to a teacher or school manager (Kelly 2004). These are collectively the 'functions' of the job, and a 'job profile' or 'job description' (which is what a job evaluation is based on) is a public narrative statement of these functions, describing the skills and know-how required to do the job successfully.

'Know-how' in data terms is the sum of technical/statistical knowledge (to analyse the data), problem-solving ability (to maximise its interpretation), and managerial and human relations skills (to oversee its utilisation).

- Technical knowledge ranges from simple familiarity with school routines to expertise in statistical modelling.
- Problem solving is the extent to which know-how is required by the incumbent to overcome the difficulties thrown up by data, so it is particularly important for data interpretation. People think with what they know, so problem solving can be thought of as a simple percentage of know-how (Kelly 2004).

---

1 There is a distinction between 'duties' and 'responsibilities', though in common parlance the terms are interchangeable. Responsibilities are the activities that define a job, whereas duties are activities done in pursuit of the responsibility. Valuing a job means concentrating on responsibilities, not duties.

- Managerial skills range from doing or directing routine activities to managing disparate groups of jobs with different and varied functions.
- Human relations skills extend to motivating, understanding and influencing sometimes reluctant colleagues to engage with the data and act on it.

Data management jobs exist to oversee whole-school data matters – school-wide analysis, checking interpretation, assuring data-informed practice and so forth – and (as we have seen in the previous chapter) to enable communication between the core and the periphery of the data network, so it is good practice in schools for tacit understandings to be made explicit so that schools have a memory of what everyone does, why and how. Job profiles are part of that process of data storage and in general they should do the following.

- Specify why each data task exists (and who does it) in terms of its primary objective of raising attainment.
- Note the accountability and impact of each data task on the mission of the school; in other words, the effect the task has on output. Accountability – answerability for results and consequences – is related to the opportunity teachers (including curriculum managers and school leaders) have to generate important outcomes for the school from engagement with data. The extent to which they are free to act is therefore inversely related to the extent to which gate-keeping or procedural control exists over the data.
- Specify the extent to which colleagues have freedom to act, and the nature and sources of control limiting their ability to take decisions.
- Bring out the technical, managerial, problem-solving and human relations skills required.
- Specify the size, scope and nature of each position answerable to the job, but define the job in its own terms and not solely in terms of how it assists or relates to other positions.
- Make it known what is needed by way of training, experience, know-how and human relations skills to do the job properly.
- Give a general idea of the magnitude of the job, and its 'prescribed' and 'discretionary' contents. The discretionary content of a data job consists of those tasks where analysis and interpretation are left to the incumbent and where the best course of action must be chosen from alternatives. It is the part that is perceived by incumbents as their 'level of work'. The prescribed content, on the other hand, consists of those tasks about which the incumbent has no choice. The discretionary element of a job is difficult to describe fully in a job profile because the relationship between the job and the person doing it is not always established, but the discretionary element is the part of the job that gives the greatest satisfaction to employees and enhances the perception of quality of work, irrespective of quantity.

The measurement of responsibility

The purpose of job evaluation and responsibility analysis is to determine appropriate status and reward for individuals in their jobs. In schools, this mostly relates to time-in-lieu or performance-related pay increments. These are very emotive issues, questioning as they do teachers' value and usefulness to others, and the greater the importance attached to the analysis and interpretation of data, the more important it is to allocate fairly the reward for leading the engagement with data at different levels throughout the school. However, before it can even be attempted it is necessary to distinguish between 'level' and 'quantity' of work. Level of work is a measure of the size and intensity of responsibility in a job; quantity of work is the amount of work done irrespective of level of responsibility. Research shows that *level* of work (rather than *quantity*) is the aspect of a job that (employees think) merits differentiation in status or reward (Jaques 1956).

In relation to schools' engagement with data, job content will change over time so it is important to have yardsticks that measure level of work which are flexible enough to adapt to changing circumstances. The most accurate and equitable approach to gauging level of work is to use the concepts of 'maximum time-span of discretion' and '*range of* level of work'.

The maximum time-span of discretion

The level of work in a job can be assessed by teasing out the discretionary content of a job, evaluating the mechanisms used to review the use of discretion by the incumbent and then discovering the maximum time that elapses during which the incumbent can use discretion in relation to his or her responsibilities. Whatever the relative sizes of the discretionary and prescribed components of a job, a period of time elapses – the 'time-span of discretion' – before the effects of discretion become apparent and the maximum for any given job is a measure of its value. For example, in one (high-value) job it may take months or a year before the impact of a certain interpretation of pupil attainment data comes to light; in another (lower-value) job, it may be noticed immediately. Data managers can keep time-span of discretion to a minimum by reviewing analyses as soon as they arrive, or they can lengthen it by postponing a review of analyses (Kelly 2004).

The prescribed element of a job should not be used as an index of importance or as a determinant of reward. Even in the simplest of jobs, like a data-entry administrator putting a decimal point in the wrong place, a tiny mistake can have huge consequences on a school-wide scale. It confuses matters to talk about the prescribed elements, reliability, accuracy and qualifications when comparing jobs. Job importance should only be judged by the amount of discretion exercised. Generally, the higher the maximum time-span of discretion, the more important the job, and time-spans of discretion decrease as one goes down the 'ranks'. A manager cannot reasonably work at a shorter time-span of discretion than a less experienced colleague, since the former must oversee or enable the latter. In education, teachers and curriculum managers with similar time-spans of discretion, irrespective of rank, typically claim parity of status and reward. Conversely, incumbents whose reward and status is perceived as being below that commensurate with their time-spans of discretion think themselves unfairly treated, and research shows these incumbents to be the major instigators of grievance procedures.

Staff data teams and the jobs they do can be grouped *by like time-spans of discretion* and an increase in an employee's time-span of discretion within the group is what defines an increase in workload. And if such an increase in workload brings the teacher to the next higher-ranking group, there should be formal promotion or greater reward. In fact, promotion can be *defined* as the movement to another group with a longer time-span of discretion.

Changes nationally in the status and remuneration of teachers and local changes in personnel are fluctuations that can subject a school to pressures that disturb it. Change cannot be managed unless and until it is recognised. Usually and unfortunately, it is noticed first by the effect it has on operations. In schools, teachers and support staff can feel dissatisfied as a result of performing well at a new higher level while being retained at an old status level, so re-grading should take place if performance warrants it. Conversely, a teacher may be unable to cope with a new position because an unrecognised promotion *has occurred*. Occasionally, amount and level of work can increase simultaneously without incumbents becoming aware of it (or rewarded for it) to such an extent that junior members of staff end up doing similar work to senior colleagues but without the status, and data-aware schools in particular need to be alert to this danger.

Range of level of work

Increased sensitivity to the concept of maximum time-span of discretion brings another evaluative concept into focus: 'range of level of work'. Range of level of work is the widest range within which work can be assigned to a teacher or school manager, from the lowest level compatible with the work merely being done, to the highest level available to be assigned. Range of level of work cannot be expanded or contracted at will. The upper level is set by the availability of data to work with, and the lower level by the fact that when an incumbent's line manager/supervisor is doing more than a certain maximum amount of reviewing, there is no time to fulfil his/her own obligations. At this lower point, it would be just as easy for the line manager to do the colleague's job as to supervise it.

The totality of work

In total, work is the sum of the prescribed and discretionary activities that teachers do in discharging their responsibilities, but what they experience as *level of* work is only the discretionary part. Discretion is required whenever there is more than one way of analysing data or whenever data is interpreted, and is therefore concerned only with those aspects of data engagement where teachers can choose from alternative ways of doing. In comparison, the prescribed portion of a job comprises those aspects of the job where the incumbent is prohibited from choosing and where prescribed rules must be followed in pursuit of the objective. The prescribed and discretionary components of a job interact as part of the totality of work. The prescribed component constitutes a boundary around the discretionary component, setting limits for it and stipulating what teachers can or cannot do with data.

The capacity to tolerate uncertainty also plays a part in a teacher's capacity to do work with school data. As tolerance of uncertainty grows, a greater capacity develops to put off decisions with the promise of something better later on. 'Time-span capacity' is the length of time an incumbent is able to tolerate the delaying effects of exercising discretion; in other words, the length of time that an incumbent can postpone a necessary event. The longer it is, the more important the job. The capacity to exercise discretion for longer or shorter periods of time is a function of an employee's ability to anticipate events that are consequent on any action. The further ahead consequences are projected in the mind's eye, the less clear they become; and the greater a teacher's time-span capacity, the greater is his/her ability to use past experience as a bridge for uncertainty. The greater the tolerance for making decisions in the face of uncertainty the more senior the position. When managers talk of being 'weighed down with responsibility' or 'spending half-term in data hell' (see Chapter 1) they are reflecting the fact that they experience too much uncertainty for too long and they feel insecure as a result.

A profile guide chart method for use in schools

The 'profile guide chart' method of job evaluation is widely regarded as the industry standard and we have developed one here for use in schools with data-related jobs. The fundamental ways in which jobs can equate with one another are arranged on scales and a 'guide chart' consists of two or more of these scales brought together in a grid. While each scale is defined only in a general way, each step on it is a progressive refinement in detail. Guide charts require an understanding of scaling techniques and an evaluation system based on them must have a number of underpinning features:

- The most important three factors in the evaluation of a job are: the knowledge required to do the job; the kind of thinking required to solve the problems commonly faced in the job; and the responsibilities assigned to the job.
- A good evaluation system should be able to rank jobs in order *and* measure their relative size; in other words, an evaluation should be able to measure the significant difference between jobs, as well as being able to order them.

- The focus should be on the nature and demands of the job itself, not on the skills and characteristics of the job-holder.

This suggests a three-factor codification with respect to what we consider common to all data jobs: 'know-how', 'problem solving' and 'accountability'. And each of these three factors has a corresponding guide chart to measure it.

Know-how

Know-how is the sum of every kind of knowledge and skill required for the acceptable performance of the job, however obtained (see Figure 11.1). Its three dimensions are *Statistical* know-how, *Managerial* know-how and *Human Relations* skills:

- *Statistical know-how* is the sum of statistical knowledge and experience in working with education and teaching data. It consists largely of specialised techniques and procedures, and can be categorised according to its variety (or width) and complexity (or depth). Exemplars are given in Figure 11.2. Typically, data interpretation jobs require a little knowledge of many things and data analysis jobs require a great deal of knowledge about relatively few things (like MLM, say). To reflect this fact, statistical know-how is on the vertical axis of Figure 11.1 and ranges from 'Basic Understanding' (A) to 'Professional Eminence' (H).
- *Managerial know-how* is the ability to integrate and harmonise the diverse functions of a job in order to produce the desired outcomes for the school. It involves, in some combination, skills in planning, organising, coordinating, executing, evaluating, directing, and controlling resources. Managerial know-how is on the upper horizontal axis of Figure 11.1 and ranges from 'Non-supervisory' (N) to 'Total' (V).
- *Human Relations skills* comprise the active person-to-person skills essential in jobs that involve work with other people. It is on the lower horizontal axis of Figure 11.1 and ranges from 'Basic' (1) to 'Critical' (3).

Problem solving

Problem solving is the original use of know-how to identify, define and resolve (mostly interpretation) problems emerging from data (see Figure 11.3). Teachers *think* about data with what they *know* about data, even in the most creative aspects of how it affects practice, so problem solving can be thought of as a simple percentage of know-how. Problem solving is diminished when results can be obtained by the automatic application of IT skills, rather than by the application of a *thinking* process to knowledge, so this chart measures the extent to which thinking processes must be applied to the job's required knowledge in order to get the results expected. It has two dimensions: 'Thinking Environment' and 'Thinking Challenge':

MANAGERIAL KNOW-HOW

GUIDE CHART FOR EVALUATING KNOW-HOW	N. Nonsupervisory — Undertakes data utilisation activities or assures that others utilise it for use in the classroom.			I. Minimal — Incumbent manages a group of data utilisation activities or performs wide range of data interpretation activities.			II. Related — Incumbent directs small team with data interpretation duties or carries out some data analysis duties.			III. Diverse — Incumbent directs a large team with data interpretation duties or manages some data analysis activities (but not for whole school).			IV. Broad — Incumbent manages wholeschool data analysis activities or sets school policy re data analysis.			V. Total — Leadership of all data management teams, policies and decisions, and responsibility for collection of data if necessary/possible.		
	1	2	3	1	2	3	1	2	3	1	2	3	1	2	3	1	2	3
A. Basic understanding: Incumbent has a basic familiarity with statistical methods.	38	43	50	50	57	66	66	76	87	87	100	115	115	132	152	152	175	200
	43	50	57	57	66	76	76	87	100	100	115	132	132	152	175	175	200	230
	50	57	66	66	76	87	87	100	115	115	132	152	152	175	200	200	230	264
B. Elementary skill/knowledge: Capable of carrying out standard statistical procedures using simple data on spreadsheets like Excel.	50	57	66	66	76	87	87	100	115	115	132	152	152	175	200	200	230	264
	57	66	76	76	87	100	100	115	132	132	152	175	175	200	230	230	264	304
	66	76	87	87	100	115	115	132	152	152	175	200	200	230	264	264	304	350
C. Intermediate skill/knowledge: Experienced in using statistics with some variation using specialist programmes like SPSS.	66	76	87	87	100	115	115	132	152	152	175	200	200	230	264	264	304	350
	76	87	100	100	115	132	132	152	175	175	200	230	230	264	304	304	350	400
	87	100	115	115	132	152	152	175	200	200	230	264	264	304	350	350	400	460
D. Extended skill/knowledge: Good at implementing whole-school data systems, with skills requiring statistical knowledge.	87	100	115	115	132	152	152	175	200	200	230	264	264	304	350	350	400	460
	100	115	132	132	152	175	175	200	230	230	264	304	304	350	400	400	460	528
	115	132	152	152	175	200	200	230	264	264	304	350	350	400	460	460	528	608
E. Diverse/specialised: Understanding & skill in a variety of activities, with command of statistical theory.	115	132	152	152	175	200	200	230	264	264	304	350	350	400	460	460	528	608
	132	152	175	175	200	230	230	264	304	304	350	400	400	460	528	528	608	700
	152	175	200	200	230	264	264	304	350	350	400	460	460	528	608	608	700	800
F. Seasoned diverse/specialised: Command of statistical theory and experienced in management.	152	175	200	200	230	264	264	304	350	350	400	460	460	528	608	608	700	800
	175	200	230	230	264	304	304	350	400	400	460	528	528	608	700	700	800	920
	200	230	264	264	304	350	350	400	460	460	528	608	608	700	800	800	920	1056
G. Broad or specialised mastery: Command of educational and statistical theory through professional development.	200	230	264	264	304	350	350	400	460	460	528	608	608	700	800	800	920	1056
	230	264	304	304	350	400	400	460	528	528	608	700	700	800	920	920	1056	1216
	264	304	350	350	400	460	460	528	608	608	700	800	800	920	1056	1056	1216	1400
H. Professional eminence: Externally recognised expertise in aspects of educational and statistical theory/practice.	264	304	350	350	400	460	460	528	608	608	700	800	800	920	1056	1056	1216	1400
	304	350	400	400	460	528	528	608	700	700	800	920	920	1056	1216	1216	1400	1610
	350	400	460	460	528	608	608	700	800	800	920	1056	1056	1216	1400	1400	1610	1852

(Left margin vertical label: STATISTICAL KNOW-HOW)

HUMAN RELATIONS SKILLS

1. Basic: Ordinary courtesy & effectiveness in dealing with colleagues.	2. Important: Influence over & understanding of teachers; management of colleagues & peers are important aspects of the job.	3. Critical: Advanced skills have been developed by incumbent in understanding & motivating people; extremely important for the job.

Figure 11.1 Evaluating data know-how in schools (adapted from: Kelly 2004)

EVALUATING KNOW-HOW	EXEMPLARS
A. Basic understanding: Incumbent has a basic familiarity with statistical methods.	Compiling class / cohort examination data.
B. Elementary skill / knowledge: Capable of carrying out standard statistical procedures using simple data on spreadsheets like Excel.	Use of spreadsheet of class results to calculate means, modes, medians etc.
C. Intermediate skill / knowledge: Experienced in using statistics with some variation using specialist programmes like SPSS.	Department-wide analysis of pupil performance data using SPSS, and engagement with FFT data returns in subject area.
D. Extended skill / knowledge: Good at implementing whole-school data systems, with skills requiring statistical knowledge.	Introducing systems of analysis and / or interpretation across the school.
E. Diverse / specialised: Understanding & skill in a variety of activities, with command of statistical theory.	Managing different data teams across the school and helping others with their data interpretation.
F. Seasoned diverse / specialised: Command of statistical theory and experienced in management.	Managing small data initiatives across the school and solving data problems that are not everyday or predictable.
G. Broad or specialised mastery: Command of educational and statistical theory through professional development.	Managing major data initiatives across the school and solving data problems that arise from the school facing challenging circumstances.
H. Professional eminence: Externally recognised expertise in aspects of educational and statistical theory / practice.	Leading data change in a school that is involved in some innovation or pilot programme, and / or leading other schools in the area or nationally.

Figure 11.2 Some examples of data know-how in schools (adapted from: Kelly 2004)

- *Thinking Environment* represents the extent to which assistance is available from colleagues and from precedent. This dimension is on the vertical axis of Figure 11.3 and ranges from 'Highly Structured' (A) to 'Abstract' (H).
- *Thinking Challenge* represents the complexity and novelty of the thinking that is required in the job. It is represented on the horizontal axis of Figure 11.3, and ranges from Repetitive (1) to Uncharted (5).

Accountability

Accountability is the extent to which teachers and managers are answerable for their actions and their consequences in relation to their engagement with data. It is the measured effect of the job on the academic outputs of the school (see Figure 11.4) and is related to the opportunity the job provides for bringing about improvement in pupil outcomes. There are three components to accountability, in the following decreasing order of importance: 'Freedom to Act', 'Job Impact' and 'Magnitude'.

- *Freedom to Act* is the degree to which personal or procedural control exists or does not exist. It is represented on the vertical axis of Figure 11.4 and ranges from 'Restricted' (R) to 'General Guidance' (H).

THINKING CHALLENGE

THINKING ENVIRONMENT

GUIDE CHART FOR EVALUATING PROBLEM SOLVING	**1. Repetitive** Identical data situations requiring the incumbent to give guidance on established best practice.	**2. Patterned** Similar data situations requiring the incumbent to make discriminating choices between options.	**3. Varied** Differing data situations requiring the incumbent to search for solutions within an area of known options.	**4. Adaptive** Variable data situations requiring analysis, interpretation, evaluative and/or constructive thinking.	**5. Uncharted** New or non-recurring path-finding data situations requiring development of imaginative approaches.
A. Highly structured: Thinking about data utilsation within detailed rules or under constant supervision from line manager.	10% 12%	14% 16%	19% 22%	25% 29%	33% 38%
B. Routine: Thinking within detailed school practice or with immediate help/examples available.	12% 14%	16% 19%	22% 25%	29% 33%	38% 43%
C. Semi-routine: Thinking within well defined established procedures. Precedence or ready assistance available.	14% 16%	19% 22%	25% 29%	33% 38%	43% 50%
D. Standardised: Thinking within diverse procedures. Precedence or access to assistance available.	16% 19%	22% 25%	29% 33%	38% 43%	50% 57%
E. Clearly defined: Thinking within a whole-school remit towards specific goals. Guided mostly by practice and precedent.	19% 22%	25% 29%	33% 38%	43% 50%	57% 66%
F. Generally defined Thinkingwithin a whole-school remit towards specific goals. Some intangible, unstructured aspects.	22% 25%	29% 33%	38% 43%	50% 57%	66% 76%
G. Broadly defined: Thinking in education/statistical concepts. Broadly towards school goals. Much intangible.	25% 29%	33% 38%	43% 50%	57% 66%	76% 87%
H. Abstract: Thinking in terms of educational philosophy or human relations theory or statistical concepts.	29% 33%	38% 43%	50% 57%	66% 76%	87%

Figure 11.3 Evaluating problem-solving in schools (adapted from: Kelly 2004)

- *Job Impact* is the degree to which the job affects outcomes. It is reckoned as being in one of four categories: 'Primary impact' (P) occurs when the job exercises control over the resources and activities that produce the improvement; 'Shared impact' (S) occurs when the job that controls the resources and activities that produce the improvement is shared equally with one other person, or where there is control of most, but not all, of

GUIDE CHART FOR EVALUATING ACCOUNTABILITY	SCHOOL SIZE 1. Very small UK School Groups 1 & 2 or 100–400 pupils				2. Small UK School Group 3 or 401–700 pupils				3. Medium small UK School Group 4 or 701–1000 pupils				4. Medium large UK School Group 5 or 1001–1300 pupils				5. Large UK School Group 6 or 1301–1600 pupils				6. Very large UK School Groups 7 & 8 or 1601 + pupils			
Impact =	A	C	S	P	A	C	S	P	A	C	S	P	A	C	S	P	A	C	S	P	A	C	S	P
R. Restricted: Data restricted to utilisation and subject to explicit instructions/constant supervision.	5 6 7	7 8 9	9 10 12	12 14 16	7 8 9	9 10 12	12 14 16	16 19 22	9 10 12	12 14 16	16 19 22	22 25 29	12 14 16	16 19 22	22 25 29	29 33 38	16 19 22	22 25 29	29 33 38	38 43 50	22 25 29	29 33 38	38 43 50	50 57 66
A. Prescribed: Data utilisation role is subject to indirect instructions or remote supervision.	8 9 10	10 12 14	14 16 19	19 22 25	10 12 14	14 16 19	19 22 25	25 29 33	14 16 19	19 22 25	25 29 33	33 38 43	19 22 25	25 29 33	33 38 43	43 50 57	25 29 33	33 38 43	43 50 57	57 66 76	33 38 43	43 50 57	57 66 76	76 87 100
B. Controlled: Data interpretation role is subject to established routines or close supervision.	12 14 16	16 19 22	22 25 29	29 33 38	16 19 22	22 25 29	29 33 38	38 43 50	22 25 29	29 33 38	38 43 50	50 57 66	29 33 38	38 43 50	50 57 66	66 76 87	38 43 50	50 57 66	66 76 87	87 100 115	50 57 66	66 76 87	87 100 115	115 132 152
C. Standardised: Interpretation role subject to standard procedures and supervision of progress.	19 22 25	25 29 33	33 38 43	43 50 57	25 29 33	33 38 43	43 50 57	57 66 76	33 38 43	43 50 57	57 66 76	76 87 100	43 50 57	57 66 76	76 87 100	100 115 132	57 66 76	76 87 100	100 115 132	132 152 175	76 87 100	100 115 132	132 152 175	175 200 230
D. Generally regulated: Data interpretation role subject to definite procedures and supervision.	29 33 38	38 43 50	50 57 66	66 76 87	38 43 50	50 57 66	66 76 87	87 100 115	50 57 66	66 76 87	87 100 115	115 132 152	66 76 87	87 100 115	115 132 152	152 175 200	87 100 115	115 132 152	152 175 200	200 230 264	115 132 152	152 175 200	200 230 264	264 304 350
E. Directed: Analysis role subject to defined policy. Directs medium-term results of others.	43 50 57	57 66 76	76 87 100	100 115 132	57 66 76	76 87 100	100 115 132	132 152 175	76 87 100	100 115 132	132 152 175	175 200 230	100 115 132	132 152 175	175 200 230	230 264 304	132 152 175	175 200 230	230 264 304	304 350 400	175 200 230	230 264 304	304 350 400	400 460 528
F. General direction: Analysis role subject to functional policies. Directs long-term results of others.	66 76 87	87 100 115	115 132 152	152 175 200	87 100 115	115 132 152	152 175 200	200 230 264	115 132 152	152 175 200	200 230 264	264 304 350	152 175 200	200 230 264	264 304 350	350 400 460	200 230 264	264 304 350	350 400 460	460 528 608	264 304 350	350 400 460	460 528 608	608 700 800
G. Guidance: Major data role subject to guidance of school policy.	100 115 132	132 152 175	175 200 230	230 264 304	132 152 175	175 200 230	230 264 304	304 350 400	175 200 230	230 264 304	304 350 400	400 460 528	230 264 304	304 350 400	400 460 528	528 608 700	304 350 400	400 460 528	528 608 700	700 800 920	400 460 528	528 608 700	700 800 920	920 1056 1216
H. General guidance: Major data role subject to guidance of national/local educational policy & law.	152 175 200	200 230 264	264 304 350	350 400 460	200 230 264	264 304 350	350 400 460	460 528 608	264 304 350	350 400 460	460 528 608	608 700 800	350 400 460	460 528 608	608 700 800	800 920 1056	460 528 608	608 700 800	800 920 1056	1056 1216 1400	608 700 800	800 920 1056	1056 1216 1400	1400 1610 1852
Impact =	A	C	S	P	A	C	S	P	A	C	S	P	A	C	S	P	A	C	S	P	A	C	S	P

(Rows R–H are labelled vertically in the left margin: FREEDOM TO ACT)

A = ancillary
C = contributory
S = shared
P = primary

Figure 11.4 Evaluating accountability in schools (adapted from: Kelly 2004)

the significant variables that bring about the improvement; 'Contributory impact' (C) occurs when the job provides advice, interpretation or support to others so that the improvement can be achieved; and 'Ancillary impact' (A) occurs when supplementary assistance, information or an auxiliary service is given in support of others. Job impact is represented on the lower horizontal axis of Figure 11.4. There are A, C, S and P categories in each of the six Magnitude categories (see below).

- *Magnitude* represents the extent to which the whole school is covered by the job. This dimension is represented on the upper horizontal axis of Figure 11.4, parallel to the impact dimension, and ranges in six steps from 'Very Small' (1) to 'Very Large' (6) and corresponds to the UK government's categorisation of schools by size.

The scales on the guide charts and the shape of jobs

The scales on the Know-how and Accountability charts (Figure 11.1 and Figure 11.4) – but not on the problem-solving chart (Figure 11.3) – are expandable to reflect the size and complexity of the school, and the nomenclature can be adjusted to suit any individual circumstance; in other words, it is possible to 'size' the charts. For each factor, the reading is a single number. The numbers on the charts increase at a rate of 15 per cent (except for very small numbers) in order to conform to two general principles of psychometric scaling:

- Weber's Law, which states that when comparing objects one perceives not *actual* difference, but the *ratio of difference* to magnitude, so the relationship between numbers is more important than the numbers themselves.
- The concept of 'Just Noticeable Difference', which states that the extent of difference required to be noticeable tends to be a specific constant percentage, so an observer must have (say) a 15 per cent difference between measures in order to notice that one job is bigger than another.

Using guide charts, jobs can be scientifically described on the basis of the relationship between know-how, problem solving and accountability, but instinctively managers *also* know the 'shape' of jobs: 'uphill', 'flat' or 'downhill'. Linking the two, we define an uphill job as one for which the accountability score is greater than the problem-solving score; a downhill job as one in which accountability is smaller than problem-solving; a flat job as one in which the two are equal in size. So an uphill job is one where results are more important than intensive thinking – a 'do' job – and a downhill job is one where the use of knowledge through thinking is more important that answerability for results – a 'think' job.

Job evaluation using guide charts is a measuring *process* not a measuring *instrument*, which is why it is possible to modify the scales to reflect the character and structure of a particular school and why the charts have the ability to absorb new information on job content over time. It is a *relative* not an *absolute* measuring process based on four beliefs: every job requires some know-how, problem solving and accountability; guide chart scales reflect degrees to which these three factors are developed and used in a job; a relative rank order can be produced for jobs, and differences between jobs can be measured that reflect their relative importance; guide charts are driven by principles, rather than by immutable scales or rules, so the process of measurement can be adapted for use in different organisations.

Checking the evaluation: 'sore thumbs' and correlations

The idea of *shape* is what gives the word 'profile' to the title of the guide charts and it controls their relative calibration; in other words, the numbering patterns on the guide charts are set such that they produce scores for the factors which, when arrayed for a given job, produce a shape or profile that is *recognisable* to the incumbent. This gives an important *post facto* check on an evaluation: the profile is studied to see that its shape *makes sense* and the score for a job is compared to scores for bigger, smaller and similar jobs to moderate the evaluation.

After a job has been evaluated, if the relationship between problem solving and accountability does not fit the incumbent's perception, there is the possibility that an error has occurred (on either side). For example, data-entry jobs should be 'do' jobs and data-interpretation jobs should be 'think' jobs. Jobs can be compared to others above and below it, in descending order say, to see if any of the scores in any of the three dimensions are overly high or low in comparison to what might be called a 'sore-thumb' check.

Guide chart job evaluation has a second check, that of 'correlation', which involves taking a sample of evaluations and comparing them with known jobs (in other schools, perhaps). A correlation factor can then be worked out that allows a correspondence to be made between the two, but it is important that two spurious effects are first eliminated from the comparison: a 'heiligenschein' or 'halo effect', where an incumbent's above-average performance in a job increases the score allocated to the job; and a 'horns effect', where an incumbent's below-average performance decreases the score. Remember: comparison should be between *jobs*, not between *job-holders*.

Three examples of evaluation using guide charts

Example 1

Highfield School is a large (1,650 pupils) comprehensive school with a sixth form of approximately 400. According to its most recent inspection report from Ofsted, it has a well-established senior management team with two deputy heads (see Figure 11.5, Panel 1). One of the deputy positions, the more junior of the two is being evaluated using the guide charts.

PANEL 1

School: Highfield School   **Ofsted:** May 2009
Type: Comprehensive
Size: 1,650   **Group:** 7–8

Salary for job:
Equivalent positions: 2 deputy heads
Membership of SMT: 7: H + 2DH + 3 Senior Teachers + operations manager

PANEL 2

Position: Deputy Head
Duties mentioned in job description:
To manage the use of data to raise achievement and monitor pupil progress.
To design & implement a new whole-school system for monitoring pupil progress.
To develop base-line testing in Year 7.
To raise teacher awareness of data systems and to gauge their effectiveness
To support teachers in their target setting.
To liaise with the curriculum deputy head.
To organise and chair meetings to discuss and disseminate data policy.
To develop study programmes to encourage pupils.
To develop links with outside data agencies (including FFT).
To develop a range of celebratory events for achievement.
To work with department heads to ensure consistency.
To carry out administration for the post.
To assist the head in preparing reports.
To reinforce rules and ethos and to deal with discipline in Year 10.

PANEL 3

Personal qualities required: None specified in job description

PANEL 4

Guide Chart Analysis

Summary: To design, explore, develop, implement, monitor & support a whole-school system for monitoring pupil progress.

Know-how: F+; III; 3   608
Problem solving: F+; 4   (57%)   347
Accountability: F; 6; C+   460   **Total:** 1415

PANEL 5

Responsibility Analysis

Discretionary element: Large
Max time-span of discretion: Greater than 1 year
Range of level of work: Wide

Figure 11.5 Example 1 of a guide chart evaluation (Highfield School, deputy headship)

The job description is specific as to the deputy's role and jointly held responsibilities. The incumbent is expected to undertake a significant amount of teaching, but this varies from year to year and (the exact whole-time equivalent) is not made explicit in the job specification. The most important managerial functions of the job include the exploration, design, development and implementation of a new whole-school data system to monitor pupil progress and attainment, and selling that system to the teaching and pastoral staff (see Figure 11.5, Panel 2).

Responsibility Analysis: The job description is a fairly thorough one and the responsibilities described in it are onerous and of fundamental importance to the mission of the school. The discretionary element of the job is 'Large' and the maximum time-span of discretion for substantive tasks such as the design and implementation of a whole-school data system is relatively long – 'in excess of one year' – so a large guide chart score can be anticipated. The range of level of work is 'Wide', from assisting the head in the preparation of official reports to the design of the whole-school system for monitoring pupil progress (see Figure 11.5, Panel 5).

Know-How: Since the job involves managing medium-size change with unpredictable problems and demands *at least* a good command of statistical theory (see Figures 11.1 and 11.2), the assessment of the Statistical Know-how required for the job is on the boundary of 'Seasoned Diverse/Specialised' (F) and 'Broad or Specialised Mastery' (G). The F+ and G– scores are the same (see Figure 11.1) so it can be scored as F+ (say).

The job involves the direction of a large diverse school-wide team and affects the entire school, so Managerial Know-how is assessed as 'Diverse' (III) (see Figure 11.1, upper horizontal axis).

Skills in motivating staff are 'Critical' to the success of the introduction of the system so this is assessed as '3' (see Figure 11.1, lower horizontal axis).

Know-how is scored as 608 (see Figure 11.5, Panel 4).

Problem solving: The job is under the head's direction towards the specific goal of developing a whole-school data system and there are many intangible aspects to the undertaking, so the Thinking Environment is assessed as being in the upper reaches of 'Generally Defined' (F) (see Figure 11.3). As the job demands interpretative and constructive thinking by the incumbent, the Thinking Challenge is assessed as 'Adaptive' (4). It is not quite (but is close to) 'Uncharted' (5) since whole-school systems can be imported from other schools. The thinking required is not path-finding, however imaginative the solution may turn out to be.

Problem solving is scored as 57 per cent. It is a percentage of Know-how and 57 per cent of 608 is 347 (see Figure 11.5, Panel 4).

Accountability: The job is subject to functional policy as the head directs the incumbent towards the job's long-term goal. As the deputy is directed by the head rather than by general school policy, the Freedom to Act is classed as 'General Direction' (F) rather than as 'Guidance' (G) (see Figure 11.4).

The Impact of the job is essentially advisory and supportive, particularly in the context of the management structure of the school, and it is not a position shared equally with another. So it is assessed as 'Contributory' (C), but at the upper end (see Figure 11.4).

The size of the school places it in the 'Very Large' category (see Figure 11.4), so the Accountability score is 460 (see Figure 11.5, Panel 4).

Example 2

Shaftesbury Road School is an 11–16 comprehensive school with 1,700 pupils, categorised as 'Very Large'. The current principal has been in place one year. The most recent Ofsted report describes the school's catchment area as 'very disadvantaged' in socio-economic terms and the school has a serious attendance problem. The inspection report identifies Key Stage 3 (KS3) as being particularly weak and recommends that it be 'reviewed and restructured'. The position of Head of KS3 is being evaluated using the guide charts.

The job description describes the position as having a mixture of pastoral and curriculum duties, but the job is primarily intended to take responsibility for all matters relating to Key Stage 3 (see Figure 11.6, Panel 2).

Responsibility Analysis: The discretionary element of the job is 'Moderate' and the maximum time-span of discretion for the job's substantive tasks is approximately 'one year'. Every year, pupil cohorts make the transition from KS2 to KS3 and from KS3 to KS4, so a modest guide chart score can be anticipated. The range of level of work is 'Medium', from managing KS3 to overseeing school visits (See Figure 15, Panel 5).

Know-how: Since the job, at its highest level of work, requires statistical skills and the ability to implement a school system for a particular year group (see Figures 11.1 and 11.2), the assessment of Statistical Know-how required for the job is 'Extended Skill/Knowledge' (D).

The job involves the direction of a large diverse school-wide team in relation to attendance, which affects the entire school, so Managerial Know-how is assessed as 'Diverse' (III) on the upper horizontal axis of Figure 11.1.

Skill in motivating staff is not critical to the job's success, but it is important that the incumbent has influence, so Human Relations Skills are assessed as 'Important' (2) (see Figure 11.1, lower horizontal axis).

Know-how is scored as 264 (see Figure 11.6, Panel 4).

Problem solving: The Thinking Environment is assessed as being at the upper end of 'Standardised' (D), as the job involves thinking within diverse procedures with assistance readily available from the head teacher and the deputy (see Figure 11.3). It is likely to involve rapidly occurring unforeseen problems, perhaps of a motivational nature, with solutions largely dictated by precedent and practice, and resolved quickly.

PANEL 1

School:	Shaftesbury Road School	**Ofsted:** January 2002
Type:	11–16 Comprehensive	
Size:	1,700	**Group:** 7–8

Salary for job:
Equivalent positions: Not documented
Membership of SMT: Not documented

PANEL 2

Position: Head of Key Stage 3
Duties mentioned in job description:
To be KS3 curriculum manager in all respects.
To coordinate the school data development plan for KS3.
To develop and enhance lines of communication with partners and parents.
To lead teams, especially the data team, at KS3.
To take charge of pupil attendance across the whole school.
To monitor underperformance across specific subgroups.

PANEL 3

Personal qualities required:
Proven management and data skills; good motivator of staff and pupils; a believer in equal opportunities; experience in more than one school; experience of mixed ability grouping.

PANEL 4

Guide Chart Analysis
Summary: Key Stage 3 manager, with responsible for data development at KS3.

Know-how:	D; III; 2	264	
Problem solving:	D+; 3 (33%)	87	
Accountability:	E+; 6; C	304	**Total:** 655

PANEL 5

Responsibility Analysis
Discretionary element:	Moderate
Maximum time-span of discretion:	1 year
Range of level of work:	Medium

Figure 11.6 Example 2 of a guide chart evaluation (Shaftesbury Road School, Head of KS3)

The job requires the incumbent to search for solutions within a fairly confined experiential area, so Thinking Challenge is assessed as 'Varied' (3).

Problem solving is scored as 33 per cent. It is a percentage of Know-how and 33 per cent of 264 is 87 (see Figure 11.6, Panel 4).

Accountability: The job is subject to school policy and practices, and the head directs the incumbent towards medium-term goals; the long end of 'Medium', as some data matters are brought forward from one year to the next within KS3. Freedom to Act is assessed as being in the upper reaches of 'Directed' (E) (see Figure 11.4).

The Impact of the job is advisory and supportive in the context of the management of the school. It is not a position shared with another, so Impact is assessed as 'Contributory' (C) (see Figure 11.4).

The size of the school places it in the 'Very Large' category (see Figure 11.4), so the Accountability score is 304 (see Figure 11.6, Panel 4).

Example 3

Eastgate High School is a medium-sized all-girls Boarding and Day school, categorised as 'Medium Small'. The job description stresses the importance of after-hours work and admissions and transition from junior schools. The position of deputy head is being evaluated using the guide charts. The duties for the post are as outlined on Figure 11.7, Panel 2.

Responsibility Analysis: The discretionary component of the job is 'Very Small' and the maximum time-span of discretion for the job's substantive tasks, as gauged from the job description, is 'less than one month'. Duties such as deputising for the head, assisting in day-to-day administration, monitoring pupil absence, arranging staff cover and lunchtime supervision, have time-spans of discretion measured in days. The range of level of work is 'Narrow' and a low guide chart score can be anticipated (see Figure 11.7, Panel 5).

Know-how: The job, at its highest level of work, involves 'Elementary Skills' (B), bordering on 'Basic Understanding' (A) (see Figures 11.1 and 11.2). The defined responsibilities merely follow standard school procedures and Statistical Know-how is assessed as B−.

The incumbent must frequently deputise for the head and the job is essentially one of being second-in-command. There is only one deputy in the school, so the Managerial Know-how is assessed as 'Broad' (IV) and the Human Relations Skills at 'Critical' (3) (see the two horizontal axes on Figure 11.1). If there is an error in this assessment, it is on the high side.

Know-how is scored as 200 (see Figure 11.7, Panel 4).

Problem solving: The Thinking Environment is assessed as being in the lower end of 'Routine' (B), confined as it is by standard school practice, with precedent and illustrative examples readily available in such a small school.

```
┌─────────────────────────────────────────────────────────────────────────┐
│                              PANEL 1                                      │
│                                                                           │
│  School:        Eastgate High School          Ofsted: January 2002       │
│  Type:          Girls 3–18 Boarding & Day                                 │
│  Size:          720                            Group: 4                   │
│                                                                           │
│  Salary for job:                                                          │
│  Equivalent positions:       None                                         │
│  Membership of SMT:          3: H + DH + Director of Studies              │
└─────────────────────────────────────────────────────────────────────────┘
```

```
┌─────────────────────────────────────────────────────────────────────────┐
│                              PANEL 2                                      │
│                                                                           │
│  Position:      Deputy Head                                               │
│  Duties mentioned in job description:                                     │
│  To deputise for the head.                                                │
│  To assist in the day-to-day running of the school.                       │
│  To help with admissions and to keep admissions data.                     │
│  To liaise with housemistresses in running the boarding section.          │
│  To monitor and keep data on pupil absence and arrange staff cover for    │
│  absent teachers.                                                         │
│  To supervise lunchtime, after-school and weekend activities.             │
│  To assist with careers guidance and health education.                    │
│  To assist in the appointment of staff.                                   │
│  To liaise with the head of the junior school to ensure a smooth          │
│  transition into Year 7 and to oversee the transfer of data from Year 6.  │
└─────────────────────────────────────────────────────────────────────────┘
```

```
┌─────────────────────────────────────────────────────────────────────────┐
│                              PANEL 3                                      │
│                                                                           │
│  Personal qualities required:                                             │
│  Commitment to the stated religious faith; be an inspiring (and           │
│  experienced) teacher; be willing to take after-school activities.        │
└─────────────────────────────────────────────────────────────────────────┘
```

```
┌─────────────────────────────────────────────────────────────────────────┐
│                              PANEL 4                                      │
│                                                                           │
│                         Guide Chart Analysis                              │
│  Summary:       To implement and support a whole school system for        │
│  progress.      monitoring pupil                                          │
│                                                                           │
│  Know-how:            B-; IV; 3        200                                 │
│  Problem solving:     B-; 2    (16%)   32                                  │
│  Accountability:      C; 3; S          66              Total:  298         │
└─────────────────────────────────────────────────────────────────────────┘
```

```
┌─────────────────────────────────────────────────────────────────────────┐
│                              PANEL 5                                      │
│                                                                           │
│                       Responsibility Analysis                             │
│  Discretionary element:              Very small                           │
│  Max time-span of discretion:        Less than 1 month                    │
│  Range of level of work:             Narrow                               │
└─────────────────────────────────────────────────────────────────────────┘
```

Figure 11.7 Example 3 of a guide chart evaluation (Eastgate High School, Deputy Head)

The job requires the incumbent to search for solutions within a fairly confined experiential area and to make discriminating choices between known things, so the Thinking Challenge is assessed as 'Patterned' (2) (see Figure 11.3).

Problem solving is scored as 16 per cent. It is a percentage of Know-how and 16 per cent of 200 is 32 (see Figure 11.7, Panel 4).

Accountability: The job is one in which duties are subject to standard procedures and, because of the short time-span of discretion, are closely monitored. Freedom to Act is assessed as being 'Standardised' (C) (see Figure 11.4).

The Impact of the job is assessed as 'Shared' (S), since activities and resources are very much shared with the head teacher (see Figure 11.4).

The size of the school places it in the 'Medium Small' (3) category (see Figure 11.4), so the Accountability score is 66 (see Figure 11.7, Panel 4).

The low evaluation score from the responsibility analysis and from the guide charts suggests that this position is not really a management job and should not require the appointment of someone at the level of deputy head.

12 A dissenting view

Challenging the complexity of UK measures

Introduction

One major advantage of value-added measures over threshold performance indicators (such as the percentage of pupils attaining five or more A*–C grades at GCSE) is that *all* students contribute to the measure, rather than just those who happen to have crossed an arbitrary threshold, which lessens the temptation for schools to focus on borderline students at the expense of those who have predicted outcomes well below or safely above the threshold. Of course, there are still technical issues unresolved at the extremes of attainment, and the risk of teachers 'playing the system' has not been completely removed, but, on balance, in the era of initiatives like 'Every Child Matters' in the UK and 'No Child Left Behind' in the US, value-added models take a clear step in a positive direction and UK models are being scrutinised by policy-makers in countries like Australia (Downes and Vindurampulle 2007) and Poland (Jakubowski 2008) as they prepare to develop their own metrics.

While most of us researching in the area of school effectiveness acknowledge the crucial benefit that VA measures have brought in capturing the progress made by students in schools, we remain critical of the fact that at practitioner level the current model is caught in the tension between having to provide *both* key public accountability measures *and* data used to steer improvement. This tension raises 'practice concerns' around three key areas: the choice of contextualising factors included in the model; issues around data and statistical modelling; and policy.

Taking account of intake: the background and rationale for included variables

In the KS2–KS4 CVA model, the variables that relate to prior attainment provide most of the model's explanatory power – typically around 50 per cent of the variance – but there are important concerns in the way these are treated. First, the model has two school-level variables that take the same value for every pupil in a given school – *level* of school prior attainment and *spread* of school prior attainment[1] – but both relate only to those pupils being modelled (i.e. those in the GCSE cohort) and not to other pupils in the school at the same time, though the latter obviously and non-trivially impacts on the learning of the former. Second, socio-economic data is included in the model, but it is not clear that the proxy measures used – typically, entitlement to free meals in school – are robust enough. And, third, there are 'subtlety issues' of concern with PLASC data.

PLASC collects contextual data annually for use in the model: on ethnicity, first language, gender, level of Special Educational Need, socio-economic indicators like FSM entitlement and deprivation measures associated with geographical location, and date of entry to school.

- Data is gathered on all the main ethnic groups, plus 'unclassified' (less than 4 per cent) for those individuals and schools who choose not to provide the information. The current range of ethnicity codes used in the CVA model is necessarily crude, especially for people of mixed background, and they ignore the 'political' subtleties of pupils claiming or denying their ethnicity, which go to the heart of whether pupils from some backgrounds feel culturally assimilated in British schools (and in British society generally). Provision exists to use an extended set of codes, but supporters of the model dismiss this possibility because extended codes are 'not universally collected' and would 'add considerably to the complexity' (Ray 2006: 22). Critics might retort that avoiding unnecessary complexity has not always been a priority for policy-makers, and that the issue is more likely to be that changing the codes would affect the consistency of the model over time, which *is* a legitimate concern (though more so for academics and policy-makers than teachers). Generally, *parents* rather than pupils provide the data on ethnicity, which (it is claimed) makes it more accurate. Typically, less than 3 per cent of pupils *change* ethnic category from year to year so it is undoubtedly good quality data, but it does raise some subtle issues. Although the PLASC-informed CVA model takes account (in the form of coefficients and standard errors calculated in the normal way) of the relative size of the various effects and how significant they are compared to the size of the school effect, the published information is not in a form that enables schools *to use the data for improvement*. The concern is one of ownership. Are teachers and head teachers aware of 'impact issues' and have they been empowered to influence the model in this respect; for example, to capture the subtlety of pupils and families denying their own ethnicity in order to 'fit in'? If '*every* child matters', what remediation is offered for the 3 per cent who change ethnicity each year, and who tells *their*

---

1   Spread of school prior attainment is included on the basis that schools with a narrow ability range 'more easily appear effective' and 'tend to have pupils with relatively high overall prior attainment' (Ray 2006: 43).

story? Sometimes, what pupils think and say about their own ethnicities says as much about race in society as the statistics. What are schools supposed to *do* with ethnic (and other similar) data in order to improve pupil outcomes, and are the assumed causalities immutable over time? If Bangladeshi girls born in September do better than Afro-Caribbean boys born in June, will this always be the case and how should teachers in the classroom act upon the information?

- Most *pupil-level* contextualising variables are simple binary (yes/no) answers to school census queries and are restricted to those for which national data is available, and in line with common practice in multivariate regression analysis a number of interaction terms are included in the model – for example, that between student ethnicity and FSM entitlement – when these have been shown to make a significant contribution to the model's explanatory power. The data on first language is essentially a binary code – 'English' and 'Other than English' – with additional 'unknown' categories. It is non-problematic data, though it might be better to distinguish between these 'other' languages, especially where a different alphabet (or none) is involved. Data collection on gender is also fairly straightforward, but like ethnicity it is unclear what *practitioners* (as opposed to researchers) are supposed to *do* with the information as a school improvement tool.

- The PLASC data on SEN is more complex as it covers a wide range of interrelated disabilities. The SEN Code of Practice offers three levels of response: 'School Action', where a teacher or coordinator provides the intervention; 'School Action Plus', where external help is sourced; and 'Statemented', where a child's educational needs are set out as entitlements by the local authority.[2] This is clear-cut in terms of action, but different local authorities attribute/distribute the categories with varying degrees of liberality and this is not taken into account in the model; nor is the fact that some schools have their VA performance over time affected by factors like the local authority closing a neighbouring special school.

- In England, children whose parents receive certain welfare benefits have entitlement to free school meals, which (as we have seen) is the main PLASC measure of social deprivation and family income. It is convenient but crude. As Ray (2006) notes, pupils who are *not* entitled to FSM vary considerably in their circumstances, just as there are degrees of deprivation within the FSM group. There is the additional problem that some parents who are entitled to FSM, from embarrassment or for cultural reasons, elect *not* to claim it, and there are other families *not* entitled to FSM who are living in very straitened circumstances. As a consequence, the continued use of such a proxy measure of deprivation is a weakness and may undermine parallel school improvement initiatives based on the model.

2 For the CVA model, the last two categories are treated as one.

Postcode data is the classifier of geographical location, which is also used to infer socio-economic status. IDACI scores are calculated by another government department, not the DfE, but it is a concern that the criteria used to define the categories *could* be manipulated to indicate success for particular government initiatives. A non-governmental index, ACORN, is used instead by FFT in its models, but whether the rationale for this is methodological or one of distrust is not known.

- There are two variables capturing mobility: a simple binary one to cater for the effect of joining a school less than two years before the end of KS4; and another for pupils joining the school outside normal times of year (i.e. *not* in July, August or September of Years 7, 8 and 9). Supporters of the model claim that this keeps the model simple and intelligible, but again it is not clear that this is always the case or that practitioners see it that way. Some variables, like 'change in FSM status from year to year', are excluded from the model – legitimately in our view – because they do not add enough to warrant the extra complexity, but other factors, like the percentage of pupils in the school from minority ethnic communities are excluded even though they appear *prima facia* to be important.

- Finally, PLASC data is collected on pupil absences and exclusions, but this data is *not* used in the CVA model because, although it would improve the model's explanatory power, it is thought that 'schools should to some extent be responsible' for the factors used (Ray 2006: 21). Here we see the recurring tensions nicely encapsulated: it is unclear whether the purpose of PLASC and its dependent CVA model is prediction, accountability or improvement. Certainly, it is proper that the model should only contain the factors/inputs that are outside the school's control so that what is left is the school effect, but it is arguable whether factors such as SEN and truancy are within or without the control of the school.

The inclusion of certain factors enhances the utility of CVA for improvement purposes, but the 'one size fits all' approach creates tensions for accountability purposes and leads to the creation of perverse incentives whereby schools can manipulate the metrics, particularly in the area of SEN and ethnicity, to get better scores. This *could* be overcome by having counterbalancing incentives elsewhere, but it is not clear that policy-makers have covered all their bases in this respect; that for every manipulation to raise false CVA scores there are equal and opposite incentives for schools *not* to do so.

Issues related to the data and statistical models used to generate VA scores

The KS National Curriculum tests used in CVA models were introduced in England to measure attainment in certain subjects, not to calculate value added. Originally, scores were reported as broad National Curriculum 'levels' and particular attention was paid to moderating the examination scripts of *borderline* students, but today, for the purpose of calculating CVA scores, a finely graded system is required in which test scores are reported to the nearest *tenth of a* level. Whether the current marking system in England is robust enough to support such fine divisions in grading *for the purpose of holding schools publicly accountable* is the question. We have applied fine-grade levels to potential school improvement applications in this book, but such applications are internal tools for use by schools to support professional judgement around individual students, not to produce a single scalar to describe the performance of a whole cohort. While the measurement error introduced by the subjectivity of the marking process will balance out during the aggregation that produces the complete national data set, the current practice of allocating all the National Curriculum tests for a single school *to a single examiner* may result in bias in the test scores for an individual school. This creates issues for the use of CVA for accountability and self-evaluation purposes. It should be possible to use electronic marking to assign randomly scanned scripts within a bank of examiners to ameliorate potential bias, but this may be no small task given the debacle over the recent introduction of electronic administration to National Curriculum tests (BBC 2008).

Second, the 'scoring system' is a concern. Pupils taking KS2 tests are given marks in English, mathematics and science, which are then converted into one of three crude overall levels: 'Level 4' is designated as the average expected attainment for age 11; 'Level 5' is above average; 'Level 3' is below average. Obviously, there is a ceiling effect for bright pupils who cannot score above a '5', though they may be operating well above that level, and since approximately one-third of pupils get the top grade, this may be significant.[3] From a school's point of view, each of the three levels is assigned a points value according to a formula and an average points score is then calculated across the three subjects. However, despite using a fine-grade system in the measure of prior attainment,[4] pupils who are scoring (or assumed to be scoring) below Level 3 receive the same number of points regardless of whether they were

3 After the experience of the 2005 CVA pilot, an adjustment was made to the 2006 scores to account for ceiling and floor effects in the predicted CVA calculations to bring them into line with the actual capped point scores observed at the extremes of the data. That said, there is clearly a limit to the capped GCSE point score ($8 \times 58 = 464$) so that a student with the same prior attainment as another but with a higher total GCSE point score will receive no extra 'credit' in his/her VA score. It is easier to make such adjustments for ceiling and floor effects in multilevel models than in median VA models.

4 The CVA models used by both DfE and FFT employ a fine-grade system. For example, when calculating KS2–KS4 CVA, the raw scores achieved in each National Curriculum test are used to calculate a decimalised level of point score. A student attaining Level 4 at KS2 under the old VA system would have been awarded a point score of 27. Using fine grades under CVA, those students only just scoring a Level 4 would get a point score of 24.0 whereas those right at the top of the Level 4 band get a point score of 29.9, which provides a continuous scale for APS.

just below the Level 3 threshold or whether they had SEN status and were not entered for the tests, so there is also a 'floor effect' to the data. The three levels are designed to be aligned over time with levels at other Key Stages – in other words, that Level 4 (say) means the same thing in any subject at any Key Stage – but as Ray (2006: 18) points out, there may be some 'misalignment' (Massey *et al.* 2003). It may be true that equivalence between KS levels is not essential for a value-added system as long as all schools take the same tests, but this is not true between years or between levels. Level 5 in Mathematics in 2001 (say) might not represent the same learning as the same level in the same subject in 2006, and a Level 3 might not represent the same level of underperformance relative to Level 4 in 2001 as it did in 2006. For school effectiveness research, this diminishes the value of any comparison of a school's CVA scores over time and for practitioners it suggests that a school can only be as good as its previous year's examination results.[5] Supporters of the current system in England claim that normalising Key Stage results so that they have the same distribution in any given year would lose the public meaning of 'levels' in terms of the learning they represent, but the same logic has not been applied to (say) GCSE and A-level examinations where equivalence across qualifications, subjects and courses is almost impossible to fathom. If the priority for policy-makers is a system that is easy for classroom teachers and parents to understand, even if that means sacrificing some robustness, then that should also apply to CVA measurement.

As discussed already, the scores generated by CVA models are calculated from the attainment of pupils, adjusting for the effect of prior attainment and taking into account a wide range of contextualising factors: ethnicity, speaking English as an additional language, gender, age, level of special educational need, entitlement to free school meals and income deprivation, late entrance to school, and being 'in care'. In England, for the KS2–KS4 CVA model, this entails trying to produce VA scores for up to 11 GCSE subjects per student adjusting for prior attainment *in only three* (English, mathematics and science) *achieved five years previously*.

In the multilevel model the residual variance is partitioned into two levels: pupil level (level 1) and school level (level 2), which are the model's random effects. It is possible to include other levels in the model – class groups within a school, for example, or groups of schools within a local authority – but this has not been done. One of the advantages of MLM, unlike OLS methods, is that it produces more robust estimates of the standard errors for factors in the model (whereas OLS methods tend to *under*estimate them), which means that judging

---

5 In the May 2007 edition of *Inspection Matters*, Ofsted stressed to school inspectors that CVA was a *relative* rather than an *absolute* measure of performance and that care should be taken when interpreting trends in CVA scores, as MLM coefficients are recalculated each year and adjustments made to the factors included in the model.

whether or not a factor is statistically significant is more rigorous. Another difference between OLS and MLM is in the way the latter 'shrinks' the value-added estimates, which depend in part on the size of the school. Application of the shrinkage factor means that the CVA score is reduced to a percentage of its raw size, closer to the mean.[6] It prevents schools at the extremes – those with residuals which suggest that they are either very effective or very *in*effective – from registering a very high or a very low CVA score. Supporters say that this is non-problematic because the raw residuals for small schools are anyway known to be poor estimates of effectiveness from one year to the next, but as we saw in Chapter 4, shrinkage causes scores to be pulled in a 'socially expected direction' and demonstrate a kind of 'statistical self-fulfilling prophecy' (Fitz-Gibbon 1991: 19).

Notwithstanding these advantages and disadvantages and the decision to opt for greater complexity within the multilevel model, 'reversions' still occur when the system goes practical. Ofsted, for example, has provided inspectors with the means to *unshrink* the data to see what the raw residuals look like. If inspectors can judge from the raw data and from their own impressions the extent to which the raw residual is 'an accurate reflection' of a school's effectiveness, why all the complexity at the practitioner level? It suggests that CVA measurement may be more aligned to the agenda of public accountability and performance tables than to the critical process of self-evaluation as espoused by the government's 'New Relationship with Schools'. This is compounded by the fact that the application of shrinkage factors causes problems in the calculation of CVA scores *for subgroups* of pupils. A recent attempt by Hillingdon Borough Council in London, for example, to assist its schools in interpreting RAISEonline outputs illustrates the problem (Thomson 2007: 41). In one sample output, the CVA score for 182 matching pupils in a cohort was 978.4; the scores for the 170 students *with* English as their first language was 978.7; while the 12 students who did *not* have English as their first language had a CVA score of 987.3. The scores for both subgroups were therefore higher than the average score for the combined cohort, which (Hillingdon Borough Council found) was very confusing information for managers and teachers who would intuitively have expected to see the scores for the two subgroups distributed around the mean for all students. What has happened is that the application of shrinkage has pulled all three residuals closer to the mean (1,000), but it has had a *greater* effect on the subgroups due to their smaller sizes.[7] The point here is not that there is a theoretical flaw in the modelling or that the system

6 Generally, OLS has a problem dealing with small cohorts so that a small school's score can only be given with a wide confidence interval. With MLM, national data is used to modify the estimate when information on the school is limited because of size.

7 In the light of such 'shrinkage discrepancies', the advice given by Hillingdon Local Authority to its schools is to avoid using RAISEonline for self-evaluation involving student subgroups, but to use FFT analyses instead for this purpose (Thomson 2007: 76).

is unfair or unjustified, but that it is necessary at practitioner level that schools be briefed extensively on issues like shrinkage to prevent a barrier of expertise growing up around the data.

Policy issues related to development of VA measures

As we saw in Chapter 2, the Value-Added National Project advised that simple and easy-to-understand measures be used in preference to slightly more robust, but much more complex, multilevel models.[8] While the logic of this approach was considered sensible at the time, 'many of the experts consulted by the DfES' favoured complexity and so 'it was decided to move ahead on this basis' (Ray 2006: 49). While multilevel models have admirably corrected for grouping effects, there has been little by way of debate as to whether the complexity added by such advancements is justified by the significance (in the vernacular sense) of the measures to practitioners. Despite opposition from some quarters, there is little doubting the benefit of MLM to effectiveness research, but if what is being measured for the public – how well pupils do at examinations and how much better or worse they do as they get older – is accepted as being only a small part of the *education* they receive in school, and if 'the school effect', though clearly non-trivial, is accepted as being relatively small, one must ask whether the obfuscation that results from the complexity of ever-more-accurate measures is worthwhile when ever fewer people can understand and interpret the results. *Ad absurdum*, if only a handful of academics understand the models to the extent of being able to challenge them, there is little use in them for professionals whose very essence lies in understanding challenges to practice and accommodating change.

Taking account of context

The first PLASC in 2002, linking individual pupils to their achievements through their Unique Pupil Numbers, afforded the opportunity to include contextual data alongside the prior attainment of pupils. The government was aware of the need to retain the confidence of stakeholders as the models pro-

---

8 At the time of the *Value Added National Project*, practitioners supported the simple approach but accepted that performance tables should contain some measures to account for different pupil intakes. As a result, the DfEE (1998a) trialled a measure of KS3–KS4 added value that compared pupil attainment at KS4 (for the 1998 cohort) with the national median KS4 attainment for pupils from the previous year. Scores for schools were then calculated as the average of these differences (Critchlow and Coe 2003). This 'median method' was easy for parents to understand and for professionals to interpret, and was consistent with how national data was presented to schools at the time (DfEE 1998b). The response to the trial was positive and although some commentators suggested that the absence of *pre*-KS3 measures was problematic, there was widespread and patient acceptance that these would be added in due course.

liferated (Miliband 2004), but slowly the voices in favour of greater complexity began to command the stage. It is difficult to see how policy-makers could have withstood the advice of pro-complexity advocates in favour of an easier-to-understand practitioner approach: the more obtuse the arguments in favour of complexity, the less anyone could contest them, least of all policy-makers who were neither statisticians nor practitioners. Somewhere in all the excitement, the importance of access for practitioners was mislaid or underestimated, and even supporters of complex modelling acknowledge that there is a difficulty 'maintaining continuity' (Ray 2006) as practitioners move to multilevel models from simpler versions. It has been suggested that these problems are largely transitional, but it seems to be more than this. A point seems to have been reached where some contextual factors are downplayed because they add too much complexity, but others are included simply because they are easy to measure. For example, FSM entitlement is still used in CVA models though the accuracy and appropriateness of its use as a proxy for economic disadvantage is questionable. Month of birth is also taken into account in CVA because by including as many factors as possible outside the school's control, the residual/difference between the model and the pupil data comes closer theoretically to 'the school effect', but month of birth is of little use to practitioners if the measures are to be used for school improvement purposes. If CVA is to be an *estimator* of future attainment, care must be taken which factors are included in order not to lower expectations; if CVA is to be used for *school improvement* purposes or to allocate funding, there is little point including factors that cannot be changed;[9] if CVA is to be used for *accountability* purposes, the model must be understandable to the extent that it does not require 'outside' expertise; and if CVA is to be used for a *combination* of the above, decisions need to be made that balance the competing claims of statistical robustness, usability and accessibility. Generally, the school effectiveness research community would welcome such a differentiation. It is not in anyone's interest to perpetuate the inappropriate use of important data.

In many ways, RAISEonline now serves as the interface between practitioners and the 'black box' of CVA prosody. Certainly, it provides schools with a better range of data and outcome measures for pupils, but is it a helpful imposition on *all* schools to use a *common* method of analysis and to have to judge performance against national patterns without fully understanding how the calculations are made and under what assumptions. The fact that data from RAISEonline is also used *for self-evaluation* merely creates the illusion of ownership, and the availability to Ofsted of the analysed data means in effect that schools are now controlled not only in *what* they do (via the National Curriculum) and in what data they collect, but in *how* they judge what they do. This in turn, it could be argued, has a de-professionalising effect on teaching and headship. The simple

---

9 Except insofar as the remaining variance is then closer to what the school adds.

fact that teachers use data is not an end in itself and it is certainly not enough to constitute a long-term strategy for school (or systemic) improvement. In particular, it is no small task to tease out the contribution made *by individual teachers*, especially in secondary schools where students change teaching groups during the school year and have had a range of different teachers for any given subject across the years of a Key Stage; and other pupils will have had access to extra tutoring both within and outside school. Yet few measures have incorporated the (intermediate) level of 'teacher' into multilevel models, though as we have seen earlier, a number of studies have suggested that the size of the teacher effect may be of the same order of magnitude as the school effect in terms of the variance partitioned to each level. While schools can justifiably be considered responsible for much of the variation at class level, such findings call into question the usefulness of a single value-added measure to inform parental choice, its long-standing rationale. While parents now have the facility, to varying extents in England, of being able to choose their children's *schools*, nowhere do they have the facility to select their children's *teachers*!

Issues of comparison and compatibility

There is an additional concern in England that the organisations that run the testing system are not independent enough of those that set policy and inspect schools, particularly when higher scores are trumpeted by policy-makers as proof that their policies are 'working'. Statistical analysis *does* indicate that the examination system in England *is testing what it claims to be testing*, but this is not the same as claiming that the tests are testing what they *should* be testing, and there is no shortage of evidence that teachers are ignoring broader educational outcomes (Volante 2004; James 2006). Given this fact and the widely held belief that pupils in England are over-tested, it is unclear why sampling is not used throughout the system, as it is in the Foundation Stage for five year olds. Why, if the tests are valid and reliable, is it necessary to test *every* child from *every* postcode and from *every* ethnic background in order to evaluate how policies are impacting on children? It should be a simple matter to arrange an appropriate sampling frame and thereby make huge savings in terms of cost and interruption. And there are additional anomalies. First, test data for KS1, KS2 and until recently KS3 is only collected for the core subjects – English, mathematics and science – which fact in itself is likely to skew both data and teaching. Admittedly, the cost of GCSE-type assessment at earlier Key Stages would be cost-prohibitive and disruptive, especially if it contained in-house elements, but one solution would be to sample externally moderated, but internally assessed, formal school examinations (rather than coursework, which some feel is losing credibility). The fact that the government does *not* address this situation is, according to Tymms and Dean (2004), evidence that it is confusing 'robustness' with 'bias'. Generally, the greater the range of evidence used to make an assessment the more robust its claims, and since classroom teachers are best placed to offer this, the government's reservation about sampling seems to be one of bias; in other words, that not all teachers will be equally exacting in their tests.

The end of the beginning: the School Report Card

CVA measures represent a huge improvement on threshold measures, both in terms of *what* is being measured (progress adjusted for prior attainment rather than raw outcomes) and *who* is being measured (*all* pupils in the cohort rather than just those who cross an arbitrary threshold). That notwithstanding, it may be that the model in England falls foul of trying to be all things to all people. Despite its complexity in that respect, in other ways it represents an *over-simplification* of the nature of school performance. Even if it *could* be measured in academic outcomes alone, across a narrow range of public examinations, school CVA scores would not capture the differential effectiveness of schools across the range of prior attainment and across the various subgroups.[10]

Value-added models meet their public audience when the shrunken residuals are used to rank schools and, as we have seen, this too causes problems (e.g. Hutchison and Schagen 2008). Admittedly, the DfE *itself* does not rank schools in its annual published performance tables, but it *is* aware that the shrunken scores it puts into the public domain *are* ranked by national and local media.[11] The one-number-fits-all approach to measuring the performance of individual schools carries with it the danger of presenting an overly simplified view of school effectiveness that belies the complexity of the metric, but does less to inform parental choice and inspection than its supporters claim. Whether or not published VA scores are accompanied by confidence intervals, and whether or not they are published as true residuals, they suggest a degree of precision in the measurement of school performance that is not justified. And, despite their complexity, the measures fail to respond adequately to competing legitimate demands: from the public for *interpretability*; from teachers for *usefulness*; and from policy-makers for *accountability*. It might be

10 The measures *could* be used to reveal differential effectiveness – by presenting each variable against the national mean performance for that category – but that would result in even greater complexity when presenting the data to a public audience. When school VA scores are published, the model imposes a ceiling on them so that they are not greater than the theoretical maximum. In response to this, Schagen (2006) has suggested standardising residuals at each prior attainment point and stretching small differences in the scale for 'extreme' pupils so that they have more chance of affecting the outcome. This is a similar approach to the one used by FFT to deal with non-linearity and ceiling effects; namely, to calculate a predicted KS4 outcome from KS2 input and then feed this back into the model as an input. Interestingly, Schagen, who is certainly no stranger to MLM, chooses to use OLS to calculate the predicted GCSE scores in the 2006 paper referenced here.

11 This practice has led to calls for the inclusion of confidence intervals in performance tables (Goldstein 2007) in the hope that their publication (as a marker of statistical significance) would be taken up by the media in their league tables, but this did not happen (cf. Chapter 3).

better if the potential of value-added measures to contribute to the data used by teachers to inform practice and improvement were not tied up so tightly with the competing demands of accountability.

In the document *21st Century Schools: a world-class education for every child*, the Secretary of State announced his intention to develop a new approach to holding schools to account: the School Report Card.

> The new School Report Card will provide stronger accountability to parents and local communities and provide the common tool for all aspects of school improvement and intervention. It will make sure that schools are held appropriately to account for their contribution to the full range of outcomes, including narrowing gaps in performance between the most and least advantaged.
>
> (DCSF 2008b: 8)

This comment suggests that the Report Card (together with the measures it summarises) will, like CVA, sit squarely on the fault-line between improvement and accountability, a prospect further emphasised by linking it to inspection: 'The School Report Card will complement Ofsted inspection reports by providing a more up-to-date assessment of performance and forming the core of the automated element of the risk assessment used by Ofsted to select schools for inspection' (DCSF 2008b: 38).

The Report Card proposal went out to consultation[12] in 2009, and the suggestion was that it would contain *a mix of measures* of school performance including:

- student progress;
- student attainment;
- wider outcomes, such as school ethos and well-being indicators;
- metrics to show how the school is 'narrowing gaps' for disadvantaged students;
- the views of students and parents.

A core issue in the consultation was whether or not all the measures included on the Report Card should be *summed* to an overall score or rating for the school. The consultation document commented:

> We are strongly attracted to including an overall score for each school on the Report Card, calculated from its scores for each of the categories

---

12 Mainly teachers and school leaders, but also governors, Local Authority education staff, representatives from voluntary community sector organisations, representatives of teacher unions, and parents and carers (DCSF 2009b).

of performance. If the School Report Card is to be clear, powerful, easily understood and easily used then we believe that it needs to bring together the different measures that it includes in this way. A single overall score would be important in simplifying and streamlining the system, by providing a single balanced measure taking account of the whole range of school responsibilities. In this way it would help ensure that the focus of public attention and accountability is on how the school is performing in the round, rather than on any single measure such as Key Stage test or GCSE results.

(DCSF 2008c: 9)

However, the consultation left respondents in the dark as to the ways in which these 'different measures' would be brought together to form the 'single overall score', though it did undertake to engage in further detailed consultation to determine the relative weighting of each performance measure and whether low performance in certain measures ('minimum standards') would place limits on the overall score attainable by a school.

The result of the consultation revealed a lack of support for the idea of an overall score (DCSF 2009b).[13] Concerns were expressed that such summary measures were too simplistic, would lead to yet more league tables, would cause unnecessary duplication of existing accountability mechanisms, would lead to a dumbing-down of the process of school choice, and would not foster partnerships between schools, which was their key purpose. Despite acknowledging that producing an overall score was 'the most controversial aspect of the consultation', the Report Cards, which will be introduced in 2011/12, are almost certain to include one. The key driver appears to be the leverage the Report Card will bring to steer the school improvement agenda in a specific direction:

We continue to believe that the inclusion of an overall – or summary – score is of great importance if the School Report Card is to deliver the improvements that we want. The inclusion of – and process of arriving at – an overall score is an important step in ensuring that there is clarity and transparency over priorities across the different performance categories for schools.

(DCSF 2009c: 7)

Whether the weighting system for the 'overall or summary' score becomes the point of leverage, reflecting the particular standards-versus-progress agenda of the day, remains to be seen.

---

13 Fifty-seven per cent of respondents were *not* in favour of either an overall score *or* a summative rating for the school. Sixty-six per cent of respondents expressed the opinion that the Report Card should include separate reporting of contextual factors for the school and 59 per cent of respondents felt that all measures on the card should be adjusted for context. A further 22 per cent believed that at least some of the measures should be contextualised.

Appendix 1
ACORN deprivation classification system

This table shows all ACORN classification categories, groups and types.

Category	Group	Type
Wealthy Achievers	Wealthy Executives	01 – Affluent mature professionals, large houses
		02 – Affluent working families with mortgages
		03 – Villages with wealthy commuters
		04 – Well-off managers, larger houses
	Affluent Greys	05 – Older affluent professionals
		06 – Farming communities
		07 – Old people, detached houses
		08 – Mature couples, smaller detached houses
	Flourishing Families	09 – Larger families, prosperous suburbs
		10 – Well-off working families with mortgages
		11 – Well-off managers, detached houses
		12 – Large families and houses in rural areas
Urban Prosperity	Prosperous Professionals	13 – Well-off professionals, larger houses and converted flats
		14 – Older professionals in detached houses and apartments
	Educated Urbanites	15 – Affluent urban professionals, flats
		16 – Prosperous young professionals, flats
		17 – Young educated workers, flats
		18 – Multi-ethnic young, converted flats
		19 – Suburban privately renting professionals

(*continued on next page*)

(continued)

Category	Group	Type
Urban Prosperity *(continued)*	Aspiring Singles	20 – Student flats and cosmopolitan sharers
		21 – Singles and sharers, multi-ethnic areas
		22 – Low income singles, small rented flats
		23 – Student terraces
Comfortably Off	Starting Out	24 – Young couples, flats and terraces
		25 – White collar singles/sharers, terraces
	Secure Families	26 – Younger white-collar couples with mortgages
		27 – Middle income, home-owning areas
		28 – Working families with mortgages
		29 – Mature families in suburban semis
		30 – Established home-owning workers
		31 – Home-owning Asian family areas
	Settled Suburbia	32 – Retired home owners
		33 – Middle income, older couples
		34 – Lower income people, semis
	Prudent Pensioners	35 – Elderly singles, purpose-built flats
		36 – Older people, flats
Moderate Means	Asian Communities	37 – Crowded Asian terraces
		38 – Low income Asian families
	Post Industrial Families	39 – Skilled older family terraces
		40 – Young family workers
	Blue Collar Roots	41 – Skilled workers, semis and terraces
		42 – Home-owning, terraces
		43 – Older rented terraces
Hard Pressed	Struggling Families	44 – Low income larger families, semis
		45 – Older people, low income, small semis
		46 – Low income, routine jobs, unemployment
		47 – Low rise terraced estates of poorly off workers
		48 – Low incomes, high unemployment, single parents

Category	Group	Type
Hard Pressed (*continued*)		49 – Large families, many children, poorly educated
	Burdened Singles	50 – Council flats, single elderly people
		51 – Council terraces, unemployment, many singles
		52 – Council flats, single parents, unemployment
	High Rise Hardship	53 – Old people in high rise flats
		54 – Singles and single parents, high rise estates
	Inner City Adversity	55 – Multi-ethnic, purpose-built estates
		56 – Multi-ethnic, crowded flats

Appendix 2

Full list of variables included in the FFT SX model, with coefficients and effect sizes

Variable	Coefficient in SX model	Effect size of variable	Variable Type (S/P)
KS4 mean score	1.04	1.43	P
SEN: School Action Plus	−67.15	0.63	P
Joined late	−60.18	0.57	P
School GDF (ACORN) rank	−0.94	0.43	S
Interaction: KS4 mean and KS2 TA differential	0.04	0.41	P
SEN: Statement	−36.13	0.34	P
SEN: School Action	−34.66	0.33	P
Gypsy/Roma	−32.51	0.31	P
FSM	−29.64	0.28	P
Bangladeshi	28.60	0.27	P
Irish heritage Traveller	−25.39	0.24	P
Black African	24.97	0.23	P
Interaction: KS4 mean and school FSM rank	0.00	0.23	
Same intake and output school	24.74	0.23	P
Chinese	23.68	0.22	P
Interaction: KS4 mean and school KS2 mean	−0.03	0.22	
EAL	23.20	0.22	P
Interaction: KS4 mean and school GDF rank	0.00	0.20	
Ethnic background not obtained	−21.01	0.20	P

Variable	Coefficient in SX model	Effect size of variable	Variable Type (S/P)
Pakistani	18.98	0.18	P
Indian	16.95	0.16	P
Gender	16.76	0.16	P
School FSM rank	0.35	0.15	S
Any other Asian	16.26	0.15	P
Any other ethnic group	14.11	0.13	P
KS2 English differential	23.34	0.13	P
Any other white	13.60	0.13	P
Ethnic background refused	−12.67	0.12	P
Months at school	0.54	0.11	P
Black Caribbean	11.07	0.10	P
Interaction: School KS2 mean and GDF rank	0.04	0.08	S
KS2 TA differential	14.23	0.08	P
Interaction: Ethnicity and school FSM rank	−0.16	0.07	
Any other black	−6.72	0.06	P
KS2 Mathematics differential	9.84	0.05	P
Mixed white/Asian	5.54	0.05	P
KS2 science differential	9.25	0.05	P
Mixed white/any other	−4.81	0.05	P
School KS2 mean	9.06	0.04	S
School KS2 SD	−24.10	0.04	S
Interaction: KS2 English and KS2 maths differentials	−15.74	0.03	P
Interaction: KS2 English and KS2 science differentials	−13.56	0.03	P
Mixed white/black African	−3.32	0.03	P
Interaction: KS2 maths and KS2 science differentials	−15.25	0.03	P
Mixed white/black Caribbean	−2.20	0.02	P

(*continued on next page*)

(*continued*)

Variable	Coefficient in SX model	Effect size of variable	Variable Type (S/P)
Interaction: School KS2 mean and FSM rank	0.01	0.02	S
Interaction: Months in school and joined late	0.99	0.02	P
Interaction: School FSM and GDF ranks	0.00	0.02	S
Age (months)	1.26	0.01	P
Irish	0.88	0.01	P

Source: Thomson and Knight (2006).

Bibliography

ASCL (2009) *ASCL Technical Annex Oct 09 for early release based on published* (9 *October*) *coefficients*, Association of School and College Leaders. Online. Available www. ascl.org.uk/mainwebsite/Resources/Document/ASCL%20Technical%20Annex %20Oct%2009%20early%20release%20-%20ver3.pdf (accessed 16 February 2010).

BBC News (2008) 'Delays hit pupils' test results'. Online. Available http://news.bbc. co.uk/1/hi/education/7489510.stm (accessed 15 February 2009).

Bernhardt, V. L. (1998) *Data Analysis for Comprehensive School-wide Improvement*, Lauchment, NY: Eye on Education.

Brandsma, H. and Knuver, J. (1989) 'Effects of school classroom characteristics on pupil progress in language and arithmetic', *International Journal of Educational Research*, 13(7): 777–88.

Brookover, W., Beady, C., Flood, P. and Schweitzer, J. (1979) *School Systems and Student Achievement*, New York: Praeger.

Brown, T. A. (2006) *Confirmatory Factor Analysis for Applied Research*, New York: The Guildford Press.

Burgess, S., McConnell, B., Propper, C. and Wilson, D. (2004) 'Girls rock, boys roll: an analysis of the age 14–16 gender gap in English schools', *Scottish Journal of Political Economy*, 51(2): 209–29.

Bush, A., Edwards, L., Hopwood Road, F. and Lewis, M. (2005) *Why Here? Report of Qualitative Work with Teachers Working in Schools Above and Below the Floor Targets: DfES Research Report RR666*, Nottingham: DfES Publications.

Castle, S. D. (1988) 'Teacher empowerment through knowledge linking research and practice for school reform', paper presented at the Annual Meeting of the American Educational Research Association, New Orleans, April 1988.

Coleman, J., Campbell, E., Hobson, C., McPartland, J., Mood, A., Weinfeld, F. and York, R. (1966) *Equality of Educational Opportunity*, Washington DC: National Center for Educational Statistics/US Government Printing Office.

Cousins, J. B., Goh, S. and Clark, S. (2006) 'Data use leads to data valuing: evaluative inquiry for school decision making', *Leadership and Policy in Schools*, 5: 155–176.

Creemers, B. and Reezigt, G. (1997) 'School effectiveness and school improvement: sustaining links', *School Effectiveness and School Improvement*, 8(4): 396–429.

Critchlow, J. and Coe, R. (2003) 'Serious flaws arising from the use of the median in calculating value added measures for School Performance Tables in England', paper presented to the 29th International Association for Educational Assessment (IAEA) Annual Conference, Manchester, October 2003.

Davies, J. and Brember, I. (1997) 'The effects of pre-school experience on reading attainment: a four year cross-sectional study', *Educational Psychology*, 17(3): 255–65.

Day, C., Sammons, P., Hopkins, D., Harris, A., Leithwood, K., Gui, Q., Penlington, C., Mehta, P. and Kington, A. (2008) *The Impact of School Leadership on Pupil Outcomes: DCSF Research Report RR018*, Nottingham: DfES Publications.

DCSF (2007a) *Intensifying Support Programme (ISP) and Social and Emotional Aspects of Learning (SEAL) Birchwood Junior School – April 2006*. Online. Available http://nationalstrategies.standards.dcsf.gov.uk/node/88432?uc=force_uj (accessed August 2009).

—— (2007b) *Case Study Raising Attainment Plans*. Online. Available http://national strategies.standards.dcsf.gov.uk/downloader/cd825bfbe0a219980ccf3a845a0216 24.pdf (accessed May 2009).

—— (2008a) *Targeted Mental Health in Schools Project – using the evidence to inform your approach: a practical guide for head teachers and commissioners*. Nottingham: Department for Children, Schools and Families.

—— (2008b) *21st Century Schools: a world-class education for every child*, Nottingham, Department for Children, Schools and Families.

—— (2008c) *A School Report Card: consultation document*. Online. Available www.dcsf. gov.uk/consultations/downloadableDocs/A%20School%20Report%20Card%20 consultation%20document%201.doc (accessed 5 June 2009).

—— (2009a) *Permanent and Fixed Period Exclusions from Schools in England 2007/08*. Online. Available http://www.dcsf.gov.uk/rsgateway/DB/SFR/s000860/SFR18_2009_ Nationaltables_FINAL.xls (accessed 27 August 2009).

—— (2009b) *A School Report Card: consultation document analysis of responses to the consultation documents*. Online. Available www.dcsf.gov.uk/consultations/downloadable Docs/21C%20Schools%20Report%20Card%20Consultation%20Report.doc (accessed 15 March 2010).

—— (2009c) *A School Report Card: prospectus*, Nottingham, Department for Children, Schools and Families.

Demie, F. (2003) 'Using value-added data for school self-evaluation: a case study of practice in inner-city schools', *School Leadership and Management*, 23(4): 445–67.

DfEE (1997) *Excellence in Schools*, London, DfEE.

—— (1998a) *1998 Value Added Pilot: supplement to the secondary school performance tables*, London: Department for Education and Employment.

—— (1998b) *The Autumn Package*, London: Department for Education and Employment.

DfES (2004) *Pupil Achievement Tracker Quick Tour*. Online. Available http://www. standards.dfes.gov.uk/performance/word/QuickStart.doc?version=1 (accessed 16 December 2006).

—— (2005) *Primary National Strategy Excellence and Enjoyment: social and emotional aspects of learning guidance*, London, Department for Education and Skills.

—— (2006a) *Achievement and Attainment Tables: LA Conference 2006*. Online. Available. www.standards.dfes.gov.uk/performance/powerpoint/presentationLAv03. ppt?version=1 (accessed 3 December 2006).

—— (2006b) *Guidance For Local Authorities On Target Setting, Part 1: LA Targets for Key Stages 2, 3, 4, Looked after Children, Minority Ethnic Groups, Attendance, Early Years' Outcomes*. Online. Available www.standards.dfes.gov.uk/ts/docs/guide1.doc (accessed 20 March 2008).

—— (2006c) *National Curriculum Assessments at Key Stage 2, and Key Stage 1 to Key Stage 2 Value Added Measures for England 2004/2005 (Final), DfES Statistical First Release.* Online. Available www.dfes.gov.uk/rsgateway/DB/SFR/s000660/Addition2. xls (accessed 20 March 2009).

—— (2006d) *Secondary Schools (GCSE and equivalent) Achievement and Attainment Tables 2006.* Online. Available www.dfes.gov.uk/performancetables/schools_06/s8.shtml (accessed 13 April 2009).

—— (2006e) *Primary National Strategy Excellence and Enjoyment: social and emotional aspects of learning Family SEAL,* London: Department for Education and Skills.

—— (2006f) *Families of Schools: May 2006 secondary schools,* London, Department for Education and Skills.

—— (2007a) *Intensifying Support Programme (ISP) and Social and Emotional Aspects of Learning (SEAL) Birchwood Junior School – April 2006.* Online. Available http://national strategies.standards.dcsf.gov.uk/downloader/32af83a099ffbd2ee58d47cfdf9e7744. pdf (accessed 26 August 2009).

—— (2007b) *Secondary National Strategy Social and Emotional Aspects of Learning,* London: Department for Education and Skills.

Downes, D. and Vindurampulle, O. (2007) *Value-added Measures for School Improvement,* Melbourne: Department of Education and Early Childhood Development.

Downey, C. and Kelly, A. (2007a) 'Are value-added scores getting the measure of school performance in the UK?', paper presented at the International Congress for School Effectiveness and Improvement (ICSEI), Potorož, Slovenia, January 2007.

—— (2007b) 'Using FFT data in the context of Every Child Matters', paper presented at Fischer Family Trust Regional Meeting, London, 28 June 2007.

—— (2008) 'Utilising value-added progress data in the context of Every Child Matters', paper presented at the 21st International Congress for School Effectiveness and Improvement (ICSEI), Auckland, New Zealand, 7 January 2008.

—— (2010) 'Investigating patterns of non-participation in post-compulsory education: a study of learner disengagement at ages 16–18 in one English Local Authority', paper presented at the 23rd International Congress for School Effectiveness and Improvement (ICSEI), Kuala Lumpur, Malaysia, 7 January 2010.

Downey, C., Kelly, A. and Brown A. (2008) 'Evaluating a programme to develop social and emotional skills in primary school students', paper presented at the 21st International Congress for School Effectiveness and Improvement (ICSEI), Auckland, New Zealand, 7 January 2008.

Downey, C. and Williams, C. (2010) 'Family SEAL: a home-school collaborative programme focusing on the development of children's social and emotional skills', *Advances in School Mental Health Promotion,* 3(1): 30–41.

Doyle, L. and Godfrey, R. (2005) 'Investigating the reliability of the Key Stage 2 test results for assessing individual pupil achievement and progress in England', *London Review of Education,* 3(1): 29–45.

Dudley, P. (1997) 'How teachers respond to pupil data', paper presented at the British Educational Research Association Annual Conference, University of York, September 1997.

—— (1999a) 'Using data to drive up standards: statistics or psychology?', in C. Conner (ed.) *Assessment in Action in the Primary School,* London: Falmer. pp. 111–23.

—— (1999b) 'Primary schools and pupil data', in G. Southworth and P. Lincoln (eds) *Supporting Improving Primary Schools: the role of Heads and LEAs in raising standards,* London: Falmer. pp. 87–106.

Earl, L., and Fullan, M. (2003) 'Using data in leadership for learning', *Cambridge Journal of Education*, 33(3): 383–94.

Edmonds, R. (1979) 'Effective schools for the urban poor', *Educational Leadership*, 37(1): 15–24.

Edmunds, L. and Stewart-Brown, S. (2003) *Assessing Emotional and Social Competence in Primary School and Early Years Settings: a review of approaches, issues and instruments (Sure Start Evidence and Research Series)*, Annesley, Nottinghamshire: DfES Sure Start.

Evans, H. (2005) 'CVA Model and Factors', paper presented at Contextual Value Added – Secondary Schools Conference, London.

Faupel, A. (2003) *Emotional Literacy: assessment and intervention, ages 7–11*, London: NFER Nelson.

FFT (Fischer Family Trust) (2004) *FFT Data Analysis Project – Value Added Development – 0304, presentation given at FFT 2004 Regional Meetings*. Online. Available – downloaded from FFT secure server (accessed 15 March 2009).

—— (2005a) *Using ACORN data in Value-Added Analyses, guidance paper*. Online. Available – downloaded from FFT secure server (accessed 15 March 2009).

—— (2005b) *FFT Technical Information Brief: KS2–KS4 contextualised value added measures, guidance paper*, Fischer Family Trust. Online. Available – downloaded from FFT secure server (accessed 15 March 2008).

—— (2005c) *Fischer Family Trust: supplement to the PANDA (KS2)*. Online. Available http://www.fischertrust.org/downloads/dap/example_analyses/England/Self_Evaluation/Guidance_KS2.pdf (accessed 13 April 2007).

—— (2005d) *Fischer Family Trust: Supplement to the PANDA (KS34)*. Online. Available http://www.fischertrust.org/downloads/dap/example_analyses/England/Self_Evaluation/Guidance_KS34.pdf (accessed 13 April 2007).

—— (2005e) *VA Methodology, Presentation Given at FFT 2005 Regional Meetings*. Online. Available – downloaded from FFT secure server (accessed 25 March 2009).

—— (2006a) *Summary: trends in estimates (England) Key Stage 2, Key Stage 3, Key Stage 4, guidance document*. Online. Available – downloaded from FFT secure server (accessed 18 March 2009).

—— (2006b) 'DfES Guidance and FFT Estimates, guidance document', obtained via personal communication on 22 March 2007.

—— (2007a) Online. Available www.fischertrust.org/performance.htm (accessed 16 March 2007).

—— (2007b) *Analyses to Support Self-Evaluation (Example – KS2)*. Online. Available www.fischertrust.org/downloads/dap/example_analyses/england/self_evaluation/Example_Junior_FFT_EvalBook_KS2.pdf (accessed 13 April 2007).

—— (2007c) *Analyses to Support Self-Evaluation (Example – KS34)*. Online. Available www.fischertrust.org/downloads/dap/example_analyses/england/self_evaluation/Example_Secondary_FFT_EvalBook_KS34.pdf (accessed 13 April 2007).

Fielding, A. and Goldstein, H. (2006) *Cross-classified and Multiple Membership Structures in Multilevel Models: an introduction and review*, Nottingham: DfES.

Fitz-Gibbon, C. T. (1990) *Performance Indicators*, Clevedon, UK: Multilingual Matters Ltd.

—— (1991) 'Multilevel modelling in an indicator system', in S. W. Raudenbush and J. D. Willms (eds) *School, Classrooms and Pupils: international studies of schooling from a multilevel perspective*, San Diego CA: Academic Press. pp. 67–84.

—— (1997) *The Value Added National Project Final Report: feasibility studies for a national system of value-added indicators*, London: School Curriculum and Assessment Authority.

Goldstein, H. (1997a) *Value Added Data for Schools: a commentary on a paper from SCAA*. Online. Available www.cmm.bris.ac.uk/team/HG_Personal/scaavadd.html (accessed 27 August 2007).

—— (1997b) 'Methods in school effectiveness research', *School Effectiveness and School Improvement*, 8(4): 369–95.

—— (2001) 'Using pupil performance data for judging schools and teachers: scope and limitations', *British Educational Research Journal*, 27(4): 433–42.

—— (2007) *Evidence and Education Policy: some reflections and allegations, paper presented to the RSS conference in York, July 2007*. Online. Available www.cmm.bristol.ac.uk/team/HG_Personal/Evidence%20and%20education%20policy.pdf (accessed August 2009).

—— (2008) 'Evidence and Education Policy: some reflections and allegations', *Cambridge Journal of Education*, 38(3): 393–400.

Goldstein, H. and Cuttance, P. (1988) 'A note on national assessment and school comparisons', *Journal of Education Policy*, 3: 197–202.

Goldstein, H., Huiqi, P., Rath, T. and Hill, N. (2000) *The Use of Value Added Information in Judging School Performance*, London: Institute of Education.

Goldstein, H. and Leckie, G. (2008) 'School league tables: what can they really tell us?' *Significance*, 5(2): 67–9.

Goldstein, H. and Sammons, P. (1997) 'The influence of secondary and junior schools on sixteen year examination performance: a cross-classified multilevel analysis', *School Effectiveness and School Improvement*, 8(2): 219–30.

Goldstein, H. and Spiegelhalter, D. J. (1996) 'League tables and their limitations: statistical issues in comparisons of institutional performance', *Journal of the Royal Statistical Society, Series A*, 159: 385–443.

Goldstein, H. and Thomas, S. (1995) 'School effectiveness and "value-added" analysis', *Forum*, 37(2): 36–8.

Goleman, D. (1996) *Emotional Intelligence: why it can matter more than IQ*, London: Bloomsbury Publishing.

Gorard, S. (2006) 'Value-added is of little value', *Journal of Education Policy*, 21(2): 235–43.

—— (2007) 'The dubious benefits of multi-level modelling', *International Journal of Research and Method in Education*, 30(2): 221–36.

Gray, J. (1996) 'Comments on value-added approaches', *Research Papers in Education*, 11(1): 3–4.

Gray, J., Goldstein, H. and Jesson, D. (1996) 'Changes and improvements in schools' effectiveness: trends over time', *Research Papers in Education*, 11(1): 35–51.

Gray, J., Goldstein, H. and Thomas, S. (2001) 'Predicting the future: the role of past performance in determining trends in institutional effectiveness at A-level, *British Educational Research Journal*, 27(4): 1–15.

Gray, J., Hopkins, D., Reynolds, D., Wilcox, B., Farrell, S. and Jesson, D. (1999) *Improving Schools: performance and potential*, Buckingham: Open University Press.

Gray, J., Jesson, D. and Jones, B. (1986) 'The search for a fairer way of comparing schools' examination results', *Research Papers in Education*, 1(2): 91–122.

Gray, J., Jesson, D. and Sime, N. (1990) 'Estimating differences in the examination performances of secondary schools in six LEAs: a multi-level approach to school effectiveness', *Oxford Review of Education*, 16(2): 137–58.

Hallam, S., Rhamie, J. and Shaw, J. (2006) *Evaluation of the Primary Behaviour and Attendance Pilot*, London: Department for Education and Skills.

Halsey, K., Judkins, M., Atkinson, M. and Rudd, P. (2005): *New Relationship with Schools: evaluation of trial local authorities and schools*, Nottingham: DfES Publications.

Harris, A., Jamieson, I. and Russ, J. (1997) 'A study of effective departments in secondary schools', in A. Harris, N. Bennett, and M. Preedy (eds) *Organizational Effectiveness and Improvement in Education*, Buckingham: Open University Press. pp. 147–61.

Hastings, C. (1993) *The New Organisation*, London: McGraw-Hill.

Haug, J. (1997) 'Physicians' preferences for information sources: a meta-analytic study', *Bulletin of the Medical Library Association*, 85(3): 223–32.

Hemsley-Brown, J. and Sharp, C. (2003) 'The use of research to improve professional practice: a systematic review of the literature', *Oxford Review of Education*, 29(4): 449–70.

Hill, P. and Goldstein, H. (1998) 'Multilevel modelling of educational data with cross classification and missing identification of units', *Journal of Educational and Behavioural Statistics*, 23, 117–28.

Hopkins, D. and Lagerweij, N. (1996) 'The school improvement knowledge base', in D. Reynolds, R. Bollen, B. Creemers, D. Hopkins, L. Stoll and N. Lagerweij (eds) *Making Good Schools: linking school effectiveness and school improvement*, London: Routledge. pp. 61–94.

Humphrey, N. (2008) '*Key issues in the evaluation of school-based SEL programmes*', paper presented at ESRC seminar series '*The school as a location for the promotion and support of mental health*', Southampton, June 2008. Online. Available http://www.abdn.ac.uk/rowangroup/documents/Neil%20Humphrey.ppt (accessed 27 October 2008).

Humphrey, N., Kalambouka, A., Bolton, J., Lendrum, A., Wigelsworth, M., Lennie, C. and Farrell, P. (2008) *Primary Social and Emotional Aspects of Learning (SEAL): evaluation of small group work*, London: DCSF/University of Manchester.

Hutchison, D. and Schagen, I. (2008) 'Concorde and discord: the art of multilevel modelling', *International Journal of Research and Method in Education*, 31(1): 11–18.

Jakubowski, M. (2008) *Implementing Value-Added Models of School Assessment*, Florence: European University Institute.

James, M. (2006) 'Test focus "hits learning skills"', BBC, 9 August. Online. Available http://news.bbc.co.uk/1/hi/education/4777737.stm (accessed 13 September 2008).

Jaques, E. (1956) *Measurement of Responsibility: a study of work, payment and individual capacity*, London: Tavistock.

Jencks, C., Smith, M., Acland, H., Bane, M. J., Cohen, D., Gintis, H., Heyns, B. and Michelson, S. (1972) *Inequality: a reassessment of the effects of family and schooling in America*, New York: Basic Books.

Jesson, D. (1996) *Value Added Measures of School GCSE Performance: an investigation into the role of Key Stage 3 assessments in schools. Interim Report, DfEE Research Studies 14*, London: HMSO.

Jesson, D. and Gray, J. (1991) 'Slants on slopes: using multi-level models to investigate differential school effectiveness and its impact on pupils' examination results', *School Effectiveness and School Improvement*, 2(3): 230–47.

Kanter, R. M. (1983) *The Change Masters: innovation for productivity in the American corporation*, New York: Simon & Schuster.

Kelly, A. (2001) *Benchmarking for School Improvement*, London: Routledge Falmer.

—— (2004) *The Intellectual Capital of Schools: measuring and managing knowledge, responsibility and reward*, Dordrecht: Kluwer Academic Press.

—— (2008) 'School Effectiveness', in G. McCulloch and D. Crook (eds) *International Encyclopaedia of Education*, London: Routledge. pp. 517–18.

Kelly, A., Downey, C. and Rietdijk, W. (2010) *Data Dictatorship and Data Democracy: understanding professional attitudes to the use of pupil performance data in schools*, Reading: CfBT.

Kirkup, C., Sizmur, J., Sturman, L. and Lewis, K. (2005) *Schools' Use of Data in Teaching and Learning: DfES Research Report RR671*, Nottingham: DfES.

Knapp, M. S., Swinnerton, J. A., Copland, M. A. and Monpas-Huber, J. (2006) *Data-informed Leadership in Education*, Seattle, WA: University of Washington Center for the Study of Teaching and Policy.

Kreft, I. G. (1996) 'Are multilevel techniques necessary? An overview including simulation studies', cited in C. T. Fitz-Gibbon (1997) *The Value Added National Project Final Report: feasibility studies for a national system of value-added indicators*, London: School Curriculum and Assessment Authority. Annex C.

Kyriakides, L. (2004) 'Differential school effectiveness in relation to sex and social class: some implications for policy evaluation', *Educational Research and Evaluation*, 10(2): 141–61.

Kyriakides, L. and Creemers, B. (2008) 'A longitudinal study on the stability over time of school and teacher effects on student outcomes', *Oxford Review of Education*, 34(5): 521–45.

Leckie, G. and Goldstein, H. (2009) 'The limitations of using school league tables to inform school choice', *Journal of the Royal Statistical Society: Series A*, 172(4): 835–51.

Luyten, H. (2003) 'The size of school effects compared to teacher effects: an overview of the research literature', *School Effectiveness and School Improvement*, 14(1): 31–5.

Maas, C. J. and Hox, J. J. (2005) 'Sufficient sample sizes for multilevel modeling', *Methodology: European Journal of Research Methods for the Behavioral and Social Sciences*, 1(3): 86–92.

McIntyre, D. (2005) 'Bridging the gap between research and practice', *Cambridge Journal of Education*, 35(3): 357–82.

McPherson, A. (1992) *Measuring Added Value in Schools, National Commission on Education, Briefing No. 1* (February), London: NCE. [Also published as: McPherson, A. (1993) 'Measuring added value in schools', *Education Economics*, 1(1): 43–51].

Mangan, J., Pugh, G. and Gray, J. (2005) 'Changes in examination performance in English secondary schools over the course of a decade: searching for patterns and trends over time', *School Effectiveness and School Improvement*, 16(1): 29–50.

Massey, A., Green, S., Dexter, T. and Hammet, L. (2003) *Comparability of National Tests Over Time: KS1, KS2 and KS3 standards between 1996 and 2001. Final Report to the QCA of the Comparability Over Time Project*, London: QCA.

Maw, J. (1999) 'League tables and the press – value added?' *The Curriculum Journal*, 10(1): 3–10.

Miliband, D. (2004) 'Personalised learning: building a new relationship with schools', paper presented by Minister of State for School Standards, North of England Education Conference, Belfast, 8 January 2004.

Moody, I. (2001) 'A case-study of the predictive validity and reliability of Key Stage 2 test results, and teacher assessments, as baseline data for target-setting and value-added at Key Stage 3', *The Curriculum Journal*, 12(1): 81–101.

Morrison, H. G. and Wylie, E. C. (1999) 'Why National Curriculum testing is founded on a methodological thought disorder', *Evaluation and Research in Education*, 13(2): 92–105.

Mortimore, P. (1998) *The Road to School Improvement*, Lisse, The Netherlands: Swets and Zeitlinger.

Mortimore, P., Sammons, P. and Thomas, S. (1994) 'School effectiveness and value added measures', *Assessment in Education*, 1(3): 315–32.

Mortimore, P., Sammons, P., Stoll, L., Lewis, D. and Ecob, R. (1988) *School Matters: the junior years*, (reprint), London: Paul Chapman.

Myers, K. and Goldstein, H. (2004) 'Opinion: adding value?', *Education Journal*, 75: 15.

National Statistics (2006) *Beginners Guide to UK Geography: Super Output Areas (SOAs)*. Online. Available www.statistics.gov.uk/geography/soa.asp#3layers (accessed 16 March 2008).

NICE (2007) *Mental Well-being of Children, Public Health Intervention Guidance*. Online. Available www.nice.org.uk/nicemedia/pdf/MentalWellbeingFieldworkReport.pdf (accessed 18 August 2009).

—— (2008) *Promoting Children's Social and Emotional Well-Being in Primary Education: NICE public health guidance 12*, London: National Institute for Health and Clinical Excellence.

Noortgate, W. V. d., Opdenakker, M.-C. and Onghena, P. (2005) 'The effects of ignoring a level in multilevel analysis', *School Effectiveness and School Improvement*, 16(3): 281–303.

Nuttall, D. (1991) 'An instrument to be honed: tables do not reflect schools' true performance', *Times Educational Supplement*, 13 September, p. 22.

Nuttall, D., Goldstein, H., Prosser, R. and Rasbash, J. (1989) 'Differential school effectiveness', *International Journal of Educational Research*, 13(7): 769–76.

OECD (1992). *Education at a Glance*, Paris: Organisation for Economic Co-operation and Development.

Ofsted (2005) *Healthy Minds: promoting emotional health and well-being in schools*, London: Office for Standards in Education.

—— (2008) *Lincoln Birchwood Junior School: Inspection report*. Online. Available www.ofsted.gov.uk/reports/pdf/?inspectionNumber=313643&providerCategoryID=409 6&fileName=\\school\\120\\s5_120508_20080305.pdf (accessed April 2008).

—— (2009) *Day Six of Exclusion: the extent quality of provision for pupils*, London: Office for Standards in Education, Children's Services and Skills.

Opdenakker, M.-C. and Van Damme, J. (2000) 'The importance of identifying levels in multilevel analysis: an illustration of the effects of ignoring the top or intermediate levels in school effectiveness research', *School Effectiveness and School Improvement*, 11(1): 103–30.

Ozga, J. (2009) 'Governing education through data in England: from regulation to self-evaluation', *Journal of Education Policy*, 24(2): 149–62.

Palardy, G. (2008) 'Differential school effects among low, middle, and high social class composition schools: a multiple group, multilevel latent growth curve analysis', *School Effectiveness and School Improvement*, 19(1): 21–49.

Prais, S. J. (2001) 'Grammar schools' achievements and the DfEE's measures of value-added: an attempt at clarification', *Oxford Review of Education*, 27(1): 69–73.

Pugh, G. and Mangan, J. (2003) 'What's in a trend? A comment on Gray, Goldstein and Thomas (2001), "Predicting the Future: the role of past performance in determining trends in institutional effectiveness at A level"', *British Educational Research Journal*, 29(1): 77–82.

QCA (1997) *The National Framework for Baseline Assessment*, London: QCA.

—— (2001) *Supporting School Improvement: emotional and behavioural development*. London: Qualifications and Curriculum Authority.

Rasbash, J., Charlton, C., Browne, W. J., Healy, M. and Cameron, B. (2009) *MLwiN Version 2.1*. Bristol: Centre for Multilevel Modelling, University of Bristol.

Ray, A. (2006) *School Value Added Measures in England: a paper for the OECD Project on the Development of Value-Added Models in Education Systems*, London: Department for Education and Skills.

Ray, A., McCormack, T. and Evans, H. (2009) 'Value added in English schools', *Education, Finance and Policy*, 4(4): 415–38.

Raykov, T. (2001) 'Estimation of congeneric scale reliability using covariance structure analysis with nonlinear constraints', *British Journal of Mathematical and Statistical Psychology*, 54: 315–23.

—— (2004) 'Behavioral scale reliability and measurement invariance evaluation using latent variable modelling', *Behavior Therapy*, 35: 299–331.

Robinson, V., Phillips, G. and Timperley, H. (2002) 'Using achievement data for school-based curriculum review: a bridge too far?' *Leadership and Policy in Schools*, 1(1): 3–29.

Rutter, M., Maughan, B., Mortimore, P. and Ouston, J. with Smith, A. (1979) *Fifteen Thousand Hours: secondary schools and their effects on children*, London: Open Books.

Sammons, P. (2007) *School Effectiveness and Equity: making connections*, Reading: CfBT.

Sammons, P. and Smees, R. (1998) 'Measuring Pupil Progress at Key Stage 1: using baseline assessment to investigate value added', *School Leadership and Management*, 18(3): 389–407.

Sammons, P., Nuttall, D. and Cuttance, P. (1993) 'Differential School Effectiveness: results from a reanalysis of the Inner London Education Authority's Junior School Project Data', *British Educational Research Journal*, 19(4): 381–405.

Sammons, P., Thomas, S. and Mortimore, P. with Walker, A., Hind, A., Smees, R., Bausor, J. and Cairns, R. (1997) *Forging Links: effective schools and effective departments*, London: Paul Chapman.

Sammons, P., West, A. and Hind, A. (1997) 'Accounting for variations in pupil attainment at the end of Key Stage One', *British Educational Research Journal*, 23(4): 489–512.

Saunders, L. (1999) 'A brief history of educational "value added": how did we get to where we are?' *School Effectiveness and School Improvement*, 10(2): 233–56.

—— (2000) 'Understanding schools' use of "value added" data: the psychology and sociology of numbers', *Research Papers in Education*, 15(3): 241–58.

Saunders, L. and Rudd, P. (1999) 'Schools' use of "value added" data: a science in the service of an art?', paper presented at the British Educational Research Association Conference, University of Sussex, Brighton, September 1999.

Saunders, L. and Thomas, S. (1998) 'Into an uncertain world', *Times Education Supplement*, 4280, 10 July, p. 26.

Sawhney, M. and Parikh, D. (2001) 'Where value lives in a networked world', *Harvard Business Review*, 79(1): 79–86.

SCAA (School Curriculum and Assessment Authority) (1994) *Value-added Performance Indicators for Schools*, London: SCAA.

—— (1997) *Making Effective Use of Key Stage 3 Assessments*, London: SCAA.

Schagen, I. (1991) 'Beyond league tables. How modern statistical methods can give a truer picture of the effects of schools', *Educational Research*, 33(3): 216–22.

—— (2006) 'The use of standardized residuals to derive value-added measures of school performance', *Educational Studies*, 32(2): 119–32.

Schagen, I. and Schagen, S. (2005) 'Combining multilevel analysis with national value-added datasets – a case study to explore the effects of school diversity', *British Educational Research Journal*, 31(3): 309–28.

Scheerens, J. and Bosker, R. (1997) *The Foundations of Educational Effectiveness*, Oxford: Pergamon.

Sharp, S. (2006) 'Assessing value-added in the first year of schooling: some results and methodological considerations', *School Effectiveness and School Improvement*, 17(3): 329–46.

Sharp, S. and Croxford, L. (2003) 'Literacy in the first year of schooling: a multilevel analysis', *School Effectiveness and School Improvement*, 14(2): 213–31.

Shen, J. and Cooley, V. (2008) 'Critical issues in using data for decision-making', *International Journal of Leadership in Education*, 11(3): 319–29.

Shkedi, A. (1998) 'Teachers' attitudes towards research: a challenge for qualitative researchers', *International Journal of Qualitative Studies in Education*, 11(4): 559–77.

Smith, D. and Tomlinson, S. (1989) *The School Effect: a study of multi-racial comprehensives*, London: Policy Studies Institute.

Sun, H., Creemers, B. and Jong, R. (2007) 'Contextual factors and effective school improvement', *School Effectiveness and School Improvement*, 18(1): 93–122.

TDA (Training and Development Agency for Schools) (2007a) *Professional Standards for Teachers – Qualified Teacher Status*, London: Training and Development Agency for Schools.

—— (2007b) *Professional Standards for Teachers – Core*, London: Training and Development Agency for Schools.

—— (2007c) *Professional Standards for Teachers – Post Threshold*, London: Training and Development Agency for Schools.

—— (2007d) *Professional Standards for Teachers – Excellent Teachers*, London: Training and Development Agency for Schools.

—— (2007e) *Professional Standards for Teachers – Advanced Skills Teachers*, London: Training and Development Agency for Schools.

Teddlie, C. and Reynolds, D. (2000) *The International Handbook of School Effectiveness Research*, London: Falmer.

Teddlie, C., Stringfield, S. and Reynolds, D. (2000) 'Context issues within school effectiveness research', in C. Teddlie and D. Reynolds (eds) *The International Handbook of School Effectiveness Research*, London, Falmer. pp. 160–86.

Thomas, S. (2001) 'Dimensions of secondary school effectiveness: comparative analyses across regions', *School Effectiveness and School Improvement*, 12(3): 285–322.

Thomas, S. and Goldstein, H. (1995) 'Questionable value', *Education*, 85(11): 17.

Thomas, S. and Mortimore, P. (1996) 'Comparison of value added models for secondary school effectiveness', *Research Papers in Education*, 11(1): 5–33.

Thomas, S., Peng, W. J. and Gray, J. (2007) 'Modelling patterns of improvement over time: value added trends in English secondary school performance across ten cohorts', *Oxford Review of Education*, 33(3): 261–95.

Thomas, S., Sammons, P. and Mortimore, P. (1997a) 'Stability and consistency in secondary schools' effects on students' GCSE outcomes over three years', *School Effectiveness and School Improvement*, 8: 169–97.

Thomas, S., Sammons, P., Mortimore, P. and Smees, R. (1997b) 'Differential secondary school effectiveness: comparing the performance of different pupil groups', *British Educational Research Journal*, 23(4): 451–69.

Thomson, D. (2007) *Using RAISEonline in self-evaluation. Understanding what the inspectors will see (secondary)*. Online. Available http://www.egfl.org.uk/export/sites/egfl/categories/data/danda/_docs/raise_online/raiseSec.pdf (accessed 30 August 2008).

Thomson, D. and Knight, T. (2006) *'Valued added models and methods: differences between KS2–KS4 CVA and FFT SX'*, presentation given at FFT 2006 Conference. Online. Available – downloaded from FFT secure server (accessed 15 March 2007).

Timperley, H. (2005) 'Instructional leadership challenges: the case of using student achievement information for instructional improvement', *Leadership and Policy in Schools*, 4: 3–22.

Treadaway, M. (2010) Personal communication, 18 February 2010.

Tymms, P. B. and Dean, C. (2004) *Value Added in the Primary School League Tables, A Report for the National Association of Head Teachers*, Durham: CEM Centre, University of Durham.

Tymms, P. B., Merrell, C. and Coe, R. J. (2008) 'Educational policies and randomized controlled trials', *The Psychology of Education Review*, 32(2): 3–7, 26–9.

Tymms, P. B., Merrell, C. and Henderson, B. (1997) 'The first year at school: a quantitative investigation of the attainment and progress of pupils', *Educational Research and Evaluation*, 3(2): 101–18.

Van Damme, J., De Fraine, B., Van Landeghem, G., Opdenakker, M.-C. and Onghena, P. (2002) 'A new study on educational effectiveness in secondary schools in Flanders: an introduction', *School Effectiveness and School Improvement*, 13(4): 383–97.

Van Landeghem, G., Van Damme, J. Opdenakker, M-C., De Fraine, B. and Onghena, P. (2002) 'The effect of schools and classes on non-cognitive outcomes', *School Effectiveness and School Improvement*, 13(4): 429–51.

Verhaeghe, G., Vanhoof, J., Valckea, M., and Van Petegem, P. (2009) 'Using school performance feedback: perceptions of primary school principals', *School Effectiveness and School Improvement*, iFirst article: 1–22.

Volante, L. (2004) 'Teaching to the test: what every educator and policy-maker should know', *Canadian Journal of Educational Administration and Policy*, 35. Online. Available www.umanitoba.ca/publications/cjeap/articles/ volante.html (accessed 17 November 2007).

Weare, K. (2004) *Developing the Emotionally Literate School*, London: Paul Chapman Publishing.

Weare, K. and Gray, G. (2003) *What Works in Developing Children's Emotional and Social Competence and Well-being?* London: Department for Education and Skills.

Wikeley, F. (1998) 'Dissemination of research as a tool for school improvement?' *School Leadership and Management*, 18(1): 59–73.

Wiliam, D. (2000) 'The meanings and consequences of educational assessment', *Critical Quarterly*, 42(1): 105–27.

—— (2001a) 'Reliability, validity and all that jazz', *Education 3–13*, October: 17–21.

—— (2001b) *Level Best? Levels of attainment in National Curriculum assessment*, London: ATL.

—— (2001c) 'What is wrong with our educational assessments and what can be done about it?' *Education Review*, 15(1): 57–62.

Williamson, J. and Fitz-Gibbon, C. T. (1990) 'The lack of impact of information: performance indicators for A Levels', *Educational Management and Administration*, 18(1): 37–45.

Williamson, J., Tymms, P. and Haddow, M. (1992) 'ALIS through the looking glass: changing perceptions of performance indicators', *Educational Management and Administration*, 20(3): 179–87.

Wohlstetter, P., Datnow, A. and Park, V. (2008) 'Creating a system for data-driven decision-making: applying the principal-agent framework', *School Effectiveness and School Improvement*, 19(3): 239–59.

Woodhouse, G., Yang, M., Goldstein, H. and Rasbash, J. (1996) 'Adjusting for measurement error in multilevel analysis', *Journal of the Royal Statistical Society, Series A*, (159): 201–12.

Yang, M., Goldstein, H., Rath, T. and Hill, N. (1999) 'The use of assessment data for school improvement purposes', *Oxford Review of Education*, 25(4): 469–83.

Zeuli, J. (1994) 'How do teachers understand research when they read it?' *Teaching and Teacher Education*, 10(1): 39–55.

Index